1937633

APR 17 2012 Me

Children and Loss

D1599105

DATE DUE

Also available from Lyceum Books

Advisory Editor: Thomas M. Meenaghan, *New York University*

Therapeutic Games and Guided Imagery
by Monit Cheung

Understanding and Managing the Therapeutic Relationship
by Fred McKenzie

Psychoeducation in Mental Health
by Joseph Walsh

The Ethics of Practice with Minors: High Stakes, Hard Choices
by Kim Strom-Gottfried

Endings in Clinical Practice:
Effective Closure in Diverse Settings, 2nd edition
by Joseph Walsh, foreword by Thomas M. Meenaghan

Secondary Traumatic Stress and the Child Welfare Professional
by Josephine G. Pryce, Kimberly K. Shackelford, and David H. Pryce

Humanistic Social Work: Core Principles in Practice
by Malcolm Payne

An Experiential Approach to Group Work
by Rich Furman, Diana Rowan, and Kimberly Bender

Short-term Existential Intervention in Clinical Practice
by Jim Lantz and Joseph Walsh

Mindfulness and Social Work
edited by Steven Hick

The Dynamics of Family Policy: Analysis and Advocacy
by Alice K. Butterfield, Cynthia J. Rocha, and William H. Butterfield

Children and Loss

*A Practical Handbook
for Professionals*

edited by

Elizabeth C. Pomeroy
University of Texas at Austin

Renée Bradford Garcia
Licensed Clinical Social Worker, Austin, Texas

LYCEUM
BOOKS, INC.

Chicago, Illinois

Copyright © 2011 by Lyceum Books, Inc.

Published by
LYCEUM BOOKS, INC.
5758 S. Blackstone Ave.
Chicago, Illinois 60637
773 + 643–1903 (Fax)
773 + 643–1902 (Phone)
lyceum@lyceumbooks.com
http://www.lyceumbooks.com

6   5   4   3   2   1   11   12   13   14

ISBN 978-1-933478-64-7

Cover photo: Sleeping angel at Recoleta cemetery, Buenos Aires, Argentina
© Jorisvo | Dreamstime.com

Library of Congress Cataloging-in-Publication Data

Children and loss : a practical handbook for professionals / edited by Elizabeth C. Pomeroy, Renée Bradford Garcia.
    p. cm.
  Includes bibliographical references and index.
  ISBN 978-1-933478-64-7 (pbk. : alk. paper)
  1. Loss (Psychology) in children.   2. Grief in children.   3. Bereavement in children.
I. Pomeroy, Elizabeth Cheney, 1955–   II. Garcia, Renée Bradford.
BF723.L68C45   2011
155.9′3083—dc22

2010029704

To all the families with children coping with grief
and the professionals who care for them
and
In memory of John L. Bradford

Contents

About the Editors

Elizabeth C. Pomeroy, PhD, LCSW, is professor and researcher at the School of Social Work, University of Texas at Austin. She is also the co-director of the Institute for Grief, Loss, and Family Survival at the School of Social Work. She is currently editor in chief of *Social Work: The Journal of the National Association of Social Work.* She teaches in the graduate social work program in the clinical concentration as well as the BSW and PhD programs. Her research has focused on the effectiveness of mental health interventions for families and persons with chronic, life-threatening illness and in the area of HIV/AIDS, FASD, and Alcohol Prevention. Her coauthored text, *The Clinical Assessment Workbook: Balancing Strengths and Differential Diagnosis* (Wadsworth/Brooks Cole, 2003), is used throughout the United States and internationally. *The Grief Assessment and Intervention Workbook: A Strengths Perspective,* coauthored with Renée Bradford Garcia, was published in 2009.

Renée Bradford Garcia, LCSW, received her master's degree in social work from the University of Michigan in 1995. She currently has a private practice near Austin, Texas, providing individual and family counseling and psychotherapy to children, adolescents, and adults. She has worked extensively at hospice organizations serving bereaved families and individuals of all ages as well as terminally ill individuals and their families. She is coauthor of *The Grief Assessment and Intervention Workbook: A Strengths Perspective,* published in 2009.

Contributors

Tamara Linseisen (LCSW; ACSW) is associate professor of clinical social work at the University of Texas in Austin. Her areas of expertise include child abuse and neglect, children's mental health issues, and foster care and adoption.

Barbara Jones (PhD) is associate professor of social work at the University of Texas in Austin, as well as co-director of the Institute for Grief, Loss, and Family Survival. Her research focuses on children's loss, bereaved parents, and pediatric palliative care and end-of-life issues. She has fifteen years of clinical experience working as an oncology social worker with children and families in medical settings. She is deeply committed to improving the quality of life for chronically and terminally ill youth and their families.

Pamela Malone (PhD; LCSW) is adjunct instructor of social work at the University of Texas in Austin, as well as a research affiliate for the Institute for Grief, Loss, and Family Survival. She specializes in working with children and adolescents in crisis, substance abuse, and grieving families. In addition to her academic work, she has a private practice and is an expert on groupwork with at-risk adolescents.

Mikki Tesh (MSW) is a doctoral student and assistant instructor of social work at the University of Texas in Austin, as well as a research affiliate for the Institute for Grief, Loss, and Family Survival. She has extensive clinical experience in hospice and end-of-life care.

Preface

Regardless of the varied settings in which helping professionals practice, they will inevitably encounter clients who are dealing with issues of grief and loss. The grief and loss experienced by children, while quite prevalent, are often overlooked or given only cursory attention. While helping professionals may have expertise in working with children and adolescents, many have had limited training in helping children work with issues of loss and grief. In the numerous presentations that the authors have conducted over the past ten years, practitioners have stated their need for practical information and techniques to assist children with a variety of grief issues. The intention of this book is to orient professionals to the different kinds of losses and the ensuing grief issues that are relevant to children and adolescents, and to provide them with a framework for understanding and intervening in these varied circumstances.

The first chapter reviews theories of grief that have laid the foundation for our current understanding of grief, particularly as it relates to the death of a loved one. In addition, we have discussed the more newly developed Strengths-Based Framework of grief developed by the editors of this volume.

Chapter 2 examines grief and loss as it is uniquely experienced by children and adolescents. We review the developmental differences in how loss is understood and experienced by youth and how this may be conceptualized with both death-related and other kinds of losses. This understanding is crucial for assessing and intervening with grieving children. Assessment methods and instruments for use with grieving youth are also discussed at length.

Subsequent chapters address issues of loss and grief that are specific to the different settings in which professionals interact with grieving youth. Each chapter addresses issues of assessment, highlights appropriate interventions, and references useful resources for the practitioner. In addition, information related to culture and ethical practice is also provided, along with case scenarios so that practitioners can apply their knowledge of grief assessment and intervention to actual clients.

In chapter 3, Linseisen addresses grief and loss issues that are predominant for children in foster care, residential treatment, and adoption settings. Disentangling the issues of grief and loss from other emotional issues can be challenging for the practitioner but essential to successful outcomes of treatment. Children in these settings are often making major life transitions at a young age without parental support or nurturance. Grief is a major issue for these children and can often lead to the disruption of placements, resulting in additional separation and loss issues for children.

The grief experienced by children whose parents have divorced is similar to other significant losses in the lives of youth. In chapter 4, Malone provides a clear explanatory framework for assessing children of divorce in terms of their strengths and risk factors. As children grieve the death of their nuclear family, they often need support from adults who understand the magnitude of the loss. Teachers, school counselors, practitioners, and other significant professionals in the youth's life can use Malone's information and interventions to help children transition to the changes in their families.

Garcia and Pomeroy, in chapter 5, discuss the ways that grief and loss affect youth in the educational sphere and how practitioners can be responsive to their needs within the school setting. The dynamics of assessing and intervening with individual children and adolescents, classroom groups, and the school as a whole are examined. With this information teachers and school counselors can be sensitive to the variety of loss issues and crises that they encounter in their professional work.

Children and adolescents in medical settings have a unique compilation of grief issues. In chapter 6, Jones and Tesh address grief and loss with the terminally ill and its impact on youth and their families. Intervening with youth in medical settings can be a challenge due to the priority of patient care. Since medical treatment is the primary focus of attention in hospitals, the impact of grief and loss is often overlooked by medical personnel. In addition, hospital professionals may lack the knowledge and expertise for intervening with youth and their families in regard to grief and loss. The authors provide a framework for examining grief and loss issues in the medical setting for nurses, child life specialists, social work practitioners, and psychologists, pastoral counselors, and other medical professionals.

The issues of traumatic and complex grief of youth in crisis are addressed by Malone in chapter 7. This section includes children who are victims of abandonment, domestic violence, natural disaster, and other emergency situations. Often these children are in transitional living situations and are facing unknown futures. In these situations, the primary focus is often on practical concerns such as living arrangements, legal issues, and physical safety. Information related to the assessment and intervention of grief, loss, and trauma issues that may underlie the more prominent challenges facing these youth will be provided.

Finally, we conclude this volume with a section on therapeutic activities that can be used with grieving youth. These activities use readily accessible materials that can be kept in a practitioner's office to creatively intervene with youth at all developmental levels. Many times youth are unable to verbally express their inner experience. However, they have a strong ability to re-create their feelings through art and play activities. It has been our experience that these useful tools can supplement other types of therapeutic approaches in a very meaningful manner.

The authors relied heavily on their clinical experiences in devising case scenarios for this book. However, any resemblance between actual clients and those presented herein is completely coincidental.

Acknowledgments

As with any large project, the authors are indebted to a number of others for their assistance and support in the process. We are grateful for the assistance of David Follmer, executive editor, and Siobhan Drummond, managing editor, for their support and expertise in the completion of this publication. Our thanks to Reese Anna Baker, editorial coordinator, Catherine Dixon, marketing coordinator, and Lily Ye and John Bobka, interns. In addition, we would like to acknowledge those who reviewed the earlier versions of this manuscript. Their insightful comments assisted us in enhancing the final text.

We would also like to thank Barbara White, dean of the University of Texas, School of Social Work, whose support throughout this project was invaluable. We are fortunate to be associated with such an energetic and collegial faculty.

Finally, this book would not be possible without the continual encouragement and unfailing support of friends and family members. We extend a special thanks to Daniel Garcia and children Tilo and Cheve, Wanda Bradford, Nancy Pomeroy Togar, and Charles and Loretta Prokop. We are grateful to the many others who cheered us on along the way.

CHAPTER ONE

Theories of Grief and Loss: An Overview

Elizabeth C. Pomeroy and Renée Bradford Garcia

Loss, and the grief it produces, occurs in various forms, in a variety of situations, and is not immune to any age group or population. Grief may be defined as a multidimensional experience that results from a significant loss of person or object. It can involve the emotional, cognitive, physical, social, behavioral, and spiritual components of a person's life. Grief and loss may result from the death of a loved one, a move to a new location, a change in household membership or family boundaries such as that which occurs with divorce, the loss of a physical ability, a role that is not fulfilled adequately (such as a mother who is unable to provide appropriate parenting), or a fundamental change in one's community as often happens with disasters.

The terms *grief, mourning,* and *bereavement* are used interchangeably due to the fact that any one of these terms does not fully define the reaction to loss (Silverman, 2004, pp. 226–241). According to Sprang and McNeil (1995), grief and mourning are the emotional and behavioral components, respectively, that comprise the bereavement process. In addition, the term *mourning* includes the psychological process of adaptation to loss and encompasses societal and cultural norms (Silverman, 2004). Grief may involve a wide variation in emotion from laughter to despair, anger to acceptance, sorrow to joy. The following diagram in figure 1.1 depicts the overlapping relationships between these concepts.

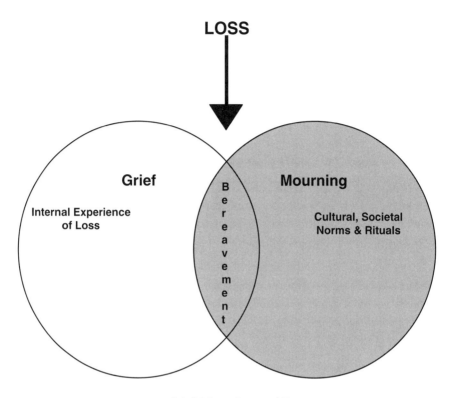

FIGURE 1.1.   *Grief, Mourning, and Bereavement*

The grief experience may vary greatly in intensity and duration, depending on the centrality of the loss in the mourner's life. Loss affects every individual in unique ways, yet there are common threads that make it a universal experience. For example, a significant loss, such as the death of a parent, results in sorrow for most children. On the other hand, some children will react with anger and other negative behaviors rather than show their sadness when a parent dies. Even losses that are different in nature may share similar grief reactions. For example, a child's experience of the death of a parent may cause the child to feel insecure and fearful and regress to behaviors of a younger child. This may also be seen in children whose parents have recently divorced as they react to the loss of their family unit as they have known it. A fundamental understanding of grief and bereavement is the first place to begin when helping children deal with any kind of loss.

While our knowledge of grief and loss was initially focused on adults, grief as it is experienced by children is a more recent field of study. With the exception of Bowlby's attachment theory, conceptual frameworks that explain the grieving process primarily refer to the experience of adult grief reactions. While there are significant differences between the ways that children and adults express their grief, understanding the original theories of grief provides a firm foundation for understanding children's grief. In this chapter, we will provide a brief overview of several theories of grief and loss. An extensive body of literature exists that provides in-depth explanations of these theoretical frameworks. The authors encourage practitioners to explore all the literature so that they may obtain an enhanced foundation in their understanding of grief and bereavement. In addition, we will present the authors' framework of grief that encompasses a person-in-environment and a strengths-based perspective.

Theories of Grief and Loss

FREUDIAN THEORY OF LOSS

In the early twentieth century, Freud provided a theory of "mourning and melancholia" that distinguished between normal and pathological mourning. He suggested that relinquishing emotional ties with the object of attachment involved obsessive remembering followed by a complete severance of emotion to the loved one and reattaching that emotion to another person. Although this other person is only a substitute for the lost loved one, the mourner eventually internalizes the reality of the loss, extinguishes the emotional energy expended on the lost loved one, and, in turn, frees it to be directed toward another. Freud also believed that the psychological identification with the lost person is internalized so that aspects of that person become part of the mourner's psychological makeup, thus making the bereavement process challenging yet survivable (Berzoff, 2004; Freud, 1976). This perspective has particular significance for children who are grieving in that a child may be able to create an identity that includes aspects of the lost loved one. In this manner, the child is able to move beyond the bereavement process while maintaining an identification with the loved one.

Freud also distinguished healthy mourning from pathological mourning and differentiated between mourning and melancholia. In both cases, the emotional experience is similar; however, with melancholia, the mourner has a lack of self-esteem, is self-critical, and eventually develops pathological melancholia, or grief. Freud postulated that this prolonged depression that accompanied the grief process was due to unconscious conflicts with the person who died that led to a more complicated mourning period. Threads of Freud's theory of mourning can be found in more recent theories and frameworks that guide current practice. Clearly, Freud's theory furthered our understanding of the grief process; however, his focus on the intrapsychic and unconscious elements of a person's psyche failed to account for environmental influences that impact the mourner's coping capacities.

ERICH LINDEMANN AND CRISIS THEORY

Following in the footsteps of Freud's theory of mourning, Eric Lindemann's research after the 1944 Cocoanut Grove Night Club disaster in which more than 500 people were killed expanded on the traditional views about the grief process (Parkes, 1964, 1970, 1972). He coined the term *grief work*, with his suggestion that resolution of grief necessitated the completion of three specific tasks. First, the mourner must relinquish the attachment to the loved one. Second, he or she must readapt to life without the presence of the loved one. Third, the person must establish new relationships with others. With Freud's psychodynamic approach as his foundation, Lindemann viewed grief work as disengagement from the deceased through an internal and solitary struggle. Only through this struggle could a person relinquish the attachment to the deceased, readjust to the environment, and develop new relationships.

Unlike Freud, Lindeman utilized empirical methods to study the process of grief and included relatively large samples of participants who had experienced a variety of losses. Based on interviews with survivors of the nightclub fire, Lindemann (Parkes & Weiss, 1983) named six characteristics of acute grief (the initial grief reaction) which are: (1) physical distress, (2) ruminations about the deceased, (3) survival guilt, (4) angry reactions to others, (5) decline in functioning, and (6) tendency to internalize characteristics of the deceased. In addition, the inability to work through the acute phase of grief, which Lindemann suggested was four to six weeks, could result in pathological or "distorted" grief reactions (Malkinson, 2007).

Lindemann's study of grief and his focus on the acute grief period led to the development of crisis theory (Malkinson, Rubin, & Witztum, 2000). Crisis theory suggested that an extreme disruption in a person's ability to function reflected a lack of adequate coping strategies and did not necessarily warrant professional treatment. This provided the basis for crisis intervention theory that is commonly practiced today, particularly in response to experiences that involve trauma and grief.

BOWLBY'S THEORY OF ATTACHMENT

John Bowlby's theory of attachment developed from his early research on infants separated from their mothers and the emotional, cognitive, developmental, and biological consequences of attachment versus separation. According to Bowlby, life-span development of attachment involves the formation of a bond (i.e., falling in love), maintenance of the attachment (i.e., loving someone), and disruption (i.e., grief and mourning) (Bowlby, 1980). He delineates over the course of three volumes how attachment behaviors maintain the affectional bond and, therefore, a state of homeostasis, or balance. When loss of the attachment figure occurs and the bond is disrupted, the person experiences stress and distress as represented by crying, clinging, and angry behaviors in an attempt to regain the connection. When these behaviors are repeatedly unsuccessful, they gradually diminish but do not stop completely.

Bowlby (1980) hypothesized that grief reactions are a reflection of this basic attachment dynamic. He further described the psychological reorganization that must take place following a loss as involving four phases. The first phase entails a period during which the mourner experiences numbness and denial that serves to deflect the anguish and despair accompanying the loss. This phase can be periodically disrupted by extreme and physically exhausting emotions. The second phase is characterized by yearning and searching, as the mourner begins to confront the loss. Common behaviors during this phase include interpreting events as signs from the loved one and seeking out evidence of the loved one's presence. When these activities are unsuccessful, anger and frustration ensue. The third phase is predominated by feelings of disorganization and desolation. The realization that the attachment bond has been severed and the activities of prior phases have failed is integrated by the mourner. The person experiences a depletion of energy and a sense of being overwhelmed. This prompts a reevaluation of the mourner's identity and self-concept that can lead to massive psychological upheaval. The final phase, according to Bowlby, involves gradual movement toward reorganization. There is growing acceptance of the permanence of the separation and the need to construct a life despite the absence of the loved one. These phases may be experienced multiple times during the bereavement process and may take days, months, or years.

In conclusion, Bowlby's theory of attachment and loss involves a cognitive behavioral framework that lends itself to modern understanding and interventions currently used in practice. Bowlby's thorough examination of attachment provides us with insight into the nature of behaviors associated with separation and loss. His work has been a foundation for our understanding of grief and the bereavement process.

KÜBLER-ROSS AND STAGES OF GRIEF

Although Lindemann was a pioneer in crisis intervention, death and dying were still taboo subjects when the United States was forced to face the mass destruction of the Vietnam War. It was the 1960s and we were a "society bent on ignoring or avoiding death" (Kübler-Ross, 1969, p. 25). Elisabeth Kübler-Ross's work was revolutionary and opened the doors to discussion about death and dying as well as grief and loss—subjects that were stigmatized and ignored in American culture during the middle of the twentieth century. Her writings originated with her professional experiences as a physician of terminally ill persons. Her first book, *On Death and Dying* (1969), included a stage model of the psychological coping process experienced by those who were dying. Later this model was applied to the grief experience and was the accepted paradigm for many years. Kübler-Ross's model included five stages of grief, which were (1) denial and isolation, (2) anger, (3) bargaining, (4) depression, and (5) acceptance.

During the stage of denial and isolation, the person has difficulty comprehending the loss and the reality that death is imminent. The person could be considered to be in a state of shock—numb to the emotional ramifications of loss. Isolation or withdrawal was noted as a common behavioral component of this initial reaction to a terminal diagnosis (Kübler-Ross, 1969).

The second stage involves anger and rage over the terminal prognosis. As the denial fades, anger takes over as the primary emotion. At times, this experience may take on irrational proportions and be difficult for others to comprehend. Often the person feels as if the terminal diagnosis is unfair or a cruel turn of fate. The stage of anger yields to the third stage, bargaining (Kübler-Ross, 1969).

During the bargaining phase, the person attempts to strike a deal with a higher being for a postponement of the inevitable death. For example, the person may secretly promise to be good in exchange for more time on Earth. Bargaining eventually leads to the fourth stage, depression (Kübler-Ross, 1969).

Depression is experienced as "a sense of great loss" (Kübler-Ross, 1969, p. 97). Kübler-Ross suggests two types of depression: reactive and preparatory. In reactive depression, the person experiences the multiple losses that are a result of the terminal illness (e.g., financial, employment, family roles, physical deterioration). In preparatory depression, the person grieves the impending losses associated with the knowledge that he or she is dying. For example, loss of significant others, loss of physical self, loss of the material world, and the final separation from others are all components of preparatory depression. In this sense, Kübler-Ross links depression and grief as similar emotional experiences.

The final stage of this model is acceptance. During this stage, the person has resolved his or her feelings of anger and sadness. Although not necessarily content, the person awaits death with "quiet expectation." Kübler-Ross suggests that during this stage the person may experience an absence of emotion and be "void of feelings." (Kübler-Ross, 1969, p. 124).

Though introduced as a model to assist health professionals understand their dying patients, Kübler-Ross's work has been applied to the experience of mourners after the death of a loved one. Kübler-Ross's framework has been considered the hallmark for understanding death and dying. Many of the elements of her model are still used by professionals today. The primary criticism of this model was the fixed and sequential aspect of the stages.

WORDEN'S TASK-ORIENTED FRAMEWORK OF MOURNING

J. William Worden (1991) developed a task-oriented, practice framework based on Bowlby's theory of attachment that emphasizes the continuum of grief as moving from the pain of separation to the adjustment of new relationships. He describes four basic tasks that must be completed for mourning to be resolved. He emphasizes the fact that these tasks are not necessarily sequential in nature and a person can move back and forth from one task to another. All of the tasks, according to Worden (1991), involve effort or work by the mourner. The four basic tasks are outlined below:

1. To accept the reality of the loss
2. To work through the pain of grief
3. To adjust to an environment in which the deceased is missing
4. To emotionally relocate the deceased and move on with life (Worden, 1991, pp. 10–18)

Worden's practice model emphasizes the need for assessment and distinguishes between uncomplicated and complicated grief. His model has been a useful guide for practitioners in the field because the tasks indicate an active approach toward the resolution of mourning. Other models, in contrast, propose phases that are passively endured by the mourner.

RANDO'S THEORETICAL FRAMEWORK OF THE GRIEF PROCESS

Therese Rando suggested that the bereavement process involves three phases that must be completed for a healthy resolution of grief. Avoidance is the first phase of this process. During this period, the mourner's task is to recognize the reality of the loss. The initial reaction to the loss of a loved one is shock, numbness, and denial, which act as a buffer against the flood of emotions that can be experienced during this time.

Rando says that this phase is therapeutic in that it serves as "emotional anesthesia" by giving the mourner time to adjust to the loss (Rando, 1993, p. 33). Some mourners may exhibit dramatic displays of emotion such as angry outbursts, screaming, and wailing. Others may seem more subdued and respond by withdrawing, isolating, and depersonalizing the experience. Rando suggests that some individuals may appear to easily accept the loss and cope by caring for other mourners. Although this initial form of avoidance is useful, it can lead to life-depleting grief reactions if they continue to compartmentalize their emotions surrounding the loss over a long period of time.

During the second phase, confrontation, the mourner responds to the loss, experiencing and expressing the emotions prompted by the grief reaction. Memories or recollections of the deceased are prominent and precipitate the relinquishing of the attachment to the loved one. This phase is considered an excruciatingly painful learning phase of grief (Rando, 1993). It is the time when the mourners are reminded through their daily interactions of their loved ones' absence. For example, when the six-year-old child waits for her older sibling in front of the school before remembering that the sibling has died, she "learns" again of the finality of the loss. When the woman passes the young mother with the baby stroller on the sidewalk, she experiences an acute sense of grief remembering that her own baby died in utero. The pain of grief experienced by the audience upon observing the empty chair placed at the high school graduation in memory of the student who would be graduating had he not died, is another example of confronting the loss. In each of these instances, Rando suggests that learning is taking place. The mourner is in effect learning how to separate from the loved one and move toward healthy adaptation. This is often considered the most emotionally painful phase of the bereavement process. Symptoms of grief during this phase affect the psychological, physiological, cognitive, social, spiritual, and behavioral functioning of mourners.

The final phase, accommodation, involves a readjustment to the world without the deceased and a placement of energy into current and future relationships (Humphrey & Zimpfer, 1996; Rando, 1993). During this phase, the mourner integrates his relationship with the deceased and simultaneously acclimates to life without the loved one. Rando states that "accommodation connotes an adaptation of one's self to make room for a particular circumstance. As such, it captures more accurately the reality that the loss can be integrated appropriately into the rest of life but that a truly final closure usually cannot be obtained, nor is it even desirable" (Rando, 1993, p. 40). Accommodation is the healthy adaptation to the loss of a loved one. It includes making room for mourning while also being able to participate in the present and hope for the future. While actively engaged in their present reality, mourners acknowledge their relationship with the deceased. This life-enhancing process allows the mourner to positively develop a life that is not hindered by the loss and provides a solid foundation upon which to move forward.

These three phases are the basis for Rando's framework of the bereavement process. She suggests that these three phases encompass all of the responses related to the grief process. Her framework combines components of attachment theory, the task-oriented model of grief, and Kübler-Ross's stages of grief. However, Rando's model moves beyond these frameworks by suggesting that mourners can move in and out of these phases and that progression does not occur in a linear fashion.

GRIEF AND THE CONSTRUCTIVIST FRAMEWORK

Another popular view of bereavement originates from a constructivist framework that views the experience of grief as one in which mourners actively search for a way to understand the loss, their changed life following the loss, and to attach some symbolic significance to the loss and its influence on their new life. The extent to which a mourner is able to make meaning of her loss is believed to influence her transition to life without the deceased. It has been purported that this conceptualization is especially relevant to those who are grieving a traumatic loss, defined as a loss that results from unexpected, horrifying, and shocking events (Neimeyer, Prigerson, & Davies, 2002). In the case of traumatic grief, research suggests that mourners who search and find some meaning in the loss as well as those who feel no need to look for significance in the loss may have better psychological outcomes compared with those who search but cannot find meaning (Neimeyer, 2000).

According to this viewpoint, the mourner's process of reconstructing her life after a death is grounded in sociological, cultural, and community influences that regulate norms around grief and bereavement. A mourner's interface with her environment provides affirmation to the grieving experience and the mourner's effort to "relearn the self" and "relearn the world" (Attig, 1996).

The mourner's process also interacts with an internal psychological component as the individual mourner attempts to adjust her internal and psychological life to the loss. Such adjustments include attempts to integrate the loss into the "personal narrative" of the mourner's life and fit the loss into a "meaningful plot structure" (Neimeyer et al., 2002).

   The construction of meaning around the death of a loved one is a very personal endeavor that varies with each individual. Often mourners will engage in activities or begin projects or organizations in memory of their loved one. Their hope is that some good, such as helping others, can come from their pain. The nonprofit, bereavement support organization For the Love of Christi is one such example. This organization was founded by parents whose daughter was killed by a drunk driver and found little support available to help them with their grief. It provides community-based grief groups for adults, children, and families. For other mourners, making meaning of the loss may take the form of significant changes in the way they live, such as attending to one's health, staying in closer touch with family and friends, and working less in order to spend more time relaxing or with family.

   While grieving adults may make meaning out of the death of a loved one, children under the age of ten are more apt to think of the loss in a more concrete manner. This is due to their cognitive and emotional level of development. It is important to recognize this framework because of its implications for adults who are caring for grieving children. On the other hand, rather than integrating a loss into a philosophical meaning of life, research has indicated that children connect a loss with their innate spirituality as well as linking the loss to present relationships and objects. For example, a child may carry a cherished object representing the loved one as a way of maintaining the relationship. In addition, a child may derive comfort connecting the death of the loved one with their spiritual belief system. For example, young children may commemorate a sibling's "heavenly birthday" by lighting candles and sharing memories of the deceased. These are concrete expressions of their loss that may bring comfort and security. As children mature and develop emotionally, the meaning they make of the loss may take on a more sophisticated form (Andrews & Marotta, 2005).

CONTINUING BONDS FRAMEWORK OF GRIEF

In the last decade, an evolving model of bereavement has emerged that reduces the emphasis on detachment from the loved one who has died and instead, focuses more attention on the internalized, ongoing relationship with the deceased. Silverman and Nickman (1996) summarize this perspective in the book *Continuing Bonds* by stating, "Survivors hold the deceased in loving memory for long periods, often forever, and that maintaining an inner representation of the deceased is normal rather than abnormal" (p. 349). For example, an adolescent internalizes the positive attributes of her father and describes her motivation to become a successful professional as related to her father's optimistic attitude toward her career goals. In this sense, the young woman's development encompassed her father's belief system and shaped her identity as a competent and goal-oriented individual who could succeed in her college education and career.

These connections that are continually held with the deceased seem to be common among mourners. This view suggests it is not pathological to have a continuing relationship with the deceased and that, in fact, it may be healthy to do so. Therefore, the bereavement process involves understanding how the continuing bond with the deceased can be maintained, enhanced, and utilized to promote a healthy response to the future for those who are no longer physically connected to the deceased person. Silverman and Nickman (1996) suggest that the centrality of the bond with the deceased may change over time; however, the relationship remains an important aspect of the person's internal life.

A Strengths-Based Framework of Grief and Loss

More recently developed is the strengths-based framework for grief and loss (Pomeroy & Garcia, 2009). While validating that grief is a negative, painful, and disruptive experience for the mourner, this perspective emphasizes the mourners' strengths and resiliencies that can be brought to bear on their unique experience of grief and loss. The strengths-based framework of grief assists practitioners in building on the inherent strengths of the individual while he or she navigates the bereavement process. It empowers a person to use his coping abilities and environmental resources in response to the death of a loved one. It views grief as a natural, normal, and potentially health-producing process that aids the individual in adjusting to the absence of the loved one.

The strengths-based framework of grief and loss draws on the perspective of social work practice developed by Saleebey (2006) and Rapp (1998), which views every client as having assets and resources that enhance his or her ability to cope with life events. People have both individual strengths and environmental strengths. Individual strengths include aspirations, competencies, and confidence (Rapp, 1998). Aspirations include goals, dreams, hopes for the future, ambitions, and positive motivation to achieve and grow. Competencies are manifested by one's unique ability to utilize talents, skills, and intellect. Confidence refers to a person's positive self-regard and her belief and tenacity in achieving goals. A person with confidence feels valuable and worthy of positive life events. Strengths are present in every individual. Some people appear to be able to capitalize on their strengths more than others.

This phenomenon may be due to a combination of biological, psycho-logical, and social factors.

Environmental strengths include resources, social relations, and opportunities. Resources include financial support, access to services, access to information, and other tangible assets. Social relations encompass friends, family, coworkers, neighbors, and others with whom one interacts. Opportunities refer to the gaps in one's life that are waiting to be filled. They represent positive events that can poten-tially change one's life.

In addition, a person maintains specific niches in life, that is, habi-tation, job, friends, and leisure activities. According to Rapp (1998), "The quality of the niches for any individual is a function of that per-son's aspirations, competencies, confidence, and the environmental resources, opportunities, and people available to the person" (p. 42). Together, a person's individual and environmental strengths influence his or her sense of well-being, empowerment, and life satisfaction (Rapp, 1998).

For clients who are grieving, the strengths perspective is a particu-larly salient framework. It builds on previous theories of grief with the addition of a lens that emphasizes the health-producing aspects that are intrinsic to the mourner, as well as the process of bereavement. Focusing on mourners' strengths rather than deficits provides the practitioner with a valuable tool that can aid in assessment and inter-vention. It effectively highlights aspects of the person and his environ-ment that can be utilized and enhanced to assist in the bereavement process and promote positive growth.

The integration of this perspective leads to a new understanding of the grief process and new insights into grief-related interventions, as outlined in the following tenets. The strengths-based framework applies to all stages of development, genders, and cultures. An explana-tion of how this framework can be applied to children is provided below.

1. Grief in response to the death of a loved one is a natural, expect-able, and potentially health-producing process that aids the indi-vidual in adjusting to the absence of the loved one.

   While historically it was believed that children didn't have the capacity to grieve, we now know that grief is a natural reaction to loss for all ages. Children's grief may look different from that of adults, but it is equally useful in helping children adjust and adapt to loss.

2. The symptoms, emotions, and behaviors associated with expected grief reactions represent a process of healthy adaptation and are not inherently pathological.

At each developmental stage, children have predictable reactions to a loss. Children may express a range of emotions that can aid them in processing the loss. While these reactions may be confusing to the child's caregivers, they may represent a healthy process of adjustment.

3. Mourners benefit by knowing that life-enhancing grief reactions are productive and beneficial. Life-enhancing grief reactions are those responses that facilitate healing within the mourner.

   As with adults, children benefit by having their grief reactions normalized and validated. Adults can play a pivotal role in assisting grieving children with understanding that their grief can be a healthy process that can alleviate the pain they are experiencing. Children can also be taught life-enhancing methods to help them cope with the loss.

4. All persons have individual and environmental strengths that can assist them as they experience grief. The mourner benefits from the reinforcement of those strengths and the encouragement to consciously employ them during the grief process.

   Due to their developmental levels, children arc often unaware of their own coping capacities as well as the environmental supports available to them. It is important for both personal and professional caregivers to teach children about their internal and external strengths and how to utilize them.

5. Environmental conditions can either help or hinder the mourner's ability to adapt to the loss and enhance the person's life.

   Environmental conditions that could help or hinder a child's ability to adjust to loss include a stable caregiving system, school and community environment, and access to additional resources as needed.

6. Many symptoms of grief, though they may be uncomfortable and are commonly regarded as negative symptoms, are healthy coping mechanisms in that they facilitate the process of separation, adaptation to change, and integration of the loss.

   Some of the uncomfortable symptoms that are commonly seen in bereaved children include crying, fear-based behaviors, regression, and withdrawal. On the other hand, children may not show visible signs of their grief, which may be disconcerting to caregivers. In both cases, children may be forming psychological safety nets in order to process the grief and move toward separation and adaptation to the loss.

7. Life-enhancing grief reactions to loss enable accommodation and adaptation to occur. They facilitate the process of psychological separation from the deceased.

In children, life-enhancing grief reactions can be facilitated by caregivers and helping professionals who are aware of children's needs for assistance with the grieving process.

8. Life-enhancing grief symptoms should not be discouraged. Rather, they should be allowed expression while being carefully monitored so that they remain helpful to the mourner's process of adaptation.

   Caregivers can assist children with life-enhancing grief symptoms by providing structure, space to express emotions, encouragement, and reassurance. On the other hand, caregivers can monitor and manage the symptoms of grief so that they don't overwhelm the child or family.

9. Grief may be considered life-depleting when the symptoms it produces significantly weaken the mourner's aspirations, competencies, and confidence. Life-depleting grief reactions are those responses and circumstances that act as impediments to the expected grieving process and interfere with the mourner's ability to live a fulfilling life.

   In children, when grief becomes an impediment to their normal development, it may be considered life-depleting.

10. Life-depleting grief reactions thwart the process of adaptation and lead to entropy.

    Children's development can be seriously compromised when they are unable to cope with loss in healthy ways.

11. Life-enhancing and life-depleting grief reactions exist on a continuum of intensity.

    Children's reactions to loss can range from mild to severe. Some children may show no outward signs of grief, while others may display intense grief reactions.

12. The experience of grief evolves over a person's lifetime and is experienced with varying levels of conscious awareness.

    Children reexperience the loss as they progress through the stages of development. At each stage of development, their awareness and perceptions of the loss change.

13. The process of grief is fertile ground for personal growth and the development or enhancement of the mourner's strengths.

    It is a common misconception that grief and loss will permanently scar children. Children have the capacity to be resilient and grow from their experience with grief.

Summary

All of the theories described in this chapter are useful for understanding the bereavement process and how it applies to children and families.

By understanding grief theory, practitioners enhance their ability to implement interventions that will benefit their clients. While a thorough understanding of the historical background and significance of grief theory is essential for good practice, the unique issues facing each client may determine the theoretical underpinning for interventions chosen.

Throughout this book, the strengths-based framework of grief will be emphasized. It can be used in conjunction with the other models presented in this chapter. Practitioners who work with children in a variety of settings will find the strengths-based framework of grief to be a useful foundation for intervening with children and families experiencing loss.

References

Andrews, C. R., & Marotta, S. A. (2005). Spirituality and coping among grieving children: A preliminary study. *Counseling and Values, 50,* 38–50.

Attig, T. (1996). *How we grieve: Relearning the world.* New York: Oxford University Press.

Berzoff, J. (2004). Psychodynamic theories in grief and bereavement. In J. Berzoff & P. Silverman (Eds.), *Living with Dying* (pp. 242–262). New York: Columbia University Press.

Bowlby, J. (1980). *Attachment and loss* (Vol. 3: Loss, sadness, and depression). New York: Basic Books.

Freud, S. (1976). Mourning and melancholia. In J. Strachey (Ed. & Trans.), *The standard edition of the complete psychological works of Sigmund Freud* (Vol. 14, pp. 243–258). New York: W. W. Norton and Company.

Humphrey, G. M., & Zimpfer, D. G. (1996). *Counselling for grief and bereavement.* Thousand Oaks: Sage.

Kübler-Ross, E. (1969). *On death and dying.* New York: Touchstone.

Malkinson, R. (2007). *Cognitive grief therapy.* Newark, NJ: W. W. Norton and Company.

Malkinson, R., Rubin, S., & Witztum, E. (Eds.) (2000). *Traumatic and non-traumatic loss and bereavement: Clinical theory and practice.* Madison, CT: Psychological Press.

Neimeyer, R. A. (2000). Searching for the meaning of meaning: Grief therapy and the process of reconstruction. *Death Studies, 24*(6), 541–558.

Neimeyer, R. A., Prigerson, H. G. & Davies, B. (2002). Mourning and meaning. *American Behavioral Scientist, 46*(2), 235–251.

Parkes, C. (1964). Recent bereavement as a cause of mental illness. *British Journal of Psychiatry, 110,* 198–204.

Parkes, C. (1970). Seeking and finding a lost object: Evidence for recent studies to bereavement. *Social Science and Medicine, 4,* 187–201.

Parkes, C. (1972). Health after bereavement: A controlled study of young Boston widows and widowers. *Psychosomatic Medicine, 34*(5), 449–461.

Parkes, C., & Weiss, R. (1983). *Recovery from bereavement.* New York: Basic Books.

Pomeroy, E. C., & Garcia, R. B. (2009). *Grief and intervention workbook: A strengths perspective.* Belmont, CA: Brooks/Cole, Cengage Learning.

Rando, T. A. (1993). *Treatment of complicated mourning.* Champaign, IL: Research Press.

Rapp, C. A. (1998). *The strengths model: Case management with people suffering from severe and persistent mental illness.* New York: Oxford University Press.

Saleebey, D. (2006). *The strengths perspective in social work practice* (4th ed.). Boston: Pearson Education.

Silverman, P. R. (2004). Bereavement: A time of transition and changing relationships. In J. Berzoff & P. Silverman (Eds.), *Living with Dying* (pp. 226–241). New York: Columbia University Press.

Silverman, P. R., & Nickman, S. L. (1996). Concluding thoughts. In P. R. Silverman & S. L. Nickman, *Continuing Bonds* (pp. 349–354). Washington, DC: Taylor & Francis.

Sprang, G., & McNeil, J. (1995). *The many faces of bereavement: The nature and treatment of natural, traumatic and stigmatized grief.* New York: Brunner/ Mazel.

Worden, J. W. (1991). *Grief counseling & grief therapy: A handbook for the mental health practitioner.* New York: Springer.

CHAPTER TWO

Children and Grief

Elizabeth C. Pomeroy and Renée Bradford Garcia

For many years, the conventional wisdom concerning bereavement was that children do not experience grief. We now know that "anyone old enough to love is old enough to grieve" (Wolfelt, 1991). Grief reactions in children and adolescents can range in intensity and are often reexperienced to varying degrees as children mature throughout their lives (Corr, Nabe, & Corr, 1994). Though children's and adolescents' experiences with loss are no less significant than those of adults, the way they grieve often looks very different. A child or adolescent's grief experience reflects different levels of cognitive development, emotional capacity, and the individual's inherent dependence on adults for care and support (Baker, Sedney, & Gross, 1992). Parents or caregivers who are also bereaved are likely to have less energy for parenting and a diminished capacity to nurture feelings of security and stability for their children. In some instances, this represents a secondary loss for the child or teen. At times, the most effective intervention on behalf of the child is to provide supportive services to the parents or caregivers. Successful grief interventions, therefore, must combine developmental knowledge of children and adolescents as well as a thorough assessment of the child's family situation. This person-in-environment framework allows practitioners to identify the internal and external strengths of the child and family to subsequently guide interventions.

Developmental Stages of Children with Death-Related Bereavement

The manner in which children process death and other losses varies depending on their developmental stage (Corr et al., 1994; Silverman & Worden, 1992). A child's ability to fully understand death is related to his or her capacity for abstract thinking in five areas: (1) the concept that all living things have a limited life span and will eventually die; (2) the notion that death is final and irreversible; (3) the idea that a deceased person's cognitive, emotional, and physical functioning end at the time of death; (4) understanding the potential causes of death, such as an accident, illness, or aging; and (5) the concept that relates to spirituality and the ability to mentally and emotionally conceptualize the post-death experience of the deceased. This construct is the basis for belief systems that describe the afterlife notions of heaven, hell, or reincarnation. This could also include beliefs that spirits of the deceased reside with us or that there is no life after death (Webb, 2002). A child's cognitive, social, and emotional development has an impact on the extent to which he or she can fully internalize these abstract ideas and subsequently influences his or her reaction to death.

Developmental Perspectives on Death

The loss of a central caregiver in the early stages of development (birth to two years) can significantly affect the infant's sense of safety and security in the world. Such a loss has the potential for the development of attachment disorders and can delay social, emotional, and cognitive development (Bowlby, 1980). In the early years, a sense of security is established by consistency and predictability in the environment. When this secure environment is disrupted by the death of a caregiver, the child may develop a variety of symptoms such as crying, writhing, rocking, biting, and other anxious behaviors (Norris-Shortle, Young, & Williams, 1993). The perception of emotional or physical abandonment during this stage of development can lead to attachment and relationship difficulties as an adult (Masterson, 1988). An inherent strength of this age is the ability to form new attachments. Infants who receive consistent caregiving are able to overcome loss and continue to grow and develop in a healthy manner. The instinctive will of infants to survive fosters resilience that enables them to recover from loss.

Children between the ages of two and five years (the second stage of development) perceive death to be a temporary condition that is reversible. Death is similar to an interruption in the daily routine, much like sleeping or being away on a trip. The child's inability to grasp the permanence of death can lead to hopes and expectations that the deceased will return. In the absence of the deceased, children often feel sad, anxious, insecure, and angry. Due to the egocentrism inherent to children of this age, they may believe that they are somehow responsible for the death or the emotional state of their family (Norris-Shortle et al., 1993). While some children may display no obvious symptoms of their grief, others may regress to an earlier stage of development. It is not unusual for children to be playing in the yard and laughing with their siblings and friends shortly following a death. On the other hand, these same children may have difficulty sleeping, cry for no apparent reason, and cling excessively to a caregiver. Other symptoms of mourning may include bedwetting, temper tantrums, and excessive whining. At this age a child's primary method of expression is play (Essa & Murray, 1994; Webb, 2002). A four-year-old whose younger brother had died in a car accident was observed digging holes and burying her boy dolls in the sandbox. Such death games are not uncommon or unhealthy for children of this age (Corr et al., 1994). Children between the ages of two and five are able to communicate their inner experience through their ability to imaginatively play and act out their feelings. They are also able to verbalize their needs and desires. These strengths provide adults with important information that can be used to help them with their grief. Again, this age group responds well to consistent nurturance and care, allowing them to successfully adapt to loss.

During the third stage of development, children between the ages of six and nine are able to comprehend the finality of death. Children of this age also begin to show a marked interest in the physiological death of the body. Fears about their own death or the death of a parent may develop. They may be reluctant to separate from caregivers due to feelings of insecurity. A child may be hyperactive, aggressive, and distracted or alternately withdrawn, sad, and despondent. It is important for practitioners to understand the grief-related nature of these symptoms and not to prematurely diagnose a more severe disorder such as ADHD or depressive disorder. At this age, a child may experience sleeping difficulties including nightmares or night terrors as well as regressive behaviors commonly noted in earlier stages of development (Essa & Murray, 1994; Webb, 2002). Elementary school–aged children are both industrious and constructive. They flourish in their ability to solve problems. In addition, they are able to use their intellect and creativity to master novel situations and tasks. The ability to empathize is an additional strength that develops at this age. These assets allow them to actively participate in their adjustment to a loss, engage in the therapeutic process, and successfully regulate the emotional upheaval that accompanies grief.

During the fourth stage of development, children between the ages of nine and twelve understand the universality and finality of death. They recognize that death is out of their control and that it has a profound impact on a family's functioning. Fears about their primary caregiver dying are exacerbated by the physical and hormonal changes characteristic of puberty. While desiring to be strong and in control of their emotions, the fluctuating mood states common to preadolescents makes it difficult for them to master these feelings. Due to their need to blend in with their peer group, preteens may feel very vulnerable. The loss of a loved one can create feelings of social isolation, loneliness, fear, confusion, and guilt. A pervasive sense of self-consciousness, common at this age, is amplified by the death of a loved one (Essa & Murray, 1994; Webb, 2002; Worden & Silverman, 1996). Children in this age group have the ability to set and achieve goals for themselves. They become capable of understanding abstract concepts such as freedom, morality, spirituality, and ethics. Their developed sense of conscience allows them to monitor and modify their behavior. With a new sense of insight they are able to understand how their feelings are connected to their behavior. Practitioners can build on this strength to assist them to control impulsive and potentially disruptive behavior patterns. At this developmental stage, children can learn life-enhancing methods for coping with loss and grief.

As children enter the world of adolescence, between the ages of thirteen and nineteen, their primary concern is to be accepted by their peer group. They may, therefore, be resistant to openly expressing mourning in the presence of close friends and family for fear of appearing weak and losing control (Rheingold et al., 2003; Ringler & Hayden, 2000). Adolescents may disguise their grief in high-risk behaviors such as using alcohol and drugs, staying out late, defying authority, skipping school, unsafe driving, and sexual promiscuity (Fleming & Balmer, 1996). While these behaviors may be exhibited often in adolescents, for teens who are mourning, they often represent a fervent need to avoid negative emotions. Bereaved teenagers may present a protective barrier of anger and withdrawal that may be difficult for a practitioner to overcome. Given the fact that adolescents are in the midst of developing their own unique identities, they have a strong internal focus and a necessary self-centeredness. These tendencies may result in feeling closely connected to the cause of death and their inability to prevent it. Thus, adolescents may assume unfounded guilt and responsibility for the death. Because adolescents can comprehend death's finality, they may experience intense sadness, confusion, worry, guilt, loneliness, and isolation (Corr et al., 1994). Bereaved adolescents may become more easily distracted, experience sleeping and eating disturbances, perform better or worse in school, and display strong emotional lability (Balk,

1983). One study indicated that an adolescent's self-concept can diminish after a death (Fleming & Balmer, 1996). Other research has shown that even two years following a death, the adolescent may experience PTSD symptoms such as shock and numbness, anxiety, depression, loneliness, and anger (Brown & Goodman, 2005).

Teenagers, like adults, may experience denial of the loss for months or years after the death (Rando, 1993). In contrast with society's stereotype of adolescents as being innately pathological, research indicates that most adolescents who lose a loved one will, in actuality, achieve greater maturity because of the loss (Fleming & Balmer, 1996). The negative stereotyping adolescents experience makes the strengths-based approach to grief and loss especially effective when working with them. During this developmental stage, adolescents' ability to fully comprehend the finality of death allows them to apply life-enhancing coping skills during the bereavement process. In addition, adolescents are able to create and develop unique ways of coping that can be most beneficial to them. Due to their greater sense of independence, practitioners can allow adolescents to be more active and directive in the therapeutic process. Adolescents are able to use grief counseling to make meaning of the loss and incorporate the experience into their lives. Adolescents may also use therapists as role models, which aids the process of identity formation and self-esteem. The importance of peers can potentially be a source of support and strength for bereaved adolescents. This reservoir of strength enables adolescents to make productive use of therapeutic interventions that can lead to successful outcomes. When adolescents are able to effectively use life-enhancing coping skills, it can produce a life-changing experience that has far-reaching ramifications for their future adult lives.

Grief Reactions to Non-Death Losses

The grief reactions of children and adolescents experiencing non-death-related losses may be similar to those who are mourning a death. Non-death losses may have either a minor or major impact on the child's emotional well-being. Non-death losses may range from a change in residence to a family divorce. While some losses may be quite tangible, other losses may be abstract and difficult to comprehend for the child. Major losses may also occur that are unexpected and traumatic. For example, an expected change in schools may elicit temporary grief reactions from a child or teen until they acclimate to the new school environment and make new friends. On the other hand, a parental divorce may be experienced as the death of a family member, even though all members are still living. This type of ambiguous loss can complicate the grieving process and make adjustment to the new reality difficult to achieve. Practitioners can refer to the earlier information provided on grief reactions in children to inform the assessment of a child experiencing non-death-related losses.

Strengths in Children and Adolescents

As stated in the strengths-based framework of grief, all individuals are endowed with individual and environmental strengths. Children and adolescents are no exception to this rule. In fact, the numerous internal and external strengths in children and adolescents can be beneficial resources at a time when they are facing the adversity of a significant loss.

In an international research study called the International Resilience Project, researchers studied resilience in children and families from thirty countries around the globe. From this large-scale research project, Grotberg (1997) uncovered twenty-six strengths that were most frequently identified as contributing to resilience among children. Some of the individual strengths that were identified included "[a] sense of being loveable, autonomy, self-esteem, hope and faith and trust, and locus of control," in addition to possessing skillfulness with "communication, problem-solving, and impulse control" (p. 6). Some of the environmental strengths, or resilience factors, that were identified included "trusting relationships, structure and rules at home, parental encouragement of autonomy, and role models" (p. 6). Many other strengths can be found in children and adolescents depending on their unique situations and personalities. From this study, Grotberg developed a practical method for classifying internal and external strengths and resources that children can readily understand. For external supports and resources that a child can access, Grotberg uses the term "I HAVE." For internal strengths, she uses the term "I AM." These inner strengths include confidence, self-esteem, and responsibility. For social skills, she uses the term "I CAN," which refers to both interpersonal and problem-solving skills. These three components of resilience correspond to Erickson's stages of development, specifically trust, autonomy, identity, initiative, and industry. Children can be aided in consciously exploring the different components of resilience. For example, the more things a child can identify under the categories "I HAVE," "I AM," and "I CAN," the more equipped they will be to deal with the death of a loved one. Table 2.1 shows some examples of how a child's strengths can be viewed using Grotberg's components of resilience.

Using this paradigm, the counselor and the child or adolescent can effectively work together to identify and enhance the child's internal

TABLE 2.1
Internal and External Strengths, Supports, and Resources

Erickson's Stage of Development	Grotberg's Component of Resilience	Examples
Trust	I HAVE	• Caregivers with unconditional love for me • Appropriate role models • Caring mentors • People who structure my environment • People who help me stay safe • People who want me to be independent
Autonomy and Identity	I AM	• A loveable person • A caring person • A person who respects myself and others • A person who takes responsibility for my actions • Hopeful for the future
Initiative and Industry	I CAN	• Find someone to talk to about my feelings • Find solutions to my problems • Exhibit self-control • Talk to someone who can help me

and external strengths and resources (taken from Pomeroy & Garcia, 2009).

To illustrate this paradigm, the following list was created by ten-year-old Tommy and his counselor after the death of his younger sister. During the sessions, the counselor and Tommy would add to this list. By the end of their work together, the list was completed as shown on p. 24.

At the end of each session, the counselor made a copy for Tommy to take home and post in his room. The counselor suggested that between sessions Tommy think about other things he could add to the list as well as keep a record of times that he used or practiced one of his strengths. As a result of this intervention, Tommy's resilience was strengthened and he was able to cope more effectively with the loss of his sister as well as his parents' grief.

Assessing Grief in Children

An accurate assessment of bereaved children and adolescents must include information from a variety of sources. While obtaining detailed

I HAVE	I AM	I CAN
A best friend	Determined to get through this	Ask Mom for time to play with me
Two parents who love me	A good friend	Tell people to stop asking me questions
A teacher who cares	Kind to my parents, friends, and pets	Kick the soccer ball in my yard
A soccer team	A person who tries hard and doesn't give up	Call a friend to come over and play
A basketball hoop	A person who will always love and remember my sister	Play video games
My dog, Rocky	A smart person	Ask my teacher for help

information from a young child is unlikely, collaborative resources can provide important and accurate information about the loss and the problems the child may be experiencing. Relevant data can be gleaned from parents or caregivers, medical and school personnel, and other adults who have central involvement in the child's life (e.g., an aunt who provides after-school child care). Three primary elements in grief assessment of a child were identified by Webb (1996). The individual child's level of functioning, the factors related to the death, and the child's support system are all key components of a grief assessment (see the Psychosocial Assessment Interview Guide later in this chapter). Initially, the practitioner wants to gather as much information as possible from the youth's parents or caregivers. This may be done over the first few sessions of counseling. Older children and adolescents may also be able to provide salient information.

If the youth is complaining of physical symptoms, a physician's referral is warranted prior to the beginning of therapy. It is recommended that the practitioner form a collaborative relationship with the youth's physician regardless of the presenting problems. If the need should arise for medical intervention, the relationship with the medical professional will have already been established. For example, a young child who presents with encopresis may have a medical problem and should be thoroughly assessed by a physician before determining that it is likely due to regression associated with loss.

Conducting an assessment with children under age thirteen most often involves play and activity therapy in order to access and observe the child's feelings and behaviors. Through various activities, such as drawing pictures of family, home, or a favorite activity, the practitioner opens the door for conversation regarding the child's experiences and relationships (Webb, 1996). The practitioner may utilize a variety of techniques in eliciting the child's feelings and perceptions. For example, some children are unable to articulate their feelings with words and need assistance developing a vocabulary for emotions. Pictures of faces that display varied emotions as well as stories about feelings may be useful in this regard. Other children need time to direct their own play before engaging in a therapeutic activity. While some children naturally make use of the available supplies in a therapeutic manner, other children require the practitioner to provide structure and direction. Practitioners should investigate the variety of published play therapy resources such as books on play therapy, games, and art projects.

Older children often possess a great deal of insight and understanding of their experience of loss. However, practitioners must develop a safe working relationship before expecting the older child to share this information. For adolescents, assessment should include perceptions of self-concept; levels of distress, anxiety, and depression; degree of loneliness; and presence of anger responses (Fleming & Balmer, 1996). For older children, practitioners should also seek to know their feelings about seeing a practitioner, their interpretation of the loss, and its impact on their ability to function. Teens often converse more easily when simultaneously involved with another activity. This may take the form of going for a walk, engaging in a board game, making something with their hands, or listening to music. In general, older children and teens are better able to express their feelings verbally if the practitioner establishes good rapport.

Grieving Children and Mental Health Issues

Due to the variety of grief reactions in children, practitioners must be astute in differentiating between grief reactions and the possibility of a more pervasive mental disorder. Symptoms of grief can mimic other emotional or behavioral disorders. However, the etiology of the symptoms is quite different. While the symptoms of mental health disorders will remain consistent over time, grief reactions in children often ebb and flow from one day to the next. On the other hand, children with emotional disorders may also experience bereavement, which can complicate the assessment and diagnostic process. For example, children are often mistakenly diagnosed with ADHD for hyperactivity, inability to focus attention, impulsivity, learning difficulties, and excessive distractibility. These symptoms, however, are also common among children who have experienced a recent loss of a loved one. Failure to recognize the context of such behavior can lead to a misdiagnosis and potentially harmful interventions. However, children who have previously been diagnosed with ADHD may also experience a grief reaction in which their ADHD symptoms are temporarily intensified. With some children it may be unclear if the behavior is caused solely by grief or if there is also an underlying mental health issue. Furthermore, it may be impossible to discern the causative factors for the emotional or behavioral symptoms with which a child presents. In these cases, it is important to obtain as much information from collaborative sources as possible. When the child has experienced a loss, it is prudent to delay diagnosing the child until grief symptoms have abated. Many times, the behavioral manifestation of grief will gradually diminish as children begin to adjust to the loss. As the grief reactions subside, it will become clearer if there are additional mental health issues that require attention.

Lucy is a six-year-old first-grader who was referred by her teacher for counseling. During the first session, she jumped on the therapist's couch, pulled out every stuffed animal from the cabinet, and threw them on the floor. She quickly moved to the top of the desk, where she grabbed the stapler and began stapling all the paper within reach. The therapist tried to engage her in conversation about school, but she often changed the subject and told the therapist that she wanted to play a game. Halfway through the game, she lost interest and grabbed another toy from the shelf and began turning like a top on the floor. After twenty-five minutes of frantic activity, the therapist decided to talk to Lucy's parents, who were in the waiting room. While Lucy's grandmother watched her in the waiting room, the parents described the traumatic event that led up to the death of Lucy's little sister. The parents divulged that Lucy's aunt was driving Lucy and her sister Dolly to a birthday party when she was hit by a drunk driver in a head-on collision. Dolly was bent over Lucy's lap when the ambulance arrived. Lucy has insisted that Dolly will be coming home from the hospital since she saw Dolly taken away by ambulance. In addition, her aunt was seriously injured and spent several weeks in the hospital but was recently discharged. Lucy has asked her aunt several times if Dolly was coming home, too. In the past month, Lucy's activity level has been highly elevated, and she had difficulty eating and sleeping. When her behavior becomes unmanageable and the parents administer consequences, Lucy dissolves into insatiable tears. In a discussion with Lucy's teacher, she suggested that the parents have Lucy evaluated for ADHD and possible medication. The parents state that they are experiencing shock and grief themselves and do not know how to help Lucy. After inquiring about previous functioning, the therapist recommends that Lucy continue in counseling for several weeks in order to conduct a thorough evaluation. The parents agree to wait before pursuing an

ADHD diagnosis since Lucy's well-child check prior to the accident was normal. As Lucy's therapy progressed, her level of activity slowed, and she was able to converse openly with the therapist. By the fifth session, Lucy began the session by asking the therapist if she knew what happened to her sister. The therapist acknowledged that she knew and asked Lucy if she understood what had happened to Dolly. Lucy told the therapist that Dolly was "living with the angels" and that she missed her. After several more sessions, it was clear that Lucy's initial emotional and behavioral functioning resulted from her grief reactions and that she clearly did not have ADHD.

Assessment Interviewing

For children and adolescents, the assessment process can take a variety of forms. One crucial element of the assessment is information obtained from the youth's parents and caregivers. This data is most often gathered through a semi-structured interview. The following guide outlines the types of information that can be useful for the practitioner working with bereaved youth. Depending on the situation and the age of the youth, some of the questions are more appropriate to ask of the parents or caregivers, while some can be asked directly of the youth, using age-appropriate language. Though the information is organized into logical sections, practitioners can use the assessment as an opportunity to build rapport with youths and their caregivers by making inquiries in a more relaxed, conversational manner. This outline, therefore, should not be used as an interview script, but as a model for the type and breadth of information that can inform interventions. In most cases, it is not possible to gather all relevant information in the initial interview. The assessment phase, therefore, may span several sessions and should continually inform interventions.

Very often a child's play or the manner in which he or she completes a therapeutic activity informs the assessment and provides clues to the kinds of information listed in this section. For example, in one case a seven-year-old boy, Joey, came to counseling after the death of his younger brother in a car accident. The mother stated that Joey got extremely upset and anxious whenever he was not with her, even if she was in another room in the home. While playing with the dollhouse and family figures, the therapist uncovered Joey's fear of his mother going to the garage to do the laundry. Upon further exploration, it became clear that Joey feared his mother would be hit by a car if she was in the garage where the laundry was done. By using the dollhouse activity, Joey was able to demonstrate his fear to the therapist even though he was unable to articulate his feelings. Observing children and family

members' body language, communication style, and patterns of interaction also provides assessment data. Practitioners should always be
mindful of the possibility that cultural differences may influence such
interactions.

Psychosocial Assessment of Grief, Loss, and Mourning

I. Descriptive and Identifying Information
   1. Name of youth
   2. Name of parent(s)/guardian(s)
   3. Address
   4. Home phone number
   5. Work phone number
   6. Date of birth of youth
   7. School grade
   8. Occupation of parent(s)/caregiver(s)
   9. Family income
   10. Youth's gender
   11. Family ethnicity
   12. Dress and appearance of child
   13. Dress and appearance of parent(s)/caregiver(s)
   14. Parents' marital/relationship status
   15. Living arrangements (include names and relationship to
       client)
   16. Religious background of family, level of involvement with a
       faith community
   17. Who do parents/caregivers rely on for support (e.g.,
       emotional, financial, childcare)?
   18. Prior losses
   19. Identified current losses

II. Description of Pre-Loss Functioning
   1. Pre-loss problems or issues
      A. Did the youth experience other psychological or
         relationship issues before the loss?
      B. For how long have the issues existed?
      C. What attempts have been made to resolve the issues? If
         it is a recurring problem, what seemed to help resolve it
         in the past?
      D. What kind of resources does the youth/family have to
         help resolve the problem? Has the family sought or
         received any treatment for this problem?
      E. Why is the youth/family seeking help now?

III. Developmental Status
   1. Cognitive functioning
      A. Does the youth exhibit normal intellectual functioning for his or her age?
      B. Has the youth been tested for cognitive abilities? If so, when, by whom, and what were the outcomes?
      C. Does the family report any developmental delays for the youth?
   2. Emotional functioning
      A. What emotions are evident for the youth in relation to the loss?
      B. How has the youth been feeling and behaving the majority of time over the past year?
      C. Has the youth's current emotional state created difficulties for the youth recently? Over the past year?
      D. How stable are the youth's emotions during the interview?
      E. Is the youth able to articulate his or her feelings in some manner?
   3. Physical functioning/medical history
      A. Does the youth's level of energy or activity seem unusual (e.g., lethargy or hyperactivity)?
      B. Does the youth display any odd or peculiar motor behaviors (e.g., motor and/or vocal tics, mannerisms, or stereotypical movements)?
      C. Does the youth have any medical conditions or problems?
      D. Has the youth been examined by a physician during the past year? What were the results of the exam?
      E. Does the youth take any prescription medications for current ailments?
      F. Does the youth take any over-the-counter (OTC) medications on a regular basis?
      G. Has the youth ever had any psychological or mental health–related treatment in the past (including inpatient, outpatient, and/or psychotropic medications)? If so, describe in detail.
      H. Does the youth present with any disabilities?
   4. Substance use
      A. Does the youth use alcohol? If so, what kind? How often?
      B. Does the youth use any other substances?
      C. Has the youth experienced any social, occupational, or legal problems associated with his or her use of alcohol and/or other drugs?

      D. Has anyone ever encouraged the youth to stop or cut back his or her use of substances?

      E. Has the youth ever been treated for a drug or alcohol problem?

      F. Do any members of the youth's household use substances? If so, describe.

IV. Relational Functioning
1. Family
      B. Who lives with the youth? What are their ages and relation to the youth?
      C. What is the youth's relationship with other family members?
      D. Who provides parenting/caregiving for the youth on a daily basis?
      E. Does the youth's presenting problem involve other family members?
      F. Is there any history of family problems? Have any family members had problems similar to the youth's current situation?
      G. Would family members be willing to participate in counseling?
2. Social support system
      A. Does the youth have close friends and/or acquaintances?
      B. Is the youth involved in a romantic relationship? If yes, describe.
      C. What is the quality of these relationships?
      D. Does the youth feel that these are supportive relationships?
      E. Are any members of his or her social support system involved in the presenting problem?
3. Spirituality
      A. Does the youth have a spiritual belief system?
      B. If so, how does this belief system impact the youth's life?

V. School/Occupational Functioning
1. School
      A. In what setting is the youth educated (e.g., preschool, public school, religious school, homebound, dropped out)?
      B. How does the youth perform academically?
      C. How does the youth feel about school?
      D. Does the youth experience difficulties regarding his or her education? If so, describe.

      E. Does the youth's presenting problem affect his or her education?

  2. Employment
      A. Is the youth employed? Unemployed?
      B. If so, where is the youth employed? Full-time? Part-time?
      C. Does the youth's presenting problem affect his or her job?

VI. Legal Problems
  1. Does the youth/family have current problems with the legal system?
  2. If so, what type of problems?
  3. Has the youth had any history of problems with the legal system?
  4. If so, what type of problems?
  5. Has the youth ever been convicted of a crime?

VII. Diversity Dynamics
  1. What is the youth's ethnicity? What is the family's ethnicity?
  2. What is the youth's nationality? If relevant, immigration status?
  3. How acculturated does the youth appear to be?
  4. What is the youth's first language? Second? Third?
  5. What are some of the family's beliefs about issues of grief and loss?
  6. Does the youth/family engage in any religious or spiritual practices?
  7. Has the youth discussed his or her sexual orientation?
  8. Does the youth/family utilize any cultural resources?
  9. Does the youth/family perceive barriers to accessing resources?

VIII. Youth's Strengths and Resources
  1. What are the youth's individual strengths?
  2. What are the youth's environmental strengths?
  3. How can these strengths be utilized to assist the youth/family in resolving the current issues?
  4. What life-enhancing versus life-depleting grief symptoms does the youth exhibit?
  5. What life-enhancing versus life-depleting coping skills does the youth's family/caregivers exhibit?
  6. What resources does the youth/family have that could be utilized to enhance coping?

      7. What agency or community resources could be utilized to intervene with the youth?

IX. The Loss Experience
    1. Has the family accurately informed the youth about the loss?
    2. Is the youth able to describe the circumstances of the loss? If so, to what level of detail?
    3. Was the loss expected? Sudden? Accidental?
    4. How did the youth find out about the loss?
    5. How did the youth react upon learning about the loss?
    6. In your opinion, was the loss inevitable? Preventable? What is the youth's perception of this?
    7. What was it like in the household and for the youth in the first hours/days/weeks after the loss?
    8. Has the youth expressed any strong feelings regarding the loss?

X. Understanding the Meaning of the Loss
    1. Tell me about the person/object/situation that is now gone.
    2. Tell me about your connection with the person/object/situation that was lost.
    3. Can you tell me what's missing in your life now that the loss has occurred?
    4. What kinds of changes have occurred in your life since the loss event?
    5. Has anything positive come out of this experience for you?
    6. Other areas to explore
       A. Can you tell me about the role that the person/object/situation played in your life?
       B. Have you experienced other losses since this one?
       C. What are some of your positive memories about _____?
       D. What are some of your less pleasant memories about _____?
       E. Can the youth articulate any deeper meaning regarding the impact of the loss on his or her life?
       F. Do you think about things you could do or say to the loved one that you have lost?

XI. Emotional and Behavioral Changes and Coping Strategies
    1. Tell me about your mood/feelings since the loss.
    2. Have you noticed any physical or behavioral changes since the loss?
    3. How has the youth been coping since the loss?
    4. What seems to have been most helpful to the youth?

5. What seems to have been unhelpful or harmful to the youth?
6. What has been the most difficult part of the loss?
7. To parents: What has been the most difficult parenting challenge since the loss?
8. What is your primary concern for the youth at this point?
9. To youth: What questions do you have about the loss?
10. To youth: What worries do you have since the loss event occurred?

XII. Social Support Systems Related to the Loss
1. How have others responded to the youth's loss?
2. How have they responded to the youth's grief reactions?
3. Does the youth have friends who have experienced similar losses?
4. How have the responses of others impacted the youth?
5. Have you been able to ask your friends and family for help when you need it? How has that felt to you?
6. What kind of support would be helpful to you right now?

XIII. Current Attachment to the Loss
1. Have you had any dreams or experiences in connection with the loss?
2. How do you feel when you encounter reminders of the loss?

XIV. Other Areas to Explore
1. How long have you been having feelings of grief?
2. How intense are your feelings of grief? Are they constant? Do they come and go throughout the day/week?
3. How has the family adjusted to the loss, incorporated it into its life?
4. Does the family talk openly about the loss?
5. How central to your life is your experience of grief right now?

XV. Other Loss Experiences
1. What other losses have you experienced in your life?
2. How did these losses affect you?
3. How did you cope with these losses?

XVI. Understanding of Grief from the Family's Cultural Perspective
1. What is your family's grief culture?
2. What are some of your family's rituals around loss?
3. How does your family's spiritual traditions affect your grief reactions?

    4. Are there specific roles that family members play when someone dies?

    5. Are there specific family values that have impacted you during this grief experience?

    6. How are you similar to and different from your family in the way you express grief?

    7. What are some of the spoken and unspoken rules about behaviors related to the bereavement period and the loss?

    8. How have your cultural and/or spiritual experiences influenced your grief experiences?

    9. Are there other topics that we need to discuss further?

Adapted and modified from Rando (1993).

Grief Assessment with Children
Using Standardized Instruments

Although there are several assessment instruments to assess grief in adults, there are few, if any, standardized instruments to measure grief in children and adolescents. Freeman, Fisher, and Abramovitz (1997) stated that this lack of standardized measures has hindered our understanding of grief in children. Therefore, you may want to use instruments that measure symptoms associated with grief. The following section will provide examples of some of the more common assessment instruments that could be used with bereaved children and adolescents. However, there are literally hundreds of scales that address specific issues relevant to this age group.

The Hogan Sibling Inventory of Bereavement (Hogan, 1990) was developed for adolescents who have lost a sister or brother. Its primary use has been for siblings whose brother or sister died following an extended illness. It has not been used in the case of sudden or unexpected death. There are no known reliability or validity studies of this instrument.

The W. T. Grant Inventory (Clark, Pynoos, & Goebel, 1994) is an instrument that was developed by a collaboration of experts in the field of childhood bereavement. Scale development resulted in four major factors identified, including avoidance, identification, affective compensation, and anticipated neediness. Studies of the reliability and validity of the instrument are underway (Freeman et al., 1997).

The Child Behavior Checklist (CBCL) (Achenbach & Edelbrock, 1983) is a self-report instrument that parents complete by reporting their observations of their child's behavior. It is appropriate for use with children four through sixteen years old. It contains 118 items that refer to specific behavioral and emotional issues, as well as two open-ended items that can be used for describing other difficulties. In addition, the social competence subscale contains up to forty items measuring the degree and quality of the child's involvement with sports, family, organizations, school, and other extracurricular activities.

The CBCL is considered one of the best scales available due to its magnitude, diversity of items, standardization, reliability, and validity (Rubin & Babbie, 2001). The scale was normed on 2,368 children in the given age range. It has a one-week test-retest reliability of .93 as well as inter-parent agreement of r = .985 for total behavioral problems and .978 for total social competencies. Studies indicate that the CBCL has internal consistency with an r = .87 (Walker, Garber, & Greene, 1991). There are profiles and specific forms of the scale for children by gender and for ages four to five, six to eleven, and twelve to sixteen (Achenbach & Edelbrock, 1983). For children under the age of four, there is the CBCL/1–5 form. The forms can be hand scored or computer scored.

The Beck Depression Inventory for Youth is the child version of the well-known Beck Depression Inventory for Adults. It is compatible with the *DSM-IV-TR* and is a twenty-item scale reflecting children's feelings of sadness, self-perceived behaviors, and negative thoughts. The inventory screens for feelings of hopelessness and suicidal ideation and is useful in clinical and school settings. It is written at the second-grade reading level (Beck, Beck, & Jolly, 2001).

Many times bereaved children also experience a lowering of self-concept and self-esteem as a result of the loss. The Piers-Harris Children's Self-Concept Scale (Piers, 1984) measures the child's own perceptions of functioning in a variety of areas such as appearance, popularity, intellectual and behavioral functioning, school functioning, and anxiety. It is an eighty-item scale with declarative statements that the child marks "yes" or "no." The instrument can be used for children ages eight to eighteen. It is designed for children with a third-grade reading level; however, for younger children, grades three to six, the administrator reads each statement aloud to the child.

This instrument has been shown to have test-retest reliabilities of .62 to .96. The internal consistency of the scale is high with alpha coefficients of .90 to .91. Studies concerning the validity of the scale indicate positive correlations between the child's self-concept and school achievement and healthy peer relationships (Kanoy, Johnson, & Kanoy, 1980; Mannarino, 1978). The scale can be obtained from Western Psychological Services and can be computerized or hand scored.

For younger children, the Hopelessness Scale for Children (HSC) (Kazdin, French, Esvelt-Dawson, & Sherick, 1983) is designed to measure thoughts concerning hopelessness, depression, and suicidal ideation (Fischer & Corcoran, 1994). Seventeen true/false statements assess the child's level of depression as well as his or her self-esteem. It can be used with children who are seven years old and older. Although reliability coefficient alphas of .70 and .71 are considered only fair, they are within the acceptable range for children's instruments. Studies have indicated that the scale can discriminate between suicidal and non-suicidal children.

Summary

Understanding bereaved children and adolescents necessitates knowledge of how grief is perceived at different developmental stages. This competency provides the context for assessing bereaved youth and a framework for guiding interventions. The psychosocial Grief Assessment Interview Guide ensures that the practitioner considers all the potential areas of a child's life that may be affected by grief and loss. Given the multitude of circumstances and situations in which a practitioner encounters children and adolescents, grief assessment and interventions may vary depending on the setting. While this chapter provides a framework for grief assessment with children and adolescents, the following chapters examine how this knowledge can be usefully applied to particular losses and settings. In addition, grief and loss interventions tailored to the various types of losses will be outlined.

References

Achenbach, T. M., & Edelbrock, C. S. (1983). *Manual for the child behavior checklist and the revised child behavior profile.* Burlington, VT: University Associates in Psychiatry.

Baker, J. E., Sedney, M. A., & Gross, E. (1992). Psychological tasks for bereaved children. *American Journal of Orthopsychiatry, 62*(1), 105–116.

Balk, D. E. (1983). Adolescents' grief reactions and self-concept perceptions following sibling death: A case study of 33 teenagers. *Journal of Youth and Adolescence, 12,* 137–161.

Beck, J. S., Beck, A. T., & Jolly, J. B. (2001). *Beck youth depression inventory.* San Antonio, TX: Psychological Corporation.

Bowlby, J. (1980). *Attachment and loss* (Vol. 3: Loss, sadness, and depression). New York: Basic Books.

Brown, E. J., & Goodman, R. F. (2005). Childhood traumatic grief: An exploration of the construct in children bereaved on September 11th. *Journal of Clinical Child and Adolescent Psychology, 34*(2), 248–259.

Corr, C. A., Nabe, C. M., Corr, D. M. (1994). *Death and dying, life and living.* Pacific Grove, CA: Brooks/Cole.

Clark, D. C., Pynoos, R. S., & Goebel, A. E. (1994). Mechanisms and processes of adolescent bereavement. In R. J. Haggerty, L. R. Sherrod, N. Garmezy, & M.

Rutter (Eds.), *Stress, risk, and resilience* (pp. 100–146). New York: Cambridge University Press.

Essa, E. L., & Murray, C. I. (1994). Research in review: Young children's understanding and experience with death. *Young Children, 49,* 74–81.

Fischer, J., & Corcoran, K. (1994). *Measures for clinical practice: A sourcebook.* (2nd ed.). New York: Free Press.

Fleming, S., & Balmer, L. (1996). Bereavement in adolescence. In C. Corr & D. Balk (Eds.), *Handbook of adolescent death and bereavement* (pp. 139–172). New York: Springer Publishing.

Freeman, L. N., Fischer, P., & Abramovitz, R. (1997). Defining grief in childhood: Test-retest reliability of the W. T. Grant childhood consortium grief inventory. Retrieved December 18, 2007, from http://www.columbia.edu/cu/csswp/research/current/grief.htm.

Grotberg, E. (1997). The international resilience project: Findings from the research and the effectiveness of interventions. Retrieved September 10, 2007, from http://resilnet.uiuc.edu/library/grotb97a.html.

Hogan, N. (1990). Hogan Sibling Inventory of Bereavement. In J. Touliatos, B. Permutter, & M. Strauss (Eds.), *Handbook of family measurement techniques* (p. 524). Newbury Park, CA: Sage Press.

Kanoy, R. C., Johnson, B. W., & Kanoy, K. W. (1980). Locus of control and self-concept in achieving and underachieving bright elementary students. *Psychology in Schools, 17,* 395–399.

Kazdin, A. E., French, N. H., Esveldt-Dawson, K., & Sherick, R. B. (1983). Hopelessness, depression, and suicidal intent among psychiatrically disturbed inpatient children. *Journal of Consulting and Clinical Psychology, 51,* 504–510.

Mannarino, A. P. (1978). Friendship patterns and self-concept development in preadolescent males. *Journal of Genetic Psychology, 113,* 105–110.

Masterson, J. F. (1988). *The search for the real self: Unmasking the personality disorders of our age.* New York: Free Press.

Norris-Shortle, C., Young, P. A., & Williams, M. A. (1993). Understanding death and grief for children three and younger. *Social Work, 38*(6), 736–742.

Piers, E. V. (1984). *Revised manual for the Piers-Harris Children's Self-Concept Scale.* Los Angeles, CA: Western Psychological Services.

Pomeroy, B. C., & Garcia, R. B. (2009). *The grief assessment and intervention workbook: A strengths perspective.* Belmont, CA: Brooks/Cole, Cengage Learning.

Rando, T. A. (1993). *Treatment of complicated mourning.* Champaign, IL: Research Press.

Rheingold, A. A., Smith, D. W., Ruggiero, K. J., Saunders, B. E., Kilpatrick, D. G., & Resnick, H. S. (2003). Loss, trauma, exposure, and mental health in a representative sample of 12–17-year-old youth: Data from the National Survey of Adolescents. *Journal of Loss and Trauma, 9,* 10–19.

Ringler, L. L., & Hayden, D. C. (2000). Adolescent bereavement and social support: Peer loss compared to other losses. *Journal of Adolescent Research, 15*(2), 209–230.

Rubin, A., & Babbie, E. (2001). *Research methods for social work* (4th ed.). Belmont, CA: Wadsworth/Thomson Learning.

Silverman, P. R., & Worden, J. W. (1992). Children and parental death. *American Journal of Orthopsychiatry, 62,* 93–104.

Walker, L. S., Garber, J., & Greene, J. W. (1991). Somatization symptoms in pediatric abdominal pain patients: Relation to chronicity of abdominal pain and parent somatization. *Journal of Abnormal Child Psychology, 19,* 379–394.

Webb, N. B. (1996). *Social work practice with children.* New York: Guilford Press.

Webb, N. B. (2002). *Helping bereaved children: A handbook for practitioners.* New York: Guilford Press.

Wolfelt, A. (1991). *A child's view of grief* [video]. Fort Collins, CO: Center for Loss and Life Transition.

Worden, J. W., & Silverman, P. S. (1996). Parental death and the adjustment of school-age children. *Omega, 33*(2), 91–102.

CHAPTER THREE

Grief and Loss for Children in Foster Care, Adoption, and Residential Treatment Settings

Tamara Linseisen, Elizabeth C. Pomeroy, and Renée Bradford Garcia

Six-year-old Jessica walked with her caseworker, Miss Lynn, up to the door of a house she had never seen before. A woman answered the door, and Miss Lynn said, "Jessica, this is Ms. Bowman, your new foster care mother." *I don't want a new foster care mother*, Jessica thought to herself. *I just want my mom!* Ms. Bowman leaned down and held out her hand to Jessica. Her white teeth shone in her big smile. "Hi Jessica!" she said in a happy sing-song voice, "Welcome to our home!" Jessica inched closer to Miss Lynn. "Go on, sweetie. It's okay," Miss Lynn said gently.

Ms. Bowman showed Jessica her room and explained that she would be sharing it with another foster child who was currently at school. Miss Lynn and Ms. Bowman talked about "appointments," "placements," "evaluations," and shuffled papers while Jessica slowly took in her new room. There were more toys than the last home, but they looked old and worn. Did that mean that things were rough around here? She had handled rough before. She could deal with "rough" as long as it was with her mom. She tried to remember her mother's hugs, her soft skin, strong arms, and the shower of wet sloppy kisses that would cover Jessie's face. "Oh, Jessie," she would say. "Oh, Jessie." This meant Mommy's rampage was over and Jessie didn't have to be afraid anymore, at least until she awoke from the long nap she was slipping into or until

Mommy's boyfriend came home. What she wouldn't give to be in her mommy's arms again!

"Jessica? Jessica? Honey, I've got to go now," Miss Lynn was saying. "I'll be back to check on you in a few weeks, okay?" Jessie panicked. She wanted to say, "No, Miss Lynn. Don't leave me here! Don't leave me by myself! Take me home with you, Miss Lynn, please?" But she knew that if she opened her mouth, she would start crying and her last foster parents didn't like it when she cried. Miss Lynn wiped the corners of her teary eyes and said, "You'll be all right, honey. You've got all of your things here with you. Where is Princess Ariel, your stuffed kitty cat? Let's find it, and that will make you feel better." Jessie managed to mutter, "Remember, it got torn up at that last place." "Oh, that's right," said Miss Lynn. "I'm sorry, Jessica. We'll try to find you another Princess Ariel, okay?" While Jessica stared blankly at her shoes, Miss Lynn continued talking but Jessica didn't really hear what she was saying. The next thing she knew she was standing at the window watching the back of Miss Lynn walk away from the house and drive off in her car.

Jessica is the face of a child's grief in the foster care setting.

Grief, Loss, and the Foster Care System

Due to the crises that surround a child being placed in foster care, the ensuing grief reactions are often overlooked or misinterpreted as a reaction to the placement or their previous abuse. Regardless of the chaotic circumstances surrounding these children, or the abuse they experienced by their family, the severance of ties from one's family and home create a sense of loss that results in a variety of grief reactions. Feelings of abandonment, hopelessness, fear, anxiety, and unpredictability dominate the lives of these children. Underlying all the changes and adjustments that a foster child must endure is an overwhelming and unrecognized sense of loss.

Children are placed into foster care via court order when it is determined that they are in imminent danger or "the parents are unable or unwilling to cooperate with the social service agency in improving the care of their children" (Crosson-Tower, 2005, p. 268). Crosson-Tower (2005) also reviewed other reasons a child might be placed into foster care by the court system. She identified the following as other considerations:

- The parents are unable to provide the child with proper care because of the hospitalization, incarceration, or physical or mental incapacity of one or both parents.

- The parents abandon their children, and an emergency placement must be arranged.
- Treatment is necessary and can only be obtained by a court order and not through the informal resource channels of social service.
- The parents are denying the child medical attention, and the lack of this attention may be life-threatening.
- The case involves death of a child or severe physical injury inflicted on the child by the parent.
- The case involves sexual abuse and state statutes indicate that sexual abuse is punishable by law (Davidson, 1997; Myers, 1998; Katner & Plum, 2002; Faller, 2003).

(Taken from Crosson-Tower, 2005, p. 268.)

Regardless of the reasons for court action, placement into foster care ignites a series of losses that may be acute yet temporary, or acute and enduring. Bourguignon and Watson (1987) recognize grief as the affective state that an individual experiences when something of significance is unexpectedly withdrawn. Some placements are short-term in nature, with parents making appropriate changes or obtaining needed support. Other family members might also step into the role of caretaker for these children, while the parent is focusing on improving parenting skills, managing anger more effectively, or gaining sobriety. Grief and loss in these situations is present and must be addressed; however, because protective factors are put into place more quickly, grief reactions are often more transient with more salient potential for resolution.

Many children in foster care are not so fortunate. Family members cannot or do not do what is necessary to facilitate reunification. These children remain in foster care longer, and when this occurs, it is more likely that children will have to be moved to emergency settings, foster homes, or more intensive placements such as residential treatment over time.

This turmoil and lack of permanency, along with the pain the child experiences when parents are unable to take her home, increases the layers of grief and loss a child might suffer in the system. Fiorini and Mullen (2006) have defined grief in a way that seems to encompass the experiences of children in the foster care system:

> Grief is an inevitable, never-ending process that results from a permanent or temporary disruption in a routine, a separation, or a change in a relationship that may be beyond a person's control. Although loss is a universal experience, the causes and manifestations of it are unique to each individual and may change over time (p. 10).

The following vignette offers a glimpse into what a number of foster children face as they develop and grow within an imperfect child welfare system.

> A clinical social worker working with a fifteen-year-old foster youth (Cindy) in a residential treatment setting sought consultation in order to provide the most effective therapeutic interventions to this grieving adolescent. The social worker indicated that Cindy's birth mother had relinquished her parental rights approximately ten years prior, when Cindy was almost five years old. Child protection officials initially became involved with the family because of chronic neglect in Cindy's home. Cindy's birth mother suffered with alcoholism, could not hold a job, offered minimal supervision to Cindy, and was unable to meet her ongoing needs.
>
> Cindy had lived in four different foster homes throughout the ten years, and this was her second placement in residential treatment. Her moves from foster homes were sometimes facilitated by what the social worker termed as "blowouts," meaning that Cindy struggled to manage her feelings both at home and at school. She had a history of self-harm, with two non-lethal suicide attempts and regular cutting on her arms and ankles. She often expressed anger and resentment about being separated from her family and constantly begged her social worker to reunite her with her birth mother. She resisted any attempts by her foster parents to form an attachment and would sabotage her placement just when the relationships began to grow. In addition, Cindy was described by her teachers as sad, lonely, withdrawn, and unapproachable. The social worker expressed frustration to her supervisor because she didn't know how to engage Cindy's cooperation. It was clear to the supervisor that Cindy was reacting to multiple losses and, like many adolescents, was burying her grief under anger, denial, and isolation.

Neither Cindy's story nor the social worker's experience is foreign to those who work in the field of child welfare. Although all foster children do not require hospitalization and residential treatment, they all do experience multiple levels of disruptions and losses. The layers of disruption depend on several factors, such as the length of time a child remains in care, the number of foster homes and out-of-home placements in which the child is placed, the number of school changes the child experiences, the family's ability to accept responsibility and make changes in their lives, the quality of foster care the child receives, and the consistent involvement of caring adults over time.

When a child enters foster care, she often will go to a temporary housing environment, either in a home or shelter. Once the child's needs are assessed and foster family options are located, the child might then be transferred to a home where she is able to stay for a longer period of time. Family members or friends are sometimes identified for temporary placement, but children may also be placed with strangers who are licensed as foster care providers. Cournos (2002) writes, "Many of the systems set up to help these children, while well-intentioned, focus exclusively on their physical well-being while ignoring their internal experience" (p.149).

A child entering foster care is experiencing many losses at the outset. Daily lives are disrupted as daily routines change. Attachments to friends in school or childcare are limited or ended without good-byes. Any temporary bonds made with teachers or other care providers are terminated. In addition, pets as well as neighborhoods are often left behind. If the children are adolescents, the losses of close friendships or memberships in certain social circles might feel devastating to them. When children are removed from their homes, they must leave many items, prized possessions, favorite activities, and important relationships behind. These multiple and layered losses can lead to intense grief reactions that may go unaddressed.

Once in foster care, a child's contact with family members often is limited to designated visitation times, and these are usually scheduled at weekly or twice-weekly intervals, depending on the age of the child and the circumstances of the child's removal from the home or family of origin. Visitation with family members is an important way to promote attachment between the children in protective care and their family members. Family members are sometimes in transient situations and cannot be reached easily for scheduling of visits, or they or the children are not physically or mentally well enough to visit on a regular basis. Safety of the child is of utmost concern during visits, and this can hinder visitation from occurring

Victor is a ten-year-old fourth-grade boy who entered foster care at the age of three. Victor had five other siblings who were from different fathers. Victor's three youngest siblings were placed in foster care due to ongoing domestic violence between Victor's mother and her boyfriend. In addition, it was suspected that the boyfriend was selling cocaine and exposed the children to pornography. Visits by the birth mother were infrequent due to her lack of transportation and the controlling behavior of her boyfriend who was prohibited from visiting the children. In addition, Victor was placed in four different foster homes over a period of seven years. Victor reacted to these circumstances by becoming ambivalent about seeing his mother, denying any desire to have a relationship with her, and remaining emotionally isolated from foster siblings or caseworkers. On the other hand, Victor expressed a desperate need to see his biological siblings. Although sibling visits were attempted, they eventually diminished in frequency due to the difficulty of coordinating between foster families. Victor continually pleaded for information about his older brother and sister, aged nineteen and twenty, who remained with his biological mother.

Multiple factors determine visitation schedules and a child's access to his parents, siblings, grandparents, other relatives, and/or fictive kin. *Fictive kin* is a term used to refer to individuals who are not related by birth, marriage, or adoption, but have a significant emotional relationship with the child. In some cases, a parent might not be allowed to visit because of reasons associated with substance abuse, poor anger management, unsafe boundaries, or other serious impairment that might represent a hazard to a child. In other situations, because the child protection system is often overwhelmed, children and their families do not visit because of transportation glitches, scheduling errors, faulty communication, inability to find third-party supervisors, or some other related logistical barrier. Siblings placed in different foster homes present a significant challenge to visitation due to geographical distances, transportation problems, and conflicting schedules of all persons involved. This comprises an additional loss that children will grieve.

As a child remains in foster care over time, grief and loss issues stretch beyond sadness related to missing their family members. Boss (2000) discusses ambiguous loss as the distress associated with the loss of a relationship in which confusion exists about that person or relationship. She further defines one category of ambiguous loss to be when the person is physically absent but psychologically present. Ambiguous loss is prominent among foster children. Foster and adoptive children have ties to and memories of family members who are not present in their lives. Ambiguous loss complicates the bereavement process because these children know that their family members are alive, keeping active the fantasy that they might go home to them one day. Boss (2000) indicates that ambiguous losses can immobilize or freeze grief, not allowing "people to achieve the detachment that is necessary for normal closure" (p. 10). This type of grief can have a significant impact on a child's well-being and future relationships.

Assessment

Fahlberg (1991) identified multiple influences on a child's reaction to separation from family members and his familiar daily routine and environment. These factors also impact a child's bereavement process. The list includes:

- The child's age and stage of development
- The child's attachment to the parent
- Past experiences with separation
- The child's perceptions of the reasons for the separation
- The child's preparation for the move
- The "parting and welcoming messages" the child receives
- The post-separation environment
- The child's temperament
- The environment from which he is being removed (p. 142)

When assessing the impact of a child's separation from his family system, it is important to obtain as much detailed information about the initial removal of the child as possible. This information might be acquired from the caseworker, foster family members, emergency shelter personnel, and case documentation, along with an interview of the child. The information above could be integrated into the Loss Experience of the psychosocial assessment in chapter 2.

Although separation from a parent is significant no matter the child's age or stage of development, the impact of loss varies at different ages. Infants are at risk for developmental regression because of changes to routine and daily rhythm. Fahlberg (1991) stated that, prior to the age in which separation anxiety begins, babies "react to the differences in temperature, noise, smell, touch, and visual stimulation that vary from household to household" (p. 144). Emotional distress of parental separation is most obvious between the ages of about six months and four years (Rutter, 1981). Babies younger than six months of age are not as selective yet in their attachments to particular caregivers, and children older than four years tend to have the cognitive capacity to understand the tenacity of relationships in the midst of separation.

Because children of preschool age often are developmentally involved in "magical thinking," children of this age often blame themselves and believe that they have been removed from the home because of their own thoughts, feelings, or behaviors. Self-blame is a possible indicator of the psychological effects of loss or separation, and it can be helpful to identify what the child believes he or she has done to facilitate the separation. Removal of latency-aged children may interfere with children's customary developmental tasks such as school achievement and learning, peer relationships, and conscience development (Fahlberg, 1991). Concrete thinking, peer difficulties, decreasing grades in school, and decreased maturity may be indicators of unresolved loss issues for these children. These children from approximately seven to twelve years of age often need more structured activities or particular tools to discuss their losses and grief responses.

In adolescence, the developmental task at hand is identity formation. Separation and loss issues can exacerbate the emotional fluctuations and lability that are more common at this age. An increase in impulsivity may also be evident in the adolescents' behaviors at home or at school. In addition, teens might seek comfort from peer relationships that are marked with the instability they feel internally or that help distract them from their pain. Adolescents typically have more advanced language abilities, abstract reasoning, and cognitive development, as well as increased maturity emotionally. Because of this, clinical interviews will likely bring forth accurate and relevant material that will aid in assessing the adolescent's current functioning. While it is clear that separation from attachment figures can have detrimental influences on developmental stages, children are simultaneously developing strengths to cope with these various transitions in their lives. Using the strengths-based framework, as outlined in chapter 1, foster care workers and practitioners can build on children's inherent resiliencies and assist and encourage them to use life-enhancing coping skills.

When children are placed in foster care and under the managing conservatorship of the state, losses become evident, and grief reactions are interspersed into all aspects of the child's daily life and emerging identity. Using the strengths-based framework to assess the child's emotional functioning will ensure that these issues are not missed or overlooked while determining the most effective treatment interventions for the foster child. Without realizing the significance of a child's bereavement process, misdiagnosis can occur and the child can be perceived as severely disturbed rather than actively mourning (Fahlberg, 1991). Traumatic loss experiences can delay development or cause regression of milestones and/or skills, so a child or adolescent must be assessed developmentally to determine his or her position on cognitive, emotional, educational, and behavioral levels. This assessment is critical in order to provide psychoeducation to all stakeholders about the foster child and is essential to accurate case planning and monitoring of progress.

Consider the following questions during the assessment phase with foster youth:

1. How many homes has the child lived in prior to coming into foster care? The more moves the child has already experienced, the less reaction she is likely to demonstrate during this separation. This child might be even more guarded than most children regarding the formation of new relationships, and her wariness to form new relationships can impact her current placements. A child's lack of emotion after multiple placements may result from ongoing grief that was inadequately addressed.

2. What are the child's perceptions of why he was removed from the home? Fahlberg (1991) suggests not telling the child that the separation is not his fault. By using the word "fault," a child may become focused on the issue of blame, and because children are self-focused, it is likely that they will blame themselves. Discussing responsibility rather than fault allows the child to focus on the specific reasons that his parent was unable to meet his needs.

3. Does the child have magical thinking about her control of the situation? Does she believe that changing her behavior or doing something special will help her to go home to her family sooner? The loss of control is an experience the child feels throughout a separation from her family. It is an example of an intangible loss, a loss that is secondary to the primary loss of the child's family but one that is critical and often overlooked by all involved with the child (Fiorini & Mullen, 2006).

4. What other intangible losses is the child experiencing? Which of these might be causing considerable grief reactions? Some examples of these are the losses of: innocence, dignity, the fantasy that "everything will be all right," identity, the dream of family, the idea of parents as powerful, community, stability, power, and trust. Though it may not be conscious, foster children may grieve these types of losses.

5. How was the child prepared for his move from his family? Were adults present who could explain the move or comfort the child about the move? How was the child introduced into his new surroundings? What was the emotional tone of the transition? All of these issues play a part in the child's adjustment to his new environment while accepting the loss from his previous placement. Just as the circumstance of a death provide important assessment information, so do the circumstances pertaining to a child's removal from the home.

6. How does the child manage crises? Is he more likely to withdraw and possibly become depressed, or does he tend to become aggressive or hyperstimulated? Are caregivers able to adapt to the child's coping strategies? How attuned are the caregivers to the child's grief? This attunement is necessary in order to help the child learn how to regulate his own emotions, especially those regarding his separation and loss.

Interventions

Regardless of a foster youth's age at time of separation from his or her primary caregivers, the child's sense of trust is affected. This impaired capacity to trust can manifest as detachment, disdain, anger, sarcasm, people-pleasing, perfection, and other relationship issues. Often, a clinician or other involved professional can misunderstand the youth's initial response to the therapeutic relationship. Some might experience anxiety or inadequacy about their ability to form a relationship with the youth. They might feel extraordinarily sad or sorry for the child. On the other hand, the practitioner might feel uniquely qualified as the only one who can understand the child. Because of the complexities involved in treating children who have experienced abuse, neglect, and related trauma, along with multiple loss, clinical supervision is a necessity for the provision of effective interventions and ethical practice. Clinical supervision provides a container for clinicians to share their responses and reactions regarding this work's intensity, and it also provides the clinician with the objectivity that is critical for sound therapeutic decision-making.

As is widely supported through Kazdin's (2005) review of relevant literature, numerous studies have suggested a strong correlation of positive outcome in psychotherapy to the quality of the therapeutic relationship. The relationship between the youth and clinician is a key factor in promoting healing of previous hurts and wounds that have had an impact on the child's ability to form trusting relationships. Crenshaw (2007) indicates that this relationship is critical when treating youth suffering the effects of trauma and grief. He goes further to promote a model that uses the "active direction, guidance, and facilitation of a therapist knowledgeable about trauma-informed therapy" to guide youth affected by trauma and grief "to develop a coherent and meaningful narrative, thereby reducing the risk of subsequent psychopathology" (p. 324). This model reflects the influence of recent neurobiological research that supports the idea that the safety provided by the secure therapeutic relationship allows the brain to regulate and integrate more complex and troubling emotions (Perry, 2005; Siegel, 1999).

The experience of bereavement changes over time, and life milestones and transitions often trigger feelings that are related to a new stage of grieving. Consider the following vignette:

> LaCretia was seeing her school counselor to prepare for her high school graduation only two months away. During her second meeting with the counselor, LaCretia burst into tears and was eventually able to share why. She stated that she found herself feeling sad and somewhat lost because only her foster parents would see her walk across the stage. LaCretia indicated that she had not been thinking much about her birth family until she realized this, and now, she sees them in her dreams and sees herself with them. The

school counselor facilitated a discussion between LaCretia and her foster mother in order for LaCretia to feel supported at home. She told her foster mother that she had not shared these feelings because "the last thing I want to do is hurt your feelings."

This situation demonstrates not only how LaCretia's graduation triggered memories and sadness associated with her loss, but it also shows one of the complex issues involved with sharing feelings regarding families of origin in substitute care. Fears of betraying birth family or foster family members often emerge, confounding attachment and grief. Work with foster youth should include activities that identify the intangible losses they have experienced.

As a general rule, adolescents are able to engage in abstract thought, which opens up several possibilities for grief interventions. Some useful communication tools with adolescents include journaling, writing letters, scaling from one to ten, using fill-in worksheets, making advantage/disadvantage lists, creating drawings, listing emotions, and utilizing Gestalt techniques (i.e., two chairs, personal fairy tales, or guided fantasies) (Fahlberg, 1991).

Holz (1984) describes a letter-writing activity that involves an adolescent composing a "Dear Abby" letter after reading a story about a child's experience in foster care. The Dear Abby letter is written to explain the child's situation and to ask for help with specific issues. The story provided could easily consist of a foster youth struggling with issues related to ambiguous and tangible loss. Either the clinician can respond as Abby, with compassion and potential solutions, or the child can be asked to respond as Abby to the foster youth in the story. This type of activity allows for creative communication while working toward resolution of bereavement.

Music is often part of an adolescent's culture, and many songs reflect grief and loss experiences. Listening to select music or reading song lyrics together with other teens in a group setting, alone at home as an assignment or in a therapeutic setting with a clinician present can facilitate grief interventions in a life-enhancing manner.

A lifebook, a historical scrapbook of a child's life made of memorabilia, words, photographs, and artwork, offers adolescents and children a chance to review their past while creatively archiving pieces of their identity. Not only can the creation of the lifebook be therapeutic, but reviewing and adding to it over time can often facilitate the expression of grief. Since identity development is a critical component of adolescent development, scrapbooking and making and filling memory boxes can also serve as therapeutic activities, especially if a trusted individual is participating in the process with the teen.

Bibliotherapy, the use of books or stories to help solve problems, also serves children and younger adolescents who are mourning. Speaking directly about loss of family and the circumstances leading up to their removal from the home can sometimes be too threatening and painful for foster youth. For this reason, reading stories or watching movie or television clips that have loss-related subject matter can help the youth to access feelings without the experience of being overwhelmed. This concept is sometimes called "being one step removed" from the intensive or more personal process.

Because preschool and elementary-aged children sometimes lack the cognitive and emotional resources to utilize some of the strategies useful with adolescents, Crenshaw (2004) developed storytelling and projective drawing strategies to create and expand meaningful dialogue between child and therapist. Fahlberg (1991) related that toy telephones, puppets, dolls, and joint storytelling often help to facilitate communication with children ages four to ten. This age group tends to do well with workbooks, games, and art activities, which can serve as strengths-based interventions.

Gardner (1971) introduced a useful technique with children from age three to twelve. The child is asked to choose a favorite animal and name him. The adult then starts telling a story about the animal that reflects the child's history. The adult shares a few sentences and then asks the child to add to the story. The goal would be for the child to have the chance to share emotions, reactions to life events, and future wishes. Because the adult will take the story back after a few sentences from the child, the adult can solicit responses to particular areas of interest or questioning with the child. This activity can work well to access feelings about multiple losses.

Children will often listen to what adults are saying about them but have difficulty hearing what is said to them specifically. For this reason, it can be helpful to use activities to access feelings. Feeling faces and lists of emotions can help children to identify feelings with prompts. Assisting children to know who their support systems are can increase their safety to mourn. Creating a visual representation of people, love objects, activities, and institutions in their lives offers a symbolic reminder of whom children can count on for support and comfort.

Fiorini and Mullen (2006) introduce an activity for children called Good-bye, Cookie Jar, in which children decorate a cookie jar and add "cookies" to the jar over time. The cookies are made of paper and are divided into three categories: memories, feelings, and wishes. This type of activity offers a tangible, experiential opportunity for children to explore some of the more intangible parts of their loss experiences.

Finally, in order to shore up a child or teen's resiliency in the face of so much loss, a self-esteem box can be constructed. Foster parents, case workers, therapists, treatment center staff, and other significant adults can write notes that they share with the child and place in the box. Notes are written about positive aspects of the child with careful attention given to the wording and tone of these notes so that they are designed to be purely positive. The goal is to provide the child with a source of positive feedback that the child can keep with them throughout all the transitions that he or she may experience.

These are some useful resources that have been reported as successful when intervening with children in the foster care system. In addition, there are other resources that are described at the end of this chapter that the practitioner may find beneficial.

Working with the Professional Team

Lee and Whiting (2007) encourage all those invested in foster children's lives to recognize that most behaviors of these children are actual signs of survival and strength. Many of the externalizing and internalizing behaviors are "active coping strategies appropriate to the children's circumstances" (p. 426). These authors go on to say that all those involved with the youth "need to appreciate how unresolved grief leads to ambivalence about and fears of interdependency, relationship testing, and self-fulfilling prophecies of non-lovableness" (p. 426). The more that caseworkers, case managers, guardians *ad litem*, foster family members, and therapists recognize the fear, hurt, anger, powerlessness, impotence, loss, and grief with which these children are coping, the more likely that these stakeholders will be able to access more empathy from within, building a capacity for patience and understanding, benefiting the children greatly.

It is recommended that team members communicate closely with each other when working with these youth. Because the children's trust has been damaged by the abuse or neglect they have suffered, they look for and sometimes create reasons not to trust adults involved in their lives. This can lead to defenses such as splitting and projection on the child's part. As a result, team members often experience compassion fatigue if they are operating in isolation rather than leaning on other knowledgeable members of the team for support and clarification.

When working with concepts of ambiguous loss, Boss (2004) highlights particular strategies to engage clients most effectively. She suggests that team members:

- Engage in active listening without judging the client.
- Offer each other support and information to understand and manage the confusion that is likely being experienced by the client.

- Allow the child space to feel angry at a parent who breaks promises, does not visit regularly, or fails to follow through with service plans.
- Lee and Whiting (2007) strongly suggest that the team members share the truth with foster youth about the reasons they are in placement and how their family members are responding. Hughes (1997) posits that withholding information from foster children can increase feelings of powerlessness and helplessness.

Residential Treatment

As a safe living environment, residential treatment aims to keep youth safe from their own dangerous behavior and facilitates psychological, emotional, and behavioral interventions in a contained atmosphere. Residential treatment is not only available for foster children; it is a modality that can be utilized for any youth who is not able to function safely in a community-based setting. All grief and loss issues addressed in this section apply to children in both foster care and residential treatment. On the other hand, because children who are in residential treatment but not in foster care return to family members, their situations are different. The foster youth's lack of family stability often exacerbates grief and loss issues, and the foster youth's resilience can be compromised. Consider the following example:

> John, a twelve-year-old Caucasian male, was placed in residential treatment because of a pattern of runaway and other dangerous behaviors. Child protection workers had become involved in his life because his mother was not able to take him home due to her own psychiatric issues. John continued to demonstrate aggressive behaviors in the treatment center, and during one episode with his therapist, he exclaimed, "Why should I try to get better? I can't go home anyway! My mother doesn't want me, and I have to live with strangers!"

John's situation is not unique. When feeling safe enough to share openly in residential treatment, children in the foster care system will often talk about the pain associated with the loss of their families and home environments. In these situations, foster youth not only suffer the loss of their families, but they also grieve the environments, cultures, values, and beliefs they knew and understood. They must adapt to new authority figures, structures, and rules that are often much more stringent than what they experienced previously. With the loss of their former support system, they must meet and adapt to new peers as well, which may or may not be a positive experience.

Therapeutic programming, individualized treatment plans, token economy, positive peer pressure, appropriate expectations, and limit-setting are considered to be components that make residential treatment work (Pazaratz, 2003). Practitioners who staff residential treatment facilities are charged with helping youngsters deal with feelings of anger and grief, particularly if they have experienced multiple placements (Pazaratz, 2003). Maintaining connection to birth or substitute family members via phone calls, letters, e-mails, and so on can be helpful to the children who are placed in residential care.

Preexisting grief issues may be exacerbated within the residential treatment environment. Children are often highly sensitive to and affected by the losses their peers experience in the setting. With the high turnover rates of both staff and residents in residential treatment environments, the loss with which these children must cope is compounded. If placed geographically far from birth or foster families, visitation can be minimal and phone calls can be short, easily interrupted, or diminished due to particular structures or systems in treatment facilities. Finally, foster youth may suffer intensified grief when watching peers reunify with their families either through visitation or discharge. These observations serve as visual reminders of what the child in foster care does not or may not have in his or her life, triggering further grief reactions for the child.

Interventions and resources mentioned later in this chapter are relevant for foster youth in residential treatment. Minimizing barriers that limit birth or foster family contact is highly recommended. Because many of these children have been traumatized, their ability to link cause and effect is often disrupted. Eliminating family contact as a consequence for negative behaviors is not beneficial to these children's capacities for attachment. Furthermore, it complicates their grief experiences in residential treatment.

Adoption

Some children in out-of-home care are not able to be returned to their birth parents. Newborns are sometimes removed from their birth parents and placed in homes that are designated as both foster and adoptive homes. This designation means that some children are placed into homes they will never leave. It is difficult to discern the impact of a newborn's removal from their birth parents. In these situations, Howe and Fearnley (2003) indicate that infants placed between birth and six months of age demonstrate minimal developmental impairments. Issues related to their adoptions tend to emerge when the child is old enough to share his or her adoption story with friends, usually in the early to middle latency years. "The child may have been raised to think of adoption in a neutral way, but other children who tease or misunderstand what adoption is about may challenge this view" (Grotevant, Dunbar, Kohler, & Esau, 2000, p. 383).

As abstract thought processes develop, young adopted adolescents have more capacity to recognize issues related to loss. These youth may find themselves asking questions related to their new awareness. They may wonder why their birth parents were unable or unwilling to do what was necessary to reunite with them, and as their identities continue to form, adoption becomes more prominent as a central theme (Grotevant, 1997). Because identity formation is a central theme during adolescence, the grief reactions can be intense during the teenage years (Smith & Howard, 1999).

Children removed from their homes do not necessarily stay in one setting following their separations from original caregivers or family members. Multiple placements are sometimes required for various reasons prior to the child's legal adoption. In most states, it is preferable or even mandated that sibling groups be placed together in foster homes or in adoptive placements. The ages of the siblings, their emotional and behavioral characteristics and needs, and the number of siblings in the group impact placement availability and goodness of fit. The following case vignette illustrates this dynamic:

> Rodderick was ready for adoption, but his caseworker kept telling him that he couldn't be placed until his older sister "worked through her issues." He wasn't sure what that meant and he wanted her to be adopted too, but he was getting tired of waiting. He and his sister had been moved from three different foster homes because of her behavior. He didn't understand why she was so mean to their foster parents and to the other kids in the home. Every time, his caseworker asked him if he wanted to move when they moved his sister, and what else could he say but yes? They had been together, just the two of them, for a long time, but he wanted to have a normal life again.

Children adopted at older ages have often suffered more trauma, placement breakdowns, and separations when they are placed in what might be called their "forever families." According to Howe and Fearnley (2003), there is growing evidence that families who adopt older children are struggling to manage the children's relationship and behavioral difficulties, particularly in "mid-to-late childhood and adolescence" (p. 371). The emotional and behavioral needs of children placed for adoption through the child welfare system vary widely. In most states, however, children whose parental rights have been terminated have experienced significant neglect, abuse, family chaos, and loss. In addition, along with the acuity or chronicity of the maltreatment, the family or family members have been unable to improve enough to have the children return home.

Chronic early maltreatment within a family or early caregiving relationship can result in children having complex trauma, also called developmental trauma (Becker-Weidman, 2009). Becker-Weidman (2009) defines the term *complex trauma* as "the dual problem of children's exposure to traumatic events and the impact of this exposure on the immediate and long-term outcomes" (p. 138). Children who have experienced complex trauma then also have experienced the loss of what many other children have without asking—emotional regulation, a safe base from which to explore, direction in life, and the ability to detect or respond to dangerous cues (Becker-Weidman, 2009).

Preliminary research has shown that children who have experienced complex trauma often have "marked discrepancies between chronological and developmental ages" (Becker-Weidman, 2009). School success, parenting, socialization, and emotional and behavioral self-regulation are likely to be affected due to this discrepancy. In the majority of cases, these children have also experienced other losses. For example, cognitive delays can prohibit a child's progress in school and lead to educational failure. Consequently, the child's self-esteem suffers, which can obstruct healthy resolution of the trauma and loss.

Complex trauma can also lead to difficulties in social relationships. For latency-aged children as well as adolescents, making and keeping friendships is a critical part of the developmental process. Children with complex trauma may subordinate themselves in an attempt to maintain friendships, befriend others who have similar problems as themselves, or withdraw from appropriate friendships completely. Children who experience problems with self-regulation of affect and behavior are likely to have problems with peers, in school, and at home. Due to a lag in development, children may lack the affective regulation that their peers have achieved, thereby becoming social outcasts. This sets the stage for multiple losses. If unrecognized or misunderstood, these losses and complex grief reactions can lead to placement difficulties and even adoption disruption.

Grief Resources for Practitioners

Few resources exist that focus on loss and grief in this population. Much of the literature on loss and children focuses on children dealing with death, and this does not allow for discussion of many of the effects of ambiguous loss experienced by foster children. The following list will acquaint practitioners with some of the more relevant resources available.

1. *Engaging Resistant Children in Therapy: Projective Drawing and Storytelling Techniques* by David Crenshaw
2. *Ambiguous Loss: Learning to Live with Unresolved Grief* by Pauline Boss
3. *The Magical Thoughts of Grieving Children: Treating Children with Complicated Mourning and Advice for Parents* by James A. Fogarty
4. *Spirit Games: 300 Fun Activities that Bring Children Comfort and Joy* by Barbara Sher
5. *Therapeutic Exercises for Children: Guided Self-Discovery Using Cognitive Behavioral Techniques* by Robert D. Friedberg, Barbara A. Friedberg, and Rebecca J. Friedberg.
6. *Children in Foster Care and Adoption: A Guide to Bibliotherapy* by John T. Pardeck and Jean A. Pardeck

Ultimately, much of the grief and loss literature discusses meaning-making as a significant component for grief resolution (Walsh-Burke, 2006). One of the biggest challenges for practitioners working with these youth is allowing the space for grieving while also supporting the child's search for meaning in all that has happened. This process is not linear, but with compassionate support and guidance, the children and adolescents can make meaning of their circumstances and choose to grow. Consider the following story as an example:

> Valerie was fifteen years old and had 150 slight, self-inflicted cuts on her arms when she arrived at the residential treatment facility. She was transferring from an inpatient psychiatric facility. Valerie indicated that she would not be forming a relationship with anybody in the treatment center, neither staff nor other kids. She stated that she had to get home to take care of her mother and that no one could stop her. Her psychomotor activity was agitated, and for the first three months, she and her therapist walked around the grounds for her therapy hour each week. Over time, Valerie began to recognize that she was too young to be responsible for her mother, and she slowly began to allow connection with her therapist. Valerie mourned the losses she felt when recognizing that she did not have a mother who could take care of her. She tearfully shared memories about painful times and remembered times of joy as well. As she grieved, Valerie began to make meaning of her life as it was and found ways

to connect with her mother that did not require her to take care of her mom. She stopped cutting and increased her communication. After fifteen months, she was discharged to a foster home with ongoing contact with her birth family.

Practitioners who are knowledgeable about disenfranchised grief will offer another facet to the grieving process for this population. Doka (1989) explains that disenfranchised grief results from loss that "cannot be openly acknowledged, publicly mourned, or socially supported" (p. 4). Being in a foster family has a stigma attached because the reasons that necessitated foster placement are generally not easy topics to discuss. Many foster youth do not have peers with whom they share their stories, and many of them keep their histories secret. This, along with the complex, confused, and suppressed feelings that the children in these situations experience, generates this state of disenfranchised grief (Webb, 2003). Practitioners must be knowledgeable about these issues in order to help the children mourn.

Common Ethical Dilemmas

Children grieve in their own ways and on their own time. It can be difficult for stakeholders to allow this process to take place without pushing, shaming, berating, or avoiding. Because of the loss of control the child has experienced as a result of the abuse and/or neglect, the separation from family members and other chaotic situations, it is even more important to honor the youth's self-determination about his grief process.

Because foster youth have experienced traumatic life events, stakeholders can overidentify or find themselves wanting to rescue them. Professional boundaries can be crossed, and disempowerment can occur. Rather than focusing on a youth's strengths and resilience, a treatment team member can concentrate on the deficits or hurts. This ultimately is not helpful to the youth and represents an ethical challenge.

Finally, although the child welfare system dutifully attempts to advocate in the best interests of children, there are multiple systemic issues that create ethical dilemmas. Youth are expected to persevere and share their life stories with multiple treatment team members over time, and this can feel like a breach of confidentiality for the youth, especially with such a high rate of staff turnover. Relationships are developed only to be disrupted because stakeholders do not always remain involved in the children's lives from beginning to end. This creates more loss issues for the youth and may exacerbate grief reactions, behavioral problems, poor coping, withdrawal, or depression. In addition, decisions for placements and placement changes are sometimes driven by legislative mandates or agency policy, rather than by the individual needs of a child. Ethical dilemmas are likely to emerge in these situations because of the competing needs of the system and the youth.

Cultural Considerations

Placement of children into the homes of well-meaning strangers is complicated by the need for consideration of and sensitivity to culture. Different family systems have their own cultural ways to manage painful feelings, separation, loss, and grief. Children who enter foster care might have other ways to define the concept of family, as well as different values and ways of seeking help, communicating with elders, and using language (Samantrai, 2004). Practitioners and foster families who understand their own cultural beliefs and experiences often will be able to identify cultural differences of the children with whom they work. Foster parents who can be open and curious about their foster youths' family culture without shaming or labeling will provide a safer environment in which the children can mourn. It is problematic and can be divisive to make assumptions about how children "should" feel or how they "should" mourn. Also, consideration of the foster child's developmental stage can help the foster parent be attuned to the child's emerging identity and cultural norms. Not all cultures value independence and autonomy, so some children might instead value collectivism and responsibility to family. For these children, it is important to recognize that their grief might show itself through guilt and anxiety of not being with and helping their families of origin.

Samantrai (2004) notes that practitioners cannot know all the details of each culture represented in their clients, so she suggests that they seek "appropriate consultation from people more familiar with the culture" and ask "the client what his cultural practices are, to what extent he believes in and uses his traditional practices, and what they mean to him" (p. 79). The following illustrates the need for cultural sensitivity in this work:

> Maria, a fifteen-year-old Latina female, was admitted into a residential treatment facility after being removed from her foster home due to persistent suicidal thoughts and self-cutting behaviors. Her therapist in the treatment center determined that Maria lacked assertiveness and that she must tell people what she needed while also looking them in the eyes. For more than eight months, Maria was told that this was

one of her primary goals, yet she was not making this change. When this goal was stated at her nine-month staffing, Maria looked everyone in the eyes and said, "My father called me 'disrespectful' and threatened to slap me if I told him anything and looked him in the eye. Y'all just don't get it. I ain't doing that!"

Clearly, the therapist was insensitive to the cultural implications of the goal she established for her client. It wasn't until the client pointed out the incongruency that the staff understood her resistance to change her behavior. This is an example of a lack of cultural competence and exploration. This lack of understanding obstructed the therapist's ability to see Maria's strengths in the context of her culture.

Summary

The grief experienced by youth in foster care, adoption, and residential treatment settings may be acute and complex. Youth are placed in these settings for a variety of reasons with the primary issue being safety concerns. The transient nature of foster care and the lack of stability place children at high risk for chronic grief reactions that can have far-reaching ramifications for their future. In the case of adoption, depending on their age, children may be separated from the only environment they have known. While residential treatment centers may provide structure and stability for the child, they may be a traumatic adjustment away from anything familiar. Oftentimes, practitioners must operate in crisis intervention mode and the issues of grief become secondary to finding a secure home for the youth. Rather than viewing the expression of grief reactions by youth as a potential strength that will eventuate in their ability to cope more effectively with a difficult situation, professionals must necessarily focus on more concrete aspects of the child's situation. Unfortunately, the foster care and residential treatment systems must focus primarily on the immediate safety and well-being of children and are limited in their ability to address the long-term consequences of family loss and disruption. Understanding grief from a strengths-based framework can enhance practitioners' abilities to intervene effectively with youth as they guide them through these transitions. This chapter provides practitioners with the tools and techniques to strengthen children's coping capacities and provide them with ways to openly mourn and resolve some of their loss issues. By developing competence in the area of grief and loss, practitioners can openly acknowledge the grief experience of children in foster care, adoption, and residential treatment settings while at the same time assist their caregivers to recognize and understand the pervasiveness of grief in the lives of these youth.

References

Becker-Weidman, A. (2009). Effects of early maltreatment on development: A descriptive study using the Vineland Adaptive Behavior Scales II. *Child Welfare, 88*(2), 137–161.

Boss, P. (2000). *Ambiguous loss: Learning to live with unresolved grief.* Cambridge, MA: Harvard University Press.

Boss, P. (2004). Ambiguous loss research, theory, and practice: Reflections after 9/11. *Journal of Marriage and Family, 66*(3), 551–566.

Bourguignon, J., & Watson, K. (1987). *After adoption: A manual for professionals working with adoptive families.* Springfield, IL: Illinois Department of Children and Family Services.

Cournos, F. (2002). The trauma of profound childhood loss: A personal and professional perspective. *Psychiatric Quarterly, 73*(2), 145–156.

Crosson-Tower, C. (2005). *Understanding child abuse and neglect* (6th ed.). Boston: Pearson Education, Inc.

Crenshaw, D. (2004). *Engaging resistant children in therapy.* Rhinebeck, NY: Rhinebeck Child and Family Center Publications.

Crenshaw, D. (2007). An interpersonal neurobiological-informed treatment model for childhood. *Journal of Death and Dying, 54*(4), 319–335.

Davidson, H. (1997). The courts and child maltreatment. In M. E. Helfer, R. S. Kempe, & R. D. Drugman (Eds.), *The battered child* (pp. 482–499). Chicago: University of Chicago Press.

Doka, K. (1989). *Disenfranchised grief: Recognizing hidden sorrow.* Lexington, KY: Lexington Books.

Fahlberg, V. (1991). *A child's journey through placement.* Indianapolis, IN: Perspectives Press.

Faller, K. (2003). *Understanding and assessing child sexual maltreatment.* Thousand Oaks, CA: Sage.

Fiorini, J., & Mullen, J. (2006). *Counseling children and adolescents through grief and loss.* Champaign, IL: Research Press.

Fogarty, J. (2000). *The magical thoughts of grieving children: Treating children with complicated mourning and advice for parents.* Amityville, NY: Baywood Publishing.

Friedberg, R., Friedberg, B., & Friedberg, R. (2001). *Therapeutic exercises for children: Guided self-discovery using cognitive-behavioral techniques.* Sarasota, FL: Professional Resource Press.

Gardner, R. (1971). *Therapeutic communication with children: The mutual storytelling technique.* New York: Jason Aronson, Inc.

Grotevant, H. (1997). Family processes, identity development, and behavioral outcomes for adopted adolescents. *Journal of Adolescent Research, 12*, 139–161.

Grotevant, H., Dunbar, N., Kohler, J., & Esau, A. (2000). Adoptive identity: How contexts within and beyond the family shape developmental pathways. *Family Relations, 49*, 379–387.

Holz, L. (1984). *Foster child.* New York: Messner.

Howe, D., & Fearnley, S. (2003). Disorders of attachment in adopted and fostered children: Recognition and treatment. *Clinical Child Psychology and Psychiatry, 8*(3), 369–387.

Hughes, D. (1997). *Facilitating developmental attachment: The road to emotional recovery and behavioral change in foster and adopted children.* Northvale, NJ: Jason Aronson, Inc.

Katner, D., & Plum, H. (2002). Legal issues. In A. P. Giardino and E. Giardino (Eds.), *Recognition of child abuse for the mandated reporter* (pp. 309–350). St. Louis, MO: G. W. Medical.

Kazdin, A. E. (2005). Treatment outcomes, common factors, and continued neglect of mechanisms of change. *Clinical Psychology: Science and Practice, 12*(2), 184–188.

Lee, R., & Whiting, J. (2007). Foster children's expression of ambiguous loss. *The American Journal of Family Therapy, 35,* 417–428.

Myers, J. (1998). The legal system and child protection. In J. E. B. Myers, S. E. Diedrich, D. Lee, K. Fincher, and R. Stern (Eds.), *The APSAC handbook on child maltreatment* (pp. 305–328). Thousand Oaks, CA: Sage.

Pardeck, J. T., & Pardeck, J. A. (1998). *Children in foster care and adoption: A guide to bibliotherapy.* Westport, CT: Greenwood Publishing Group.

Pazaratz, D. (2003). Skills training for managing disturbed adolescents in a residential treatment program. *Clinical Child Psychology and Psychiatry, 8*(1), 119–130.

Perry, B. (2005). Applying principles of neurodevelopment to clinical work with maltreated and traumatized children: The neurosequential model of therapeutics. In N. B. Webb (Ed.), *Working with traumatized youth in child welfare.* New York: Guilford Press.

Rutter, M. (1981). *Maternal deprivation reassessed.* London. Penguin Books.

Samantrai, K. (2004). *Culturally competent public child welfare practice.* Pacific Grove, CA: Brooks/Cole-Thomson Learning.

Sher, B. (2002). *Spirit games: 300 fun activities that bring children comfort and joy.* San Francisco: Jossey-Bass.

Smith, S., & Howard, J. (1999). Promoting successful adoptions: Practice with troubled families. Thousand Oaks, CA: Sage Publications.

Siegel, D. (1999). *The developing mind.* New York: Guilford Press.

Walsh-Burke, K. (2006). *Grief and loss: Theories and skills for helping professionals.* Boston: Pearson Education, Inc.

Webb, N. (2003). Play and expressive therapies to help bereaved children: Individual, family and group treatment. *Smith College Studies in Social Work, 73,* 405–422.

CHAPTER FOUR

Children and Adolescents Growing Up in the Shadow of Divorce

Pamela A. Malone

Seven-year-old Dakota looks for his parents in the stands as he walks up to bat. He spots his dad sitting on the bottom bench of the bleachers, looking very intense and serious as he watches Dakota. Then he catches sight of his mom and her boyfriend sitting at the very top of the bleachers. *Great*, he thinks to himself, *she brought Stan.* As he gets into formation and waits for the pitch, he hears his mother's laughter. *She's not even watching me!* Dakota thinks. *She's too busy with Stan.* He's so distracted by his parents' presence that he swings and misses the first two pitches. He hits the third pitch, but it's a pop fly and is caught—"Out!" the ump yells. Dakota looks to the ground as he heads back to the dugout, not wanting to see the disappointment on his father's face or see his mom having the time of her life even though he just bombed. He hears Stan's voice saying, "That's okay, Dakota! You'll get it next time!" Dakota doesn't look up, but his face gets hot, and he can feel the tension in the bleachers between his mom and dad. His dad hates Stan, so Dakota pretends to not like him, too. *Why couldn't Mom come without Stan?* Dakota wonders. *Can't we at least pretend we're a normal family for a couple of hours?*

After the game, Dad runs down his list of things Dakota needs to work on to improve his game. Dakota listens silently, wishing he could have done something his dad would be proud of. As he is gathering his things, Stan comes by and praises Dakota for his game and mentions some positive things that he did. Dakota smiles broadly and then catches a glimpse of his dad watching him. He quickly drops the smile and ducks his head into his bat bag, pretending to look for something. He's staying at his mom's house this weekend, so he goes to say good-bye to his dad. Dad gives him a big hug and that sad look that Dakota knows so well. "Why don't you ask your mom if you can come home with me—just for a little while?" Dakota remembers that his mom had promised ice cream after the game and he was really looking forward to it, but Dakota doesn't want to hurt his dad's feelings. His chest aches with worry. He knows that if he asks Mom, it will start a fight between her and Dad. But he also knows Dad is alone and really sad, and if Dakota went with him, he could cheer him up. Dakota is stuck. There is no solution that feels right, and he freezes, not knowing what to do.

Later that night, he is lying in bed at his mom's house. As usual, he feels like crying. He wonders what his dad is doing. Is Dad feeling as lonely as he is right now? Does he have the same empty feeling in the pit of his stomach, like someone has died? He begins to feel scared. What if the house catches on fire and he can't get down from his bunk bed fast enough to get out? What if a bad guy comes to the house and breaks in? Ever since his dad left, Dakota has these nightly worries. He longs for the time before the divorce. Life was so much easier then. Fantasies of Mom and Dad together again start playing through Dakota's mind as he drifts to sleep.

Dakota is the face of a child's grief in the midst of divorce.

Introduction

Each year approximately 1 million children in the United States experience the divorce of their parents, and 20 million children currently live with just one parent (U.S. Bureau of the Census, 2009). Half of all divorces in the United States involve children and adolescents, and about 40 percent of children will experience their parents' divorce (Amato, 2000). "The increase in marital dissolution has had major implications for the settings in which children are nurtured and socialized" (Amato, 2000, p. 1269). Although many children and adolescents survive the impact of their parents' divorce with resilience and good coping skills, and develop into well-adjusted individuals (Kelly, 2007), there are many who experience divorce as a significant loss that can lead to grief reactions. This chapter focuses on the children and adolescents who struggle with the change, transition, and loss caused by the time preceding, during, and following parental divorce. The formative years for these children and adolescents are largely influenced by their parents' divorce.

Reactions to separation and divorce may vary among children and adolescents depending on their ages and the specific circumstances. The severity and duration of negative responses is also dependent on the presence of a variety of protective (life-enhancing) factors and risk factors (Amato, 2000). Children and adolescents enduring parental divorce may experience phases of grieving similar to those associated with death and dying (Shulman, 2005). Similar to the death of a parent, divorce affects children and adolescents by putting them at higher risk for a number of affective disorders and mental health problems, both during childhood and into adulthood (Luecken & Appelhans, 2005). Divorce represents the termination of the family unit and is often characterized as a painful loss. The period during a divorce may involve tremendous emotional distress, confusion, relationship strain, and life upheaval for both children, adolescents, and their parents (Emery & Forehand, 1994). Divorce involves the revision of a life plan that a child or an adolescent has come to expect and depend on (Bernstein, 2006). Children and adolescents may perceive their parents' divorce as "unexpected, unwelcome, and unpredictable" (Booth & Amato, 2001) as that which was familiar transforms into an unknown and uncertain future. Divorce can have a lingering and subtle effect that nonetheless powerfully impacts childhood and adolescence.

Children's Responses to Divorce

Children's reactions to divorce depend on many variables, including the child's age, the family's level of psychosocial functioning prior to divorce, the parents' ability to focus on the needs of their children despite their own emotions of anger, frustration, and loss, as well as the basic nature of each parent-child relationship (Clarke-Stewart, Vangell, McCartney, Owen, & Booth, 2000; Cohen, 2002). Parental separation often precedes divorce by months and sometimes years. Marital conflict may also precede divorce for some period of time, exposing children and adolescents to negative emotions, arguments, and perhaps violence. Children are very vulnerable during this time period in response to high parental distress (Cohen, 2002). Marital dissolution when there is overt conflict may result in behavior problems in children (Davies & Cummings, 1994).

Infants and children younger than three years tend to absorb the emotional responses of their caregivers and react to their distress, grief, and preoccupation. They often exhibit irritability, separation anxiety, increased crying, fearfulness, sleep problems, gastrointestinal upset, aggression, and regressive behavior (Clarke-Stewart et al., 2000). Children four to five years of age tend to blame themselves for their parents' distress, unhappiness, and divorce. They may become clingy, fear abandonment, and experience nightmares. In addition, they may have behavioral problems, difficulty with task orientation, and trouble adjusting to preschool (Clarke-Stewart et al., 2000). Children this age can also become overwhelmed by their custodial parent's emotional reactions of sadness, anger, and frustration (Christ, 2000). Developmentally, their early preoperational cognitive abilities make it difficult for them to understand the meaning of divorce and the permanence of their parents' separation (Christ, 2000).

School-aged children may show aggression, have temper outbursts, and report feeling rejected by the absent or noncustodial parent. They can exhibit moodiness, preoccupation, decreased school performance, and feel somehow to blame for their parents' divorce (Clarke-Stewart et al., 2000; Cohen, 2002). These children experience profound sadness, which has the potential to develop into depression. Children at this age also struggle with divided loyalties to each parent. There may be evidence of psychosomatic symptoms such as headaches, stomachaches, sleep problems, and joint pain as a response to anger, guilt, feeling unloved, loneliness, loss, and grief. Defiance may occur at home as they test rules and limits as a way of needing to feel in control (Cohen, 2002).

At all developmental stages, children of divorce may experience grief reactions that can lead to anxiety and adjustment problems. Divorce can cause increased sensitivity to loss, a general sense of vulnerability to abandonment, and fear of losing the noncustodial parent (Luecken & Appelhans, 2005). Even children who appear to successfully cope with the challenges brought on by their parents' divorce report having unhappy thoughts, feelings, and memories about the divorce (Emery & Forehand, 1996).

Adolescents' Responses to Divorce

Adolescents are often thrust into premature autonomy as they attempt to deal with negative feelings about the divorce and their de-idealization of each parent (Cohen, 2002). Their anger, confusion, and sense of betrayal combined with the challenge of adolescent development makes dealing with parental divorce quite daunting. Young adolescents, twelve to fourteen years old, may immerse themselves in activities to distract themselves from their grief. They often strive to avoid all emotional expression, particularly any public display of their feelings (Christ, 2000). Middle adolescents, fifteen to seventeen years old, describe intense emotions that interfere with enjoying their normal routines, including school and extracurricular activities (Christ, 2000). In response to their parents' divorce, adolescents often feel different from their peers, experience self-blame, and have a heightened sensitivity to interpersonal relationships (Davies & Cummings, 1994). They may exhibit externalizing behavior such as substance abuse, poor school performance, somatic complaints, inappropriate sexual behavior, depression, anxiety, aggressive behavior, and delinquent behavior as a response to the bereavement caused by their parents' divorce (Clarke-Stewart et al., 2000).

As a result of their parents' divorce, many adolescents refuse to risk the trust and vulnerability involved in being close to someone again. They tend to remain vigilant to other possible losses, particularly in regard to relationships, and are vulnerable to affective disorders, especially during times of high life stress (Luecken & Appelhans, 2005).

Adolescents may embrace the concept of having a damaged identity due to being the child of divorce, dismiss parental efforts to help alleviate their stress, isolate themselves from the family, and develop symptoms that act as reminders that parents have hurt them (Bernstein, 2006). They may not be ready to relinquish feelings of anger, distrust, and hurt.

Gender Differences

Boys and girls may be affected differently when they experience their parents' divorce and may manifest their grief in dissimilar ways (Videon, 2002). The impact of parental divorce in very early childhood "affects girls more strongly than boys emotionally, and boys more strongly than girls intellectually" (Clarke-Stewart et al., 2000, p. 323). Girls adapt more quickly post-divorce than boys, who continue to exhibit emotional distress, academic difficulties, lower self-esteem, and behavior problems (Clarke-Stewart et al., 2000).

In general, boys tend to have more problems than girls following parental divorce, and are more negatively impacted than girls (Cherlin et al., 1991; Clarke-Stewart et al., 2000). Problems for boys related to divorce are demonstrated by aggression, acting out, depression, cognitive errors, and conduct problems (Mazur, Wolchik, Virdin, Sandler, & West, 1999; Sun, 2001). Some boys evidence increased aggression following parental divorce, which typically begins prior to the divorce (Amato, 2000; Emery & Forehand, 1996). Substance abuse and psychological problems tend to increase after divorce in boys (Doherty & Needle, 1991; Sun, 2001). However, it is suggested that some of these problems may have existed for years prior to the divorce (Amato, 2000). Until adolescence, boys may have more adverse reactions to the stressors brought on by divorce (Ge, Lorenz, Conger, Elder, & Simons, 1994).

Loyalty conflicts are evidenced more in girls who report feeling that parents put pressure on them to take sides during parental conflicts (Amato & Afifi, 2006). Girls often feel caught in the middle (Amato & Afifi, 2006). There is also evidence of more substance abuse among daughters of divorced parents (Doherty & Needle, 1991).

Life-Enhancing Factors

Life-enhancing factors are elements that strengthen and bolster children and adolescents, enabling them to cope with their loss and grief when parents divorce. Life-enhancing factors buffer children's and adolescents' responses to divorce-related stressors. They "act like shock absorbers and weaken links between divorce-related events" and the experience of stress (Amato, 2000). There are multiple life-enhancing factors that lessen the negative impact of divorce, which are characterized by three categories as outlined in table 4.1, to include individual life-enhancing factors, familial life-enhancing factors, and environmental life-enhancing factors.

INDIVIDUAL LIFE-ENHANCING FACTORS

Several individual life-enhancing factors have been identified that increase positive functioning in children and adolescents following their parents' divorce. These include attitudes or coping styles, cognitive abilities, social skills, interpersonal awareness, feelings of empathy, internal locus of control, sense of humor, and an optimistic view of the future (Cohen, 2002; Emery & Forehand, 1996; Stolberg & Garrison, 1985).

Children's and adolescents' beliefs and feelings about their parents' divorce may moderate or mediate its effects or impact on them (Amato, 2000; Emery & Forehand, 1996). If they do not blame themselves and they are able to understand that their parents' problems are not caused by them, they more easily adjust to the divorce. Coping styles that involve open exploration and communication of their feelings about the divorce and their parents allow children and adolescents to identify and adapt to the divorce. On the other hand, children who become withdrawn and silent about the divorce and employ avoidant coping strategies may develop complex grief reactions. Children and adolescents cope differently due to varying cognitive abilities and developmental tasks depending on their age and life experiences (Emery & Forehand, 1996).

Good social skills are important life-enhancing factors for children and adolescents as they navigate their parents' divorce (Aseltine, 1996; Hetherington, 1999). Social skills include communication, problem-solving, decision-making, self-management, and peer relations abilities that allow children and adolescents to initiate and maintain positive social relationships with others. Social competence is related to peer acceptance, teacher acceptance, and success in school and extracurricular activities. These skills include the ability to share, to allow others to talk without interrupting, taking turns, and possessing some degree of flexibility. In addition, the ability to appropriately manage anger and tolerate frustration enables children and adolescents to connect with other children, adolescents, and adults in a healthy and positive manner.

Children and adolescents who possess interpersonal awareness know and understand their thoughts, feelings, and behaviors (Amato, 2000). This translates to their awareness of how their actions impact others and helps them regulate their behavior. They are more easily able to understand that their parents' divorce was not caused by them and that there are times when adults can no longer live together. This awareness leads to feelings of empathy, which allows them to understand why people, especially their divorced parents, behave the way they do. Also, empathy helps children and adolescents read and interpret nonverbal cues.

Another life-enhancing factor for children and adolescents is a high internal locus of control (Aseltine, 1996; Hetherington, 1999; Kim, Sandler, & Jenn-Yum, 1997). These children and teens do not feel as though they are at the mercy of whatever occurs in life but believe that they have some amount of control over the outcome or of their response to it. Children and adolescents with greater degrees of internal locus of control possess a positive sense of self that does not depend on external reinforcement.

A sense of humor is an emotional and social tool that children and adolescents can rely on to help them through adverse life events such as parental divorce (Erickson & Feldstein, 2007). This includes seeing things from a variety of perspectives, being spontaneous, and exhibiting unconventional thinking. These youth recognize the absurd, enjoy the playfulness of life, and do not take themselves too seriously. There are physical and emotional benefits of humor that support the immune system, help children and adolescents connect with others, serve as a coping mechanism, and increase hope (Schuurman & DeCristofaro, 2009).

Maintaining an optimistic view of the future is another life-enhancing factor that leads to better outcomes of parental divorce for children and adolescents (Cohen, 2002). Children and adolescents who hold positive beliefs about the divorce tend to think more positively, develop active problem-solving abilities, and exhibit fewer psychological symptoms (Mazur et al., 1999). This suggests that attention to the positive outcomes of divorce leads to better adjustment in children and adolescents.

FAMILIAL LIFE-ENHANCING FACTORS

There are several important enhancing factors within family life that focus on the relationship between children and adolescents and their divorced parents, as well as the relationship between the divorced parents themselves. These factors include the existence of supportive and caring parents, a positive parent-child/adolescent relationship, parental cooperation and harmony, a supportive relationship with at least one parent, consistent parental rules and discipline, the maintenance of a normal household routine, and continued contact with the noncustodial parent (Cohen, 2002; Emery & Forehand, 1996; Stolberg & Garrison, 1985).

Children and adolescents tend to cope better with divorce if their parents exhibit supportive and caring behavior toward them. Although the family constellation changes during divorce, the parent-child/adolescent relationship must remain positive, strong, and consistent. This allows children and adolescents to continue to feel loved, cared for, supported, and that no matter what happens the relationship is a reliable reality. A positive relationship with at least one parent mitigates against the difficulties that can occur in response to parental divorce, even if the relationship with the other parent is not good (Emery & Forehand, 1996). In addition, frequent and consistent contact with the noncustodial parent predicts better adjustment to divorce (Emery & Forehand, 1996). Maintaining positive parent-child/adolescent relationships enables children and adolescents to develop a healthy attachment, trust, and security in future relationships.

Parental cooperation and harmony act as a life-enhancing factor buffering children and adolescents from the grief and other sources of distress in divorce. Children and adolescents tend to have better relationships with their divorced parents, grandparents, stepparents, and siblings when parents remain cooperative and cordial following the divorce (Ahrons, 2006). The emotional climate around the transition between parental households needs to be smooth and consistent. This decreases the possible stress and discomfort they may feel as they maneuver back and forth between two different parents in two different household environments.

If children receive consistent parental rules and discipline, maintain a normal routine, and experience continued parental acceptance and caring, then they are in a better position to survive the divorce with healthier levels of functioning both at home and at school (Cohen, 2002; Emery & Forehand, 1996). Maintaining these norms increases feelings of safety, security, and lets children and adolescents know what to expect on a daily basis.

Continued contact and interaction with the noncustodial parent has positive effects on children and adolescents. Contact with noncustodial fathers, for instance, predicts higher academic achievement and fewer behavior problems (Ahrons & Tanner, 2003; Amato, 2000).

LIFE-ENHANCING FACTORS IN THE ENVIRONMENT

Life-enhancing factors in the environment include a supportive network of extended family, friends, and peers. In addition, positive and successful school experiences, a feeling that teachers understand, a connection to the school community and to teachers, a connection to the neighborhood community, and a connection to a religious community make a difference for children and adolescents experiencing parental divorce (Cohen, 2002; Emery & Forehand, 1996; Stolberg & Garrison, 1985).

A supportive network of extended family members, friends, and peers enables children and adolescents to cope with the loss that divorce entails (Amato, 2000). This network can help them understand and adapt to the changes brought on by divorce. This support is crucial especially if they are enduring an uncooperative and disharmonious parental divorce. This network can provide a healthy retreat away from the conflict.

Children and adolescents who have positive and successful school experiences cope better with their parents' divorce. Success may be evidenced by good grades and/or involvement in extracurricular activities, which provides children and adolescents an arena where they can master and have some control over the outcome. Connection to the school community and to teachers is an important life-enhancing factor in that it provides them a place to be engaged, away from the home environment. Positive attention and understanding shown by teachers is associated with positive child and adolescent adjustment following divorce (Emery & Forehand, 1996).

Connection to the neighborhood community also provides an outlet for children and adolescents. A neighborhood swimming pool, basketball court, or park can offer another setting in which they can connect with friends and peers. If a family is involved in a religious community, this is another available support network that allows children and adolescents a place to retreat to and gain additional support.

TABLE 4.1
Life-Enhancing Factors

Individual	Familial	Environmental
Attitudes or coping style	Supportive and caring parents	Supportive network of extended family
Cognitive abilities	Positive parent-child/ adolescent relationship	Supportive network of friends and peers
Social skills	Supportive relationship with at least one parent	Positive and successful school experiences
Interpersonal awareness	Parental cooperation and harmony	Feeling that teachers understand
Feelings of empathy	Consistent parental rules and discipline	Connection to school community and teachers
Internal locus of control	Maintenance of a normal routine	Connection to neighborhood community
Sense of humor	Contact with noncustodial parent	Connection to religious community
Optimistic view of the future		

(Cohen, 2002; Emery & Forehand, 1996; Stolberg & Garrison, 1985)

Risk Factors

Risk factors are elements that deter children and adolescents from developing healthy coping skills in regard to parental divorce. The multiple factors that increase and amplify life-depleting reactions to the changes and challenges that divorce may bring are characterized by three categories in table 4.2 to include individual risk factors, familial risk factors, and environmental risk factors.

INDIVIDUAL RISK FACTORS

The individual risk factors that contribute to a child or adolescent's life-depleting reactions related to their parents' divorce include having a difficult temperament, poor coping skills, poor social skills, a lack of interpersonal awareness, an external locus of control, lacking a sense of humor, and presenting a very serious outlook (Cohen, 2002; Emery & Forehand, 1996; Stolberg & Garrison, 1985).

A difficult temperament has been associated with more emotional and adjustment problems in children following parental divorce (Emery & Forehand, 1996). Adaptation to change in these children

TABLE 4.2
Risk Factors

Individual	Familial	Environmental
Difficult temperament	Interparental conflict and hostility	No or limited contact with extended family members
Poor coping skills	Poor parenting skills	Nonexistent network of supportive friends or peers
Poor social skills	Reduced or no contact with noncustodial parent	School performance problems
Lack of interpersonal awareness	Lowered family income	Learning difficulties
External locus of control		Negative relationships with teachers
Lack of sense of humor		No community connection
Very serious outlook		

(Cohen, 2002; Emery & Forehand, 1996; Stolberg & Garrison, 1985)

appears to be problematic especially with the increase in stress. Therefore, personality types may have an impact on how children and adolescents cope with parental divorce. Consideration must also be made regarding the parents' personality types. For example, antisocial parents are more apt to divorce and are most likely to have temperamentally difficult children (Lahye et al., 1988).

Children and adolescents who exhibit poor or life-depleting coping skills tend to adjust poorly to their parents' divorce. Avoidant behavior, distraction, and self-blame are the most prevalent manifestations of poor coping skills (Amato, 2000; Emery & Forehand, 1996). Some children and adolescents distract themselves with school work, video games, or music to the point of isolation. Initial or elevated levels of substance use or abuse can occur as a further method of distraction and escape (Doherty & Needle, 1991; Sun, 2001). Children and adolescents who distract themselves and avoid discussing their grief about their parents' divorce are apt to hold in negative emotions, isolate from family and friends, and become anxious or depressed. They may blame themselves for the dissolution of the family unit, believing they are the cause of their parents' divorce (Amato, 2000). Many children and adolescents who self-blame ruminate about how they could have been better at school, more helpful at home, and wish they had not been born.

Children and adolescents who are deficient in social skills have difficulty interacting with others (Aseltine, 1996; Hetherington, 1999). They may misread social or communication cues, and often do not show appropriate behavior in social settings. Displaying poor social skills may cause rejection by other children, adolescents, or adults, particularly teachers. This may contribute to or exacerbate already existing learning problems or conflicts in the classroom. Poor social skills detract from children's and adolescents' ability to obtain needed support from friends and peers as they experience parental divorce.

Children and adolescents who lack interpersonal awareness do not have a good understanding of their thoughts and feelings, or the motives affecting their behavior. They may have limited capability to connect their actions with how others react to them and have difficulty self-regulating their behavior. Their ability to read nonverbal cues is limited, and they may easily misread others' behavior. This makes it more difficult for them to understand that their parents' divorce is not caused by them.

Children and adolescents who maintain an external locus of control tend to believe that things happen due to chance or fate (Aseltine, 1996; Hetherington, 1999; Kim et al., 1997). They do not see themselves as having control over events in their lives. They perceive that reinforcement comes from the external world rather than from within themselves. Academic or extracurricular achievements are viewed as due to luck or being at the right place at the right time. When a divorce occurs, children with an external locus of control feel like powerless pawns in an overwhelming conflict. This can lead to low self-esteem, hopelessness, and depression.

When children and adolescents lack a sense of humor, they are at a disadvantage for coping and managing the adverse events of life (Erickson & Feldstein, 2007). It limits their ability to look at life events from a variety of perspectives, and they tend not to be very spontaneous. Their outlook on life is very serious, which makes it difficult for them to relax. Serious children and adolescents tend to be vigilant, as if waiting for negative events to occur. They are apt to personalize their responsibility, particularly around their parents' divorce, and catastrophize about the possibility of adverse outcomes (Mazur et al., 1999).

FAMILIAL RISK FACTORS

Familial risk factors that impact children and adolescents of parental divorce include interparental conflict and hostility, poor parenting skills, reduced or no contact with the noncustodial parent, and lowered family income (Cohen, 2002; Emery & Forehand, 1996; Stolberg & Garrison, 1985).

The existence of interparental conflict and hostility is more strongly related to children's adjustment than the actual divorce (Clarke-Stewart et al., 2000; Emery & Forehand, 1996). Conflict disrupts the ability to parent well and can lead to children's problematic behavior. High levels of interparental conflict and hostility expose children to negative models of interpersonal relationships, which can lead to more aggression and acting out behavior. When divorced parents remain hostile and speak badly of one another, children and adolescents become conflicted about loyalty to their parents, often siding with one or the other (Ahrons, 2006; Amato & Afifi, 2006). This can lead to a sense of fragmentation because children and adolescents may feel the need to keep their relationship with each parent completely separate. In addition, parents' anger with each other can diminish a parent's involvement with the child/adolescent (Ahrons, 2006).

Children do not function as well when poor parenting skills exist. These may include limited affection, lack of consistency, erratic routines, and feelings of rejection. Poor monitoring and supervision, dispensing of harsh discipline, increased parent-child conflict, and the use of poor problem-solving can lead to life-depleting reactions in children and adolescents to divorce (Amato, 2000; Emery & Forehand, 1996). Poor parenting skills may have existed prior to the divorce or emerge as a result of the divorce.

Reduced or no contact with one of the parents is also a risk factor (Amato, 2000). This of course, is dependent on the parent's pre-divorce relationship with the children. If the relationship was problematic and conflictual, then disengagement may act as a protective factor. However, if the pre-divorce parent-child/adolescent relationship was positive, caring, and supportive, then risk is created when that relationship is diminished to the point of reduced or no contact (Videon, 2002).

Another risk factor pertains to the socioeconomic status of children post-divorce. In the majority of families, divorce tends to deprive children of much of the resources provided by dual income families (Fischer, 2007). Lowered family income, especially if it is severe and leads to economic hardship, contributes to stress and depression in parents, and psychological and academic problems in children and adolescents (Amato, 2000; Clarke-Stewart et al., 2000; Sun, 2001). A decline in socioeconomic status increases other negative life events such as moving from a bigger to a smaller house or apartment, living with relatives, and a change in neighborhood and schools. This impacts children's and adolescents' friendships, support systems, and extracurricular activities. These divorce-incurred negative life events represent significant losses to children and adolescents that can potentially lead to prolonged grief reactions.

ENVIRONMENTAL RISK FACTORS

There are several environmental risk factors that deter children and adolescents from healthy adaptation to parental divorce. These include no or limited contact with extended family members, a nonexistent network of supportive friends or peers, school performance problems, learning difficulties, negative relationships with teachers and the school community, and a lack of connection to a community or neighborhood, (Cohen, 2002; Emery & Forehand, 1996; Stolberg & Garrison, 1985).

Sometimes divorce causes reduced contact with extended family members (Emery & Forehand, 1996). This is particularly true if interparental conflict involves extended family members taking sides in the divorce, which can heighten conflict. Children and adolescents may lose this important support system of people who can help them navigate the changes in their lives. This is a group of people who perhaps know, understand, and love them, which includes grandparents, aunts, uncles, cousins, and other relatives. Children and adolescents are also at risk if they do not have a supportive network of friends or peers to help them normalize and validate their thoughts and feelings. Friends and peers offer distraction and normalcy.

Divorce can exacerbate any school performance problems that children and adolescents may have been facing pre-divorce, especially in areas of reading and math achievement (Emery & Forehand, 1996). Any existing learning difficulties may worsen in response to the stress of parental divorce, and new academic problems may arise. This can make school a stressful and adversarial environment.

Children and adolescents who have negative relationships with teachers, principals, or the school community in general may find the school environment stressful and dread attending school (Amato, 2000). This risk factor can lead to more school problems, absences, and even school dropout. The dual challenge of parental divorce and poor school relationships can seem insurmountable.

Another environmental risk factor involves children and adolescents having no connection to their community, neighborhood, or religious organization. This can add to a sense of loneliness and isolation, particularly as they experience the unraveling of their family.

Assessment Methods with Children and Adolescents

The overall mental health of children and adolescents can more accurately be measured than specific cognitive and emotional components (Emery & Forehand, 1996). However, there are several measurement instruments available to practitioners that are easy to administer, score, and evaluate, and that provide information about the emotional experience of children and adolescents coping with parental divorce. These measurement instruments can be used together or separately, depending on the areas practitioners need to assess. Listed below are seven such instruments, which can be found in *Measures for Clinical Practice* (Fischer & Corcoran, 2007).

1. The Children's Beliefs about Parental Divorce Scale (CBAPDS) is a thirty-six-item yes/no objective scale designed to measure children's problematic beliefs about their parents' divorce. It includes statements about the thoughts and feelings children have about themselves and their separated parents. Practitioners can gain useful information about children's experiences of peer ridicule and avoidance, fear of abandonment, maternal blame, hope of parents' reunification, and self-blame. It is recommended for children in grades three to six, and adolescents in grades seven to nine.

2. The Child's Attitude toward Father (CAF) and Mother (CAM) scales are twenty-five-item instruments designed to measure the extent, degree, and/or severity of problems a child may have with either parent. These scales measure the degree of contentment that children have in their relationship with their parents. Scores can alert practitioners that children are experiencing severe stress with the possibility of some type of violence being used to deal with stressors and problems. It is recommended for use with children ages twelve and up.

3. The How I Feel (HIF) is a thirty-item self-report measure designed to assess emotional arousal and regulation of children ages eight to twelve. It is based on the premise that a child's ability to regulate or control emotions that occur with social interactions increases his or her capacity for adaptive coping. This measurement instrument can benefit practitioners in understanding the interplay between arousal and control in social-emotional adjustment in children, particularly as they navigate their parents' divorce.

4. The Norwicki-Strickland Locus of Control Scale (N-SLCS) is a forty-item yes/no questionnaire designed to measure whether a child/adolescent has an internal or external locus of control. This can inform practitioners about whether or not this is an individual risk factor or an individual protective factor. It is recommended for children in grades three and above.

5. The Children and Adolescent Social and Adaptive Functioning Scale (CASAFS) is a twenty-four-item questionnaire designed to measure social functioning of children and adolescents. It includes subscales of school performance, peer relationships, family relationships, and home duties/self-care. This measurement instrument can benefit practitioners to identify areas of

strengths to be maximized and deficits to be targeted for treatment. It is recommended for children and adolescents in grades eight and above.

6. The Adolescent Coping Orientation for Problem Experiences (A-COPE) is a fifty-four-item questionnaire designed to measure and record behaviors adolescents determine helpful in managing problems or difficult situations that happen to them or their family members. Practitioners can utilize the results to assess an adolescent's coping strategy during or following parental divorce. It is recommended for adolescents in both middle school and high school.

7. The Inventory of Parent and Peer Attachment (IPPA) consists of three twenty-five-item questionnaires that measure attachment to parents and peers. The three separate scales measure attachment to mother, father, and close friends. Attachment to these significant others is an important source of security, considering the attachment issues potentially created by parental divorce. It is recommended for ages ten to twenty.

Practitioners are cautioned not to assume that all children and adolescents who experience divorce of their parents are symptomatic in response. Resilience plays a key role as children and adolescents grow and develop. Divorce is not always a sufficient explanation of symptoms. It is beneficial to perform a thorough assessment to determine if presenting symptoms are related to divorce and its impact, as well as to rule out any other mental health issues. Each member of a divorcing family can experience varying degrees of both distress and adjustment at different points in time throughout the divorce process (Amato, 2000). One child may experience stress prior to the divorce, another during the disintegration of the marriage, and still another post-divorce. Meeting with the divorced parents, together or separately, depending on their ability to cooperate and co-parent without hostility, is advantageous in gathering useful information about the child's or adolescent's previous and current behaviors, academic performance, mood, and developmental milestones.

Interventions with Children and Adolescents

Interventions with children and adolescents should focus primarily on adjustment and constructively modifying their response to the outcomes of divorce. Pre-divorce parental conflict and hostility cannot be undone; however, practitioners can help children and adolescents identify and understand their perceptions of these interactions (Stolberg & Garrison, 1985). Providing a supportive environment for direct discussion helps reduce the impact of divorce on children and adolescents and guide them through reframing their perception of divorce (Zambelli & DeRosa, 1992). Children and adolescents learn to discuss the losses that divorce has created in their lives and to recognize and develop coping strategies.

BIBLIOTHERAPY

The use of literature may be a life-enhancing intervention for both children and adolescents. Books for children that deal with themes of divorce and its subsequent changes and losses enable them to explore and discuss their behaviors, distressing thoughts, and feelings of grief. Bibliotherapy can be a non-threatening way for the practitioner to enter into the confused world of the child (Christenbury, Beale, & Patch, 1996). Their sense of isolation and being different from other children may be reduced if they realize other children, even if they are only characters in a book, have had similar experiences (Ayyash-Abdo, 2001). This allows children to identify with the characters and to vicariously share their experiences (Zambelli & DeRosa, 1992). It is an effective method for practitioners to engage children in discussing their lives before, during, and after their parents' divorce.

The use of literature with adolescents allows them to identify, acknowledge, and normalize their own grief reactions to their parents' divorce. Many books aimed at adolescents explain the consequences of divorce, how to develop the necessary coping skills, and ways of altering their social environment in order to adapt to the changes and losses created by divorce.

There are limitations to the utilization of bibliotherapy with children and adolescents. It should be used as an adjunct to working with the practitioner rather than the main treatment approach. Practitioners can refer to appendix B at the end of this chapter for a list of therapeutic children's books relevant to parental divorce.

ARTWORK

Making art can be therapeutic and cathartic for children and adolescents as they maneuver through parental divorce. Children and adolescents can be encouraged to make drawings or paintings, or construct collages. Children can have difficulty verbalizing the inner turmoil caused by divorce. Feelings of confusion, frustration, anger, and grief may be evoked by and expressed through artistic activities (Ayyah-Abdo, 2001). Children can be asked to draw specific pictures about their family and about themselves. They can be encouraged to draw each parent's household and their place in it. Also, providing children and adolescents the opportunity to draw during a therapy session often allows them to speak more freely about their thoughts and feelings. It serves to provide a safe activity on which to focus while discussing a potentially emotional topic.

Adolescents can be encouraged to draw or write, both during sessions and outside of sessions. They will often keep a journal of prose, poetry, ideas, and drawings that express their thoughts and feelings. Adolescents are often willing to share these with the practitioner as an invitation to their world, which opens up an avenue for expression and exploration about their reactions to parental divorce.

Interventions with Families

Families experience grief and loss in response to divorce. Practitioners can work with families in the aftermath of divorce by helping them mourn the loss of attachments and of life plans that must be revised (Bernstein, 2006).

Practitioners can aid divorcing parents to consider the impact of their post-divorce interactions on children and adolescents by helping them realize that parent-child relationships continue throughout the course of their lives (Ahrons, 2006). An ex-spouse can still be a valued member of a child's or adolescent's family, and practitioners can help post-divorce parents achieve a mutually respectful relationship (Bernstein, 2006). Family therapy has the potential of bridging painful gaps in post-divorce families when practitioners utilize methods such as thinking systematically, listening with sensitivity and respecting the voice of each family member, and creating a safe and secure environment (Bernstein, 2006).

When the mother is the custodial parent after divorce, the father may often feel unimportant in the child's life. It is imperative that practitioners emphasize to fathers the importance of continued contact with their children. Early intervention with divorcing fathers has shown to significantly increase their involvement and improve relationships with their children even years later (Ahrons & Tanner, 2003; Cookston, Braver, & Griffin, 2007; Cowan, Cowan, Pruett, & Pruett, 2007). It is also important to work with mothers to help them recognize the benefits and needs of children's relationships with their fathers. Clearly, maintaining the child-parent relationship should be pursued if there has been no history of abuse.

Practitioners can be of great benefit to parents who maintain hostile relationships by pointing out the damage to children and adolescents incurred by painful loyalty conflicts (Ahrons, 2006; Amato & Afifi, 2006). Power struggles between divorced parents cause inordinate amounts of stress on children and adolescents. These need to be recognized, defused, and diminished. Practitioners can help divorced parents develop effective co-parenting skills to minimize conflicts and build an increased resilience within the family. Amicable divorces allow children and adolescents to maintain relationships with each parent and their extended families (Ahrons, 2006). The bond between each parent and their children can be strengthened and supported over time (Shulman, 2005).

   Either parent may be overwhelmed by the changes divorce brings. There may be lingering feelings of anger, fear, sadness, and grief, as well as problems with depression and anxiety. Maintaining anger toward the ex-spouse may serve as a method of diverting a devastating depression or an all-encompassing grief (Bernstein, 2007). Practitioners can work with either parent to manage thoughts and feelings related to divorce and issues of co-parenting. Also, the relationship between children and adolescents and either parent can undergo changes and even become problematic. They may experience more closeness or more distance, changes in strictness, increased responsibility in the family, and more autonomy (Emery & Forehand, 1996). The oldest child is often thrust into the role of a secondary parent. Either parent can have difficulty maintaining parental authority, completing the myriad tasks of running a household, and giving affection toward their children (Emery & Forehand, 1996).

Group Interventions

Groups for children and adolescents of divorce focus on many of the commonly occurring stressors associated with parental divorce and offer strategies on effectively coping with these strains (Holmes & Sprenkle, 1996). Groups are designed to alleviate misconceptions, negative cognitions, and troublesome symptoms related to divorce. Essential group components include providing support, giving information about divorce and ensuing reactions, and ensuring a safe environment for discussion and expression of feelings. Group practitioners can teach communication skills, social skills, relaxation skills, anger management skills, and problem-solving skills (Holmes & Sprenkle, 1996). Benefits of group involvement include reduction in feelings of shame and isolation, decreased anxiety, increased assertiveness, and development of positive feelings about their families, themselves, and their parents (Emery & Forehand, 1996; Stolberg & Garrison, 1985). Feelings of anger, confusion, betrayal, self-blame, frustration, and grief are typical as children and adolescents confront the losses caused by divorce. An important aspect of group work is the normalization of thoughts, feelings, and behaviors as peers discuss similar experiences regarding the multiple changes, transitions, and losses that divorce brings into their lives. Groups help to replace the support systems that children and adolescents may have lost due to their parents' divorce. Group involvement promotes a move from parent-child focus to one of peer-group relatedness (Zambelli & DeRosa, 1992). Group members "learn to use others as a valid source of social comparison of their emotions and ideas . . . there is a move from one-way assistance (i.e., parent-child focus) to interpersonal relations that are based on reciprocity, intimacy, mutuality of trust, and interdependence (i.e., peer-group relatedness)" (Grunebaum & Solomon, 1982).

The following is from a booklet titled *Tips for Kids Living in Changing Families*, which was created by a group of adolescents experiencing separation and loss in their families (Malekoff, 2004, p. 182):

- Don't hide it all inside. Otherwise you will get very sad.
- Think about it, or it will hit you all at once and when you least expect it.
- Don't feel like what happened is your fault.
- Just because your parents can't stand each other, doesn't mean they can't stand you.
- If you're angry, control your temper and don't hurt anyone.
- If you're upset, don't take it out on yourself or anyone else.
- If you're sad, show your feelings to someone you feel close to.
- Go to a therapy place if you don't have anyone to talk to.
- Don't be afraid to cry.
- Try not to be pessimistic. Be optimistic.
- The only thing to fear is fear itself.
- As long as there is love in your family, that's all that counts.

This information, constructed by adolescents, is valuable for other youth because it originates from the perspective of those directly affected by divorce. Practitioners can use the group setting to encourage members to learn from each other and formulate their own life-enhancing responses to divorce.

Common Ethical Dilemmas

Practitioners who work with children, adolescents, and families at any stage of parental divorce will often encounter competing agendas and needs from the different members of the family. There is, therefore, the potential for conflicts of interest and other ethical dilemmas to arise during any intervention process. This situation is especially salient when the legal system is involved.

Custody battles can be contentious and hostile. Children can often get caught in the middle of this conflict. Practitioners can unknowingly find themselves being asked by parents to conduct child and adolescent psychosocial assessments for the purpose of gaining custody of the youth. Parents may attempt to manipulate the process in order to influence the outcome of the assessment. Practitioners, therefore, must be careful that any findings they report to a third party are not biased and are based solely on the practitioner's observations. If ongoing therapy for the parents is warranted, it is highly recommended that each parent has a separate therapist from the child.

Another ethical dilemma that can occur when working with families and divorce involves the issues of neutrality and confidentiality. While providing a safe and confidential environment for children to express their inner thoughts and feelings, the practitioner must remain objective and not display favoritism toward one parent. This allows youths to resolve their own feelings about the relationships within the divorced family system. While each parent has the right to information about the youth's progress in therapy, the practitioner must also keep specific dialogue with the youth confidential unless there is a danger to self or others.

It is important that practitioners stay up-to-date with their state's laws and statutes with regard to mandatory reporting of abuse. Practitioners have a professional and legal responsibility to report any suspicion of neglect and/or physical/sexual abuse to a child protection agency. This must be done without hesitation, even though an investigation may cause even more disturbance, confusion, and pain to an already challenged family system.

While these are general ethical considerations, there are many unique circumstances that could arise that create ethical dilemmas for the practitioner. Quality consultation or supervision is highly recommended, especially for practitioners who have limited experience in this area.

Cultural Considerations

Practitioners who work with children, adolescents, and their families must be aware of cultural issues related to divorce and parenting. As the population continues to diversify, it is important to note the value that different cultural groups often place on the family unit (Schwartz &

Finley, 2005). Considerations of ethnicity and race, culture, religion, country of origin, gender and sexual identity, and each family's system of values and norms should be assessed when developing and implementing grief-related interventions.

Examples of factors that contribute to divorce include age at marriage, age at first birth, presence of a young child in the marriage, religion, geography, educational attainment, socioeconomic status, and differences in age between husband and wife (Kposowa, 1998). Within different cultures are varying views and social sanctions regarding marriage and divorce. In some cultures divorce is highly stigmatized, whereas in other cultures it is widely accepted. In this way, the cultural background of a family may influence post-divorce adjustment, including changes in social, familial, and occupational status. For example, in some cultures, divorced women may be shunned by their families and friends, which can add to the losses that their children experience. Children in these situations may also face rejection by their peers. In addition, in some cultures a divorced woman may not be able to secure a means of living, making it virtually impossible to care for her children. There has been a dearth of research on multicultural factors that may impact children of divorce. From a clinical perspective, the relevance of these issues warrants further study. Despite this lack of information, practitioners need to be aware of the potential influence that culture may have in children's grief experience with divorce. Often the best practice is for practitioners to become active learners and allow the families to teach them about the implications that divorce has within their respective cultures.

The term *family* encompasses a range of meanings, which can include many different configurations of people. Families are "variable, fluid forms that are structured by and around the individuals within them" (Gabb, 2005, p. 587). This may include people who are biologically related and those who combine as a family based on affection, respect, similar life goals, and numerous other reasons. Many more families are blending biological and non-biological ties, with lesbian, gay, bisexual, and transgender people creating innovative ways to plan and define families (Allen, 2007).

Of particular consideration is the impact that separation, or "same-gender relational breakup," has on children of lesbian-headed families, or "lesbian parent families" (Allen, 2007; Gabb, 2005). This is also true of gay male co-parents, whether the children or adolescents are adoptive or biologically related. Without "legal rights and a parent identity," lesbian co-mothers and gay male co-fathers, particularly if they are not the birth mother or biological father, often lose connection and access to the child or adolescent they co-parented (Abrams, 1999; Gabb, 2005). When lesbian mothers and gay male fathers separate, the "other mother" or "other father" must often negotiate visitation rights with the biological parent. Likewise, the child or adolescent can painfully miss the former relationship and is further isolated from support and understanding due to the loss of the other mother or other father (Allen, 2007). The child's or adolescent's loss can be further compounded by estrangement and conflict between the former couple. Allen (2007) describes this as "fractured parent-child ties" which causes ambiguous loss, confusion, sadness, uncertainty, and a great deal of mourning. Intimate adult partnerships may end, but relationships with children and adolescents need consistency and continuity (Amato, 2000). Practitioners and nontraditional families can work together to manage the relationship losses in order to create a smooth and less painful transition.

CASE EXAMPLE

"Forever Caught in the Middle"

The following case example illustrates how a conflictual parental divorce affects a boy's life from childhood through adolescence. Concepts in this chapter are incorporated in the case example:

Travis is a sixteen-year-old boy whose parents divorced when he was seven years old. His parents agreed on joint custody, and he splits his time equally between the two households, spending a week at a time with each parent. His father remarried when he was eight years old, and his mother remarried when he was nine. Neither of his stepparents have children. He is an only child within two different families. Travis's parents fought verbally and physically throughout his early years. He describes going to his bedroom and curling up in a ball "to be as small and insignificant as possible." Whenever he perceived conflict in either household, he retreated to his bedroom and "holed up" until things calmed down. Travis had avoided all conflict within his two families, at school, and with friends up until the past two years.

Travis did well academically in elementary and middle schools. He caused no problems in school and "followed all the rules, like everyone expected." Teachers liked him since he was quiet, compliant, and did his homework. High school presented a different challenge. He failed a couple of courses during his freshman and sophomore years but did pass them in summer school. Both sets of parents were very unhappy with him, particularly his father.

Travis has played baseball "like forever since I can remember." This was something he and his father had as a common interest. Travis has been on select teams, playing year round. His father invested a great deal of money in baseball instruction clinics, camps, and select teams. However, Travis did not make the team in high school, and could not try out his sophomore year due to failing grades.

He describes his father as extremely authoritarian, raging whenever Travis does not meet his expectations. Travis is often grounded from activities with friends, driving, and from his cell phone. Weeks with his father and stepmother involve chores, homework, isolation, and avoidance of his father. Travis basically shuts down. Weeks with his mother and stepfather are completely different. Travis is rarely grounded and has been given many freedoms "to be a teenager." He is encouraged to socialize with friends, can drive his car, and always has his cell phone.

Although his parents no longer engage in physical altercations, they continue to "fight over everything about my life." Both biological parents pay equally for costs involving Travis unless it is something extra that either parent wants to invest in. His father paid for costs associated with baseball and his mother paid for guitar lessons over the years. Both parents split the cost for private school tuition in elementary and middle school. His parents argued extensively over which high school he would attend. His father wanted him to attend public school in their neighborhood, and his mother preferred he continue in private school. Travis also preferred attending the private high school since the majority of his friends and peers would be there. These are friends and peers he has known since kindergarten. His father "won that one because of the money. He never lets me forget how much I cost. Why did they even have me if I cost so much?" Travis is tired of being caught in the middle, in between his parents. He feels they fight over him and that he is the cause of their continued strife, his father's rage, and his mother's sadness.

Over the past two years Travis has shifted from being quiet, compliant, and obedient to being loud, argumentative, and stubborn, and does not hold back his anger. However, this happens only at school and when he spends his week at his mother's home, and never during the week with his father and stepmother. He has punched his fist through walls at his mother's house, yelled at her to the point of bringing her to tears, and got in his car and driven away.

Travis harbors a lot of anger and resentment, especially toward his father. He has begun to dislike anyone in an authority position, including teachers, whom he has been giving a hard time. He states that teachers do not understand him and that "they are stupid."

Travis's mother and stepfather brought him to the initial session midway through his freshman year in high school. His father gave his consent for treatment but refused invitations to join his son in a session. Individual therapy, along with some family intervention was the focus. One of the main areas for work with Travis, his mother, and his stepfather was the setting of appropriate and consistent limits. He had been given too much freedom "to be a teenager," and his mother admitted to trying to make up for "his horrible childhood" by giving him whatever he wanted when he wanted it. There were some initial power struggles as Travis adjusted to the new household rules. The therapy helped Travis become aware of how his behaviors were manifestations of his feelings of loss related to his parents' divorce. Travis was seen individually throughout his freshman year.

During his sophomore year, Travis was referred to an adolescent support group co-led by a female and male practitioner. The group consisted of four boys and five girls, all of whom had experienced their parents' divorce. Some had stepparents, some had a single parent, and others were negotiating relationships with a second stepparent. Travis met two boys and a girl who also expressed their anger by hitting things and throwing objects. The group discussed less destructive methods of releasing anger while validating the reality and commonality of the feeling. Group members were encouraged to keep a journal and bring in any writings or drawings that conveyed their thoughts, feelings, and behavior between group sessions. Travis produced a number of drawings revealing a talent that he had kept hidden from his parents. His drawings were dark and foreboding yet extremely detailed and precise. He explained the emotions attached to his drawings, and group members responded with understanding, empathy, and acknowledgment of entertaining some of the same thoughts.

The practitioners taught the group members relaxation skills to be practiced in times of stress. Travis grasped the concepts involved and successfully used the skills to calm himself whenever he felt angry and misunderstood. He envisioned a safe and secure place while breathing deeply. This worked for him while he endured his father's rages and during stressful times at his mother's house. However, retreating to his bedroom and drawing was the most beneficial stress reducer for him, and particularly sharing them with the group.

Travis will begin his junior year of high school with some new skills. He plans to continue group participation, individual therapy, and to use drawing as a means of emotional expression. He has come to the realization that his father may never change but that employment of his newfound skills can help him remain calm. He is still angry and frustrated about being caught in the middle of his parents' continued plans for him but expresses his feelings in more constructive ways.

Summary

Parental divorce is often experienced as a significant loss for children and adolescents. Though they are not involved in the decision to divorce, their lives are affected tremendously. Though this can provoke intense feelings of frustration and powerlessness in youth, there are often numerous strengths that can be called upon to help buffer the effects of this kind of loss. Children of divorce can learn how to use life-enhancing strategies for coping with the many transitions and feelings of loss that accompany divorce. While parental divorce can resolve many of the life issues confronting adults in the family, it is often the beginning of a grief experience for the children and teens involved.

Often, the grief response that is evoked by divorce goes unnoticed until other behavioral and emotional symptoms surface. It is important for practitioners to recognize that grief extends to divorce situations and may follow youth into their adult lives.

References

Abrams, N. (1999). *The other mother: A lesbian's fight for her daughter.* Madison: University of Wisconsin Press.

Ahrons, C. R. (2006). Family ties after divorce: Long-term implications for children. *Family Process, 46*(1), 53–65.

Ahrons, C. R., & Tanner, J. L. (2003). Adult children and fathers: Relationships 20 years after parental divorce. *Family Relations, 52*(4), 340–351.

Allen, K. R. (2007). Ambiguous loss after lesbian couples with children break up: A case for same-gender divorce. *Family Relations, 56,*175–183.

Amato, P. R. (2000). The consequences of divorce for adults and children. *Journal of Marriage and Family, 62*(4), 1269–1287.

Amato, P. R., & Afifi, T. D. (2006). Feeling caught between parents: Adult children's relations with parents and subjective well-being. *Journal of Marriage and Family, 68*(1), 222–235.

Aseltine, R. H. (1996). Pathways linking parental divorce with adolescent depression. *Journal of Health and Social Behavior, 3*(2), 133–148.

Ayyash-Abdo, H. (2001). Childhood bereavement: What school psychologists need to know. *School Psychology International, 22*(4), 417–433.

Bernstein, A. C. (2006). Re-visioning, restructuring, and reconciliation: Clinical practice with complex post-divorce families. *Family Process, 46*(1), 67–78.

Booth, A., & Amato, P. R. (2001). Parental predivorce relations and offspring post-divorce well-being. *Journal of Marriage and Family, 63*(1), 197–212.

Capaldi, D. M., & Patterson, G. R. (1991). The relation of parental transition to boys' adjustment problems: 1. A linear hypothesis, and 2. Mothers at risk for transitions and unskilled parenting. *Developmental Psychology, 27*(3), 489–504.

Cherlin, A. J., Furstenberg, F. F., Chase-Lansdale, P. L., Kiernan, K. E., Robins, P. K., Morrison, et al. (1991). Longitudinal studies of effects of divorce on children in Great Britain and the United States. *Science, 252*(5010), 1386–1389.

Christ, G. (2000). Impact of development on children's mourning. *Cancer Practice 8*(2), 72–81.

Christenbury, L., Beale, A. V., & Patch, S. S. (1996). Interactive bibliocounseling: Recent fiction and nonfiction for adolescents and their counselors. *School Counselor, 44*(2), 133–145.

Clarke-Stewart, K. A., Vangell, D. L., McCartney, K., Owen, M. T., & Booth, C. (2000). Effects of parental separation and divorce on very young children. *Journal of Family Psychology, 14*(2), 304–326.

Cohen, G. J. (2002). Helping children and families deal with divorce and separation. *Pediatrics, 110*(5), 1019–1023.

Cookston, J. T., Braver, S. L., & Griffin, W. A. (2007). Effects of the Dads for Life intervention on interparental conflict and coparenting in the two years after divorce. *Family Process, 46*(1), 123–137.

Cowan, C., Cowan, P., Pruett, M., & Pruett, K. (2007). An approach to preventing coparenting conflict and divorce in low-income families: Strengthening couple relationships and fostering fathers' involvement. *Family Process: Special Issue: Divorce and Its Aftermath,* 109–121.

Davies, P. T., & Cummings, E. M. (1994). Marital conflict and child adjustment: An emotional security hypothesis. *Psychological Bulletin, 116*(3), 387–411.

Doherty, W. J., & Needle, R. H. (1991). Psychological adjustment and substance use among adolescents before and after a parental divorce. *Child Development, 6*(2), 328–337.

Emery, R. E., & Forehand, R. (1996). Parental divorce and children's well-being: A focus on resilience. In R. J. Haggerty, L. R. Sherrod, N. Garmezy, & M. Rutter (Eds.), *Stress, risk, and resilience in children and adolescents: Processes, mechanisms, and interventions* (pp. 64–99). New York: Cambridge University Press.

Erickson, S. J., & Feldstein, S. W. (2007). Adolescent humor and its relationship to coping, defense strategies, psychological distress, and well-being. *Child Psychiatry and Human Development, 37*(4), 255–271.

Fischer, J., & Corcoran, K. (2007). *Measures for clinical practice and research: A sourcebook* (Vol. 1: Couples, families, and children). New York: Oxford University Press.

Fischer, T. (2007). Parental divorce and children's socio-economic success: Conditional effects of parental resources prior to divorce, and gender of the child. *Sociology, 41*(3), 475–495.

Gabb, J. (2005). Lesbian m/otherhood: Strategies of familial-linguistic management in lesbian parent families. *Sociology, 39*(4), 585–603.

Ge, X., Lorenz, F. O., Conger, R. D., Elder, G. H., & Simons, R. L. (1994). Trajectories of stressful life events and depressive symptoms during adolescence. *Developmental Psychology, 3*(4), 467–483.

Grunebaum, H., & Solomon, I. (1982). Toward a theory of peer relationships: On the stages of social development and their relationship to group psychotherapy. *International Journal of Group Psychotherapy, 32*(2), 223–307.

Hetherington, E. M. (1999). Should we stay together for the sake of the children? In E. M. Hetherington (Ed.), *Coping with divorce, single parenting, and remarriage: A risk and resiliency perspective* (pp. 93–116). Mahwah, NJ: Erlbaum.

Holmes, G. R., & Sprenkle, L. T. (1996). Group interventions in schools. *Journal of Child and Adolescent Group Therapy, 6*(4), 203–223.

Kelly, J. B. (2007). Children's living arrangements following separation and divorce: Insights from empirical and clinical research. *Family Process, 46,* 35–52.

Kim, L., Sandler, I. N., & Jenn-Yum, T. (1997). Locus of control as a stress moderator and mediator in children of divorce. *Journal of Abnormal Child Psychology, 25*(2), 144–155.

Kposowa, A. J. (1998). The impact of race on divorce in the United States. *Journal of Comparative Family Studies, 29*(3), 329–548.

Lahye, B. B., Hartdagen, S. E., Frick, P. J., McBurnett, K., Connor, R., & Hynd, G. (1988). Conduct disorder: Parsing the confounded relationship to parental divorce and antisocial personality. *Journal of Abnormal Psychology, 97*(3), 334–337.

Luecken, L. J., & Appelhans, B. (2005). Information-processing biases in young adults from bereaved and divorced families. *Journal of Abnormal Psychology, 114*(2), 309–313.

Malekoff, A. (2004). The use of "program" in group work: Cultivating a sense of competence, belonging, and creativity. In A. Malekoff, *Group work with adolescents: Principles and practice* (pp. 164–185). New York: Guilford Press.

Mazur, E., Wolchik, S. A., Virdin, L., Sandler, I. N., & West, S. G. (1999). Cognitive moderators of children's adjustment to stressful divorce events: The role of negative cognitive errors and positive illusions. *Child Development, 70*(1), 231–245.

Schuurman, D. L., & DeCristofaro, J. (2009). Adolescents, humor, and death. In D. E. Balk & C. A. Corr (Eds.), *Adolescent encounters with death, bereavement, and coping* (pp. 141–153). New York: Springer Publishing.

Schwartz, S. J., & Finley, G. E. (2005). Fathering in intact and divorced families: Ethnic differences in retrospective reports. *Journal of Marriage and Family, 67*(1), 207–215.

Shaw, D. S., Winslow, E. B., & Flanagan, C. (1999). A prospective study of the effects of marital status and family relations on young children's adjustment among African-American and European-American families. *Child Development, 70*(3), 742–755.

Shulman, L. (2005). Healing the hurts: A short-term group for separated, widowed, and divorced single parents. In A. Gitterman & L. Shulman (Eds.), *Mutual aid groups, vulnerable & resilient populations, and the life cycle* (pp. 448–468). New York: Columbia University Press.

Stolberg, A. L., & Garrison, K. M. (1985). Evaluating a primary prevention program for children of divorce. *American Journal of Community Psychology, 13*(2), 111–124.

Sun, Y. (2001). Family environment and adolescents' well-being before and after parents' marital disruption: A longitudinal study. *Journal of Marriage and Family, 63*(3), 697–713.

U.S. Bureau of the Census (2009). America's families and living arrangements: 2007, 1–21. www.census.gov.

Videon, T. M. (2002). The effects of parent-adolescent relationships and parental separation on adolescent well-being. *Journal of Marriage and Family, 64*, 489–503.

Yongmin, S., & Yuanzhang, L. (2007). Racial and ethnic differences in experiencing parents' marital disruption during late adolescence. *Journal of Marriage and Family, 69*(3), 742–762.

Zambelli, G. C., & DeRosa, A. P. (1992). Bereavement support groups for school-age children: Theory, intervention, and case example. *American Journal of Orthopsychiatry, 62*(4), 484–493.

APPENDIX A

Listed below is contact information for the persons and organizations from which to obtain the measurement instruments described in the

Assessment Methods with Children and Adolescents section (Fischer & Corcoran, 2007).

1. The Children's Beliefs about Parental Divorce Scale (CBAPDS):
   Professor Larry Kurdek
   Wright State University
   Department of Psychology
   Dayton, OH 45435-001
2. The Child's Attitude Toward Father (CAF) and Mother (CAM) scales:
   WALMYR Publishing Company
   PO Box 12217
   Tallahassee, FLA 32317-2217
   (850) 383-0045
3. The How I Feel (HIF) scale:
   Dr. Tedra Walden
   E-mail: tedra.walden@vanderbilt.edu
4. The Norwicki-Strickland Locus of Control Scale (N-SLCS):
   Dr. Stephen Norwicki Jr.
   Department of Psychology
   Emory University
   Atlanta, GA 30322
5. The Children and Adolescent Social and Adaptive Functioning Scale (CASAFS):
   Dr. Jeannie Sheffield
   E-mail: jeannie@psy.uq.edu.au
6. The Adolescent Coping Orientation for Problem Experiences (A-COPE):
   Family Stress Coping and Health Project
   1300 Linden Drive
   University of Wisconsin–Madison
   Madison, WI 53706
   (608) 262-5070
7. The Inventory of Parent and Peer Attachment (IPPA):
   Mark T. Greenberg, PhD
   Department of Psychology, NI-25
   University of Washington
   Seattle, Washington 98195
   Instruments and a short manual are available for $5.

APPENDIX B

The following is a list of books available for children and adolescents experiencing their parents' divorce:

Beyer, R., & Winchester, K. (2001). *What in the world do you do when your parents divorce?* Minneapolis, MN: Free Spirit Publishing, Inc.

Blume, J. (1978). *It's not the end of the world.* Scarsdale, NY: Bradbury Press.

Boyd, C. (1983). *Chevrolet Saturdays.* New York: Simon and Schuster.

Brotherton, M. *Split: A graphic reality check for teens dealing with divorce.* Sisters, OR: Multnomah Books.

Brown, L. K., & Brown, M. (1990). *Dinosaurs divorce: A guide for changing families.* Boston: Little, Brown & Company.

Cassella-Kapusinski, L. (2006). *Now what do I do? A guide to help teenagers with their parents' separation or divorce.* Skokie, IL: ACTA Publications.

Coleman, W. L. (1998). *What children need to know when parents get divorced.* Minneapolis, MN: Bethany House.

Danziger, P. (1997) *The divorce express.* New York: Putnam Publishing Group.

Fields, J. (2003). *Children's living arrangements and characteristics: March 2002* (Current Population Report P20–547). Washington, DC: U.S. Census Bureau.

Gardner, R. (1985). *The boys and girls book about divorce.* New York: Bantam Doubleday Dell Publishing Group.

Girard, L. (1987). *At Daddy's on Saturdays.* Morton Grove, IL: Albert Whitman & Company.

Goff, B. (1985). *Where is Daddy?: The story of a divorce.* New York: Beacon Press.

Grunsell, A. (1990). *Divorce. Let's talk about it.* London: Watts Franklin.

Holub, J. (2001). *Cinderdog and the wicked stepcat.* Park Ridge, IL: Albert Whitman.

Holyoke, N., & Nash, S. (1999). *Help! A girl's guide to divorce and stepfamilies.* Middleton, WI: Pleasant Company Publications.

Johnson, J. (1999). *Everything you need to know about your parents' divorce.* New York: Rosen Publishing.

Johnson, J., & O'Neill, C. (1998). *How do I feel about my stepfamily?* Brookfield, CT: Copper Beach Books.

Kimball, G. (1994). *How to survive your parents' divorce: Kids' advice to kids.* Chico, CA: Equality Press.

Lansky, V. (1998). *It's not your fault, Koko Bear: A read-together book for parents & young children during divorce.* Minnetonka, MN: Book Peddlers.

Lindsey, J. W. (2000). *Do I have a daddy?* Buena Park, CA: Morning Glory Press.

MacGregor, C. (2004). *The divorce helpbook for teens.* Atascadero, CA: Impact Publishers.

Mayle, P. (1980). *Divorce can happen to the nicest people.* Indianapolis, IN: MacMillian Publishing Company.

Moser, A., & Melton, D. (2000). *Don't fall apart on Saturdays!: The children's divorce survival book.* Kansas City, KS: Landmark Editions, Inc.

Osman, T. (1990). *Where has Daddy gone?* Nashville, TN: Hambleton-Hill Publishers.

Prokip, M. (1996). *Divorce happens to the nicest kids.* Warren, OH: Alegra House Publishers.

Ransom, J. F. (2000). *I don't want to talk about it: A story about divorce for young children.* Washington, DC: American Psychological Association.

Rogers, F., & Judkis, J. (1996). *Let's talk about it: Divorce.* Pittsburg, PA: Family Communications, Inc.

Rubin, J. (2002). *My mom and dad don't live together anymore*. Washington, DC: American Psychological Association.

Schab, L. M. (2008). *The divorce workbook for teens: Activities to help you move beyond the breakup*. Oakland, CA: Instant Help Books.

Spelman, C., & Parkinson, K. (2001). *Mama and daddy bears divorce*. Morton Grove, IL: Albert Whitman & Company.

Stern, E. S., Stern, Z., & Stern, E. (1997). *Divorce is not the end of the world: Zoe's and Evan's coping guide for kids*. New York: Ten Speed Press.

Stinson, K. (1988). *Mom and Dad don't live together anymore*. Westport, CT: Firefly Books.

Trueit, T. S. (2007). *Surviving divorce: Teens talk about what hurts and what helps*. New York: Scholastic Books.

Winchester, K., & Beyer, R. (2001) *What in the world do you do when your parents divorce? A survival guide for kids*. New York: Magination Press.

CHAPTER FIVE

Grief and Loss among Children and Adolescents in the School Setting

Renée Bradford Garcia and Elizabeth C. Pomeroy

Fifteen-year-old Gina sits on the sidelines at the school dance, watching her friends on the dance floor laughing and being silly. Even Scott is having a good time, and he appears to be flirting. Gina is uncomfortable watching Scott with someone else. Scott was dating Lori, Gina's best friend, when she died in a car accident seven months ago. It looks like Scott is already over it, and it makes Gina angry that he can move on so easily. *Lori was so into Scott*, Gina thinks, *and he doesn't even seem to care anymore.* In fact, to Gina it seems that hardly anyone cares.

Right after the accident, there was high drama at school. Everyone was crying in the hallways and talking about it in class. It all felt so unreal to Gina, like she had gone numb all over and was just floating through the halls, unable to feel or respond. All around her, students were crying while her eyes stayed dry. *What's wrong with me that I can't cry?* she wondered. *I was closer to Lori than any of these people!* Some of the people who were the most emotional hardly knew Lori! And then there was Felicia. Felicia had been really rude to Lori when she was alive. Lori and Gina decided she was jealous that Lori was dating Scott. But after the accident, Felicia was telling everyone that she and Lori were best friends! Nothing could be further from the truth, and yet Felicia was getting a whole lot of extra attention, especially from the guys who were trying to console her. Even now, just the mention of her name makes Gina boil with anger. Seeing her in algebra class every day makes it almost unbearable.

Gina is beginning to think that something is wrong with her. After all, it has been seven months and no one even mentions Lori anymore. Yet for Gina, everywhere she looks there are reminders of Lori. There isn't a day that goes by when memories of the accident don't wash over her like a flood, making it almost impossible to get through the day. She feels like she is screaming for help, but nobody is listening and nobody cares. To make matters worse, Gina's sixteenth birthday is looming, and she can't imagine turning sixteen without her best friend there to celebrate with her. Lori would never turn sixteen. How could Gina be happy about her birthday, knowing that her best friend since kindergarten would never grow up?

Gina is the face of an adolescent's grief in the school setting.

Introduction

In the school setting, practitioners will encounter students experiencing a myriad of losses, including loss of friendships, death of a family member, death of a peer, parental separation and divorce, relocation from a different school or community, and tragic community events that cause bereavement and grief reactions (Heath et al., 2008; Holland, 2008). It is essential that practitioners give attention to the effects of bereavement in the school setting, as it is the child's and adolescent's primary "workplace." School is where children and teens are expected to perform at their optimal intellectual, emotional, social, and behavioral capacity. As Webb (1996) states, "Any attempt to help a child must *always* consider the nature of the child's functioning in school" (p. 181). The circumstances of the loss and the unique nature of the school community may influence the degree to which the school environment is life-enhancing and/or life-depleting for the child or adolescent. For example, while smaller school settings may have greater capacity to attend to the needs of a bereaved child, this support can sometimes backfire and become overwhelming or intrusive to the child and family. Large schools, which are more impersonal, may allow for greater anonymity but lack the personal support from others that can be healing to a bereaved child or teen.

In some cases, school represents a safe harbor that fosters the child's feelings of stability (Schlozman, 2002; Heath et al., 2008). The predictable routine, focused activities, presence of consistent adults, and socialization with friends can provide respite from the changes and reminders of loss that a child or teen may be facing in his home. At times, however, school may trigger grief reactions as children compare themselves with peers who do not have losses. In addition, for children who have preexisting social or academic difficulties, the additional stress brought on by grief can exacerbate the problems at school.

Children may experience a wide variety of losses from the time they enter kindergarten until they graduate from high school. Losses can range from predictable developmental changes and normal life transitions to traumatic, unexpected events. School-based practitioners need to be sensitive to all types of losses children might experience, even those that are considered a normal part of growing up. Due to the increased number and intensity of stressors that families currently face, children may have exaggerated responses to seemingly minor changes. These strong reactions may be particularly prevalent among children who are living with multiple changes or losses. Bereaved children may be preoccupied with thoughts related to the loss and have trouble concentrating and completing academic assignments. They may resist attending school or, conversely, dedicate more time and attention to their school work (Westmoreland, 1996). For some children, grief reactions are manifested in behavior problems in the classroom (Heath et al., 2008). If a child with such difficulties is not assessed for loss-related issues, the root of the problem may go unaddressed, and a cycle of frustration and difficulty in school ensues. In its extreme form, students may lose interest in school and drop out. One key to helping such students involves efforts to retain them in school (Holland, 2008). Some children who have had major losses in their lives may utilize the school environment as a safety net for their bereavement process and appear to be coping well with the loss. In either case, school-based practitioners need to be aware of the potential impact that a loss may have on a child's social and academic functioning.

In a study of school-age children who have lost a parent, Worden (1996) found that these children had more social difficulties, lower levels of self-worth and self-confidence, were more anxious and more likely to withdraw socially than their non-bereaved peers. These differences, however, were most prominent two years after the loss had occurred. School-based practitioners, therefore, must learn to be attuned to changes in behavioral, attitudinal, emotional, and academic functioning and consider the possibility that bereavement may be a factor in the child's performance even for losses that occurred some time in the past. School-based practitioners must help the school community recognize that grief and loss can have a major impact on the child's success or failure in school. A team approach involving parents, teachers, community resources, and school-based practitioners can protect children and teens from falling through the cracks of the educational system. The school-based practitioner can facilitate collaboration among all parties to ensure that communication remains open and interventions are smoothly implemented.

Assessment

Psychosocial assessments should be conducted in order to inform and direct grief-related interventions (NASW, 2002). Because there are multiple points of intervention at schools, assessments of bereaved children in the school community may be done at an individual (micro), class (mezzo), or school-wide (macro) level, depending on the circumstances. For example, a child whose parent has been incarcerated may benefit from individualized attention, which can shelter him from some of the social stigma surrounding such a loss. A class that has suffered the death of a classmate or teacher may benefit from interventions directed toward the class as a whole. Children who attend school in a community that has experienced a tragic event, such as a natural disaster, may benefit from school-wide interventions. All assessments should be able to identify students who are at high risk for having major difficulties with the loss so that additional support and assistance can be provided.

Assessments can be informed by children or teens, their family members, teachers, school nurses, school counselors, and school administrators. At the micro level, assessments should include a psychosocial history of the individual student and his family, the circumstances of the loss, level of functioning both before and after the loss, the student's strengths and resources, an understanding of the loss from the student's cultural perspective, and other loss experiences.

When interventions target the mezzo, or class level, assessments should gather information about the culture and customs of the class, cohesiveness of the students, the degree to which different students were affected by the loss, concerns and behaviors of parents and caregivers in reaction to the loss, academic expectations and workload, as well as strengths and resources.

If the entire school has been affected by a loss, an assessment at the macro level will be helpful. Information that would inform this assessment would include the culture of the school community, resources that are available, the counseling capacity of the school, the openness of school leadership to support school-based interventions, cultural differences within and among the faculty and student body that influence perceptions about the loss, other losses the community has experienced, and the degree of cohesiveness of school personnel. In addition, assessments should also consider the amount of direct exposure to the event experienced by students, rumors circulating about the event, other behavioral reactions that have formed around the event, as well as parental concerns and behaviors.

IDENTIFYING STUDENTS IN NEED OF SERVICES

Identifying students in need of grief support is an important, though often challenging endeavor. Some students may actively seek support from a teacher and consequently be directed to the school-based mental health practitioner. It is important that school-based practitioners be visible in the school community so that students and parents can easily access them for assistance. For those students who are reluctant to seek help on their own initiative or for students who are unaware that they are in need of assistance, additional efforts may be required to ensure that these students can be offered services. Such efforts may include educating teachers and parents about behaviors that may indicate the need for additional support. In some situations, it may be appropriate for teachers to talk to students in their classes or create assignments, such as an essay or art activity, that might elicit a student's reaction to the loss. One way of identifying students who may need services is to assess those who were closest to the loss either by physical proximity or the relationship with the persons involved. Practitioners should also remember, however, that students who were at risk prior to the loss may also be negatively affected even if their relationship to the loss was more distant.

It is important for school personnel to recognize behavioral cues that may be related to a loss. While adolescents may conceal their grief reactions, which can develop into more serious emotional problems, children may act out their feelings in ways that are misinterpreted by adults. For example, children or adolescents who have experienced multiple losses, including family, peer, or even pet loss, may react strongly to other stressors that may or may not be related to the loss experience. They may appear to be hypersensitive and overreactive. Other signs that could indicate that children or adolescents are in need of services include changes in academic functioning, changes in sleeping and eating habits, school avoidance, withdrawal, disengagement from normal activities, increased anger or irritability, difficulty concentrating, and substance use. These behaviors could indicate that the grief reaction has progressed to depression.

In addition, bereaved children or adolescents may also experience teasing or harassment by peers that could overwhelm their coping skills, placing them at even higher risk for severe emotional disturbances or self-destructive behaviors. School personnel must be aware that this type of response from peers could lead to suicidal or homicidal

behaviors. School officials should notify parents immediately upon suspicion of such harassment. Steps to curtail this dynamic should be
implemented and monitored continually. It is also important to remain
aware that gossip and rumors surrounding bereaved children and their
loss can occur in many forms, including physical, emotional, and verbal, and may take place via cell phones and computers.

Chapter 2 provides more information on standardized assessment
tools that can be used with students.

Interventions

Schools can play a pivotal role in helping bereaved students (Holland,
2008; Schlozman, 2003). Well-designed school-based programs are able
to supersede insurance, monetary, and transportation limitations that
would otherwise prevent many students from receiving grief support
services (Garrison, Roy, & Azar, 1999). The school-based mental health
professional can be a valuable source of support for students who are
experiencing grief. This person should be someone students identify as
a trustworthy adult who can assist with emotional and resource needs.
School staff may refer individual students to the practitioner; students
may initiate contact with the school-based practitioner themselves; or
a child's caregivers may request that the practitioner meet with their
child. Ideally, the practitioner's office is at the school and is accessible
to students during school hours. It is viewed by the entire school community as a psychologically safe place within the school that can be
accessed whenever a student feels the need for support. This perception
results from rapport-building that the practitioner engages in with students, and this trust is essential to the success of interventions (Ayyash-
Abdo, 2001). Many teachers understand that students have emotional
as well as academic needs and will facilitate a child's request to leave
class in order to speak to a counselor.

Due to the constraints inherent in the school structure, there will
likely be student needs that are beyond the scope of what the school-
based practitioner can provide. Therefore, it is important that school-
based practitioners maintain knowledge of community resources that
assist with such needs (Holland, 2008). Practitioners can also direct students and caregivers to information that will help them as they experience their grief. For example, pamphlets and flyers on such topics as
expected symptoms of bereavement for children/teens, tips for parenting a bereaved child, divorce from a child's view, and characteristics of
a depressed child can be valuable to caregivers.

MICRO-LEVEL INTERVENTIONS

At the micro, or individual level, school-based interventions may take the form of individual or family counseling, crisis intervention, resource linkage and referral, and brokering. Effective interventions with students often involve working with the student's parents or caregivers (Ayyash-Abdo, 2001). In fact, it is often the school-based professional who alerts parents to their child's emotional pain and need for help. The practitioner helps parents attend to their child's needs and access additional services. School-based practitioners can also provide assistance directly to the student's family in the form of information, referrals, and emotional support. They may also provide family counseling, which can assist parents in understanding how their child experiences the loss, communicating about the loss appropriately with their child, and promoting healthy functioning of the family members while under stress (Ayyash-Abdo, 2001). In addition, there may be situations in which the most useful intervention for an individual child is for the child's caregivers to get support for their own loss issues. School-based practitioners can respectfully and skillfully help parents understand the connection between their bereavement and their child's behavior and refer them to appropriate resources.

Interventions with individual students may also take the form of brokering with students and their teachers. A child or teen who is bereaved may find it difficult to meet the academic demands of school due to grief reactions resulting from the loss. School-based practitioners can assist students in negotiating assignment deadlines and academic workloads with their teachers. For example, fourteen-year-old Susie's grades began to decline when her parents began negotiating their divorce. After visiting with Susie, the school-based practitioner learned that the increased tension in the house and the uncertainty of her future living situation were making it difficult for her to sleep and concentrate on her homework. She had many assignments that were turned in incomplete or not at all, and she scored poorly on several tests. The school-based practitioner met with Susie and her teachers to discuss her grades and assignments. Together they were able to identify creative and attainable ways for Susie to fulfill her academic requirements. Because they had an understanding of Susie's home situation, the teachers were willing to be flexible with her. It is important that such brokering is done with the student's permission and involvement so that her confidentiality is not violated. Likewise, while it is beneficial for practitioners to facilitate this process, they must not overtake it to the point of excluding either the student or teachers from the negotiations. Allowing students to remain at the center of such discussions provides them with experiences of self-efficacy, opportunities to learn important social skills, and the potential to develop deeper connections with other supportive adults. Ideally, after the initial meetings, students will feel empowered to approach teachers with academic issues without the help of the practitioner.

School-based practitioners can also help bereaved students link into the broader school community by steering them toward healthy activities and supportive groups of people such as school clubs, teams, projects, and assisting school office staff. Helping students integrate into the school community and find their niche can help facilitate the grief task of accommodating to the loss and putting energy toward current and future relationships (Humphrey & Zimpfer, 1996; Rando, 1993).

MEZZO-LEVEL INTERVENTIONS

Mezzo-level interventions at schools can include support groups, classroom discussions and activities, as well as faculty and parent information or training sessions.

Support Groups   A valuable role of the practitioner who provides services in schools is to help children connect with other bereaved students. This is often accomplished by facilitating support groups among students throughout the school who are experiencing similar losses. Doing so allows students opportunities for mutual support, decreases isolation, and provides a normalizing effect as students see that others are having symptoms and experiences similar to their own. Support groups for children who have had a significant loss, such as the death of a parent, can be particularly beneficial. Due to the strain that such a loss puts on the parenting capacity of the surviving parent, support groups can provide such children with a "surrogate support system" that assists in the healthy development of the child (Zambelli & DeRosa, 1992, p. 484).

With administrative support, these groups can occur during school hours in a confidential location. Groups that are held during class time always have the potential of interrupting academic instruction or testing. Thus, it can be helpful to alternate meeting times so that students do not miss the same class each week. This also facilitates greater cooperation from teachers in allowing their students to leave class to attend the group.

Though there are common elements of grief in all types of losses, separate groups should be formed for specific types of losses, such as loss due to death, divorce, a parent who is incarcerated, a parent who is deployed by the military, or victims of natural disaster. Information about the group can be made available to parents, teachers, and students with instructions on how to sign up or refer someone to the group. For groups that may be stigmatized by other students, such as a parent's incarceration, flyers can be posted in strategic locations, such as bathroom stalls. It is helpful to do an individual intake with each student to explain the group, generate interest, and assess for group appropriateness. At this time, students can also be given parental consent forms that must be signed and returned. Another method of recruiting group members may be to invite students who have been identified as having a relevant loss to a short informational presentation during which the group is explained.

Once six to ten group members have been identified, and the group schedule and location has been confirmed, passes should be prepared and delivered so that students will be excused from class to attend the group. A closed group that accepts no new members after the second week is most effective as it allows group members to become more trusting of one another, thus increasing the depth of personal information that is shared. Sufficient group time for processing all group members' thoughts and feelings ranges from sixty to ninety minutes, but school constraints may place limits on this time frame. If the group facilitator is an outside professional who has been brought in to lead the group, it is beneficial to have an appropriate staff person, such as a school counselor, to be the co-facilitator. This makes it easier to manage logistical matters and problems that may arise. It also facilitates learning for the staff person on handling grief issues with students as well as allowing students to connect with a supportive person who is accessible on campus between sessions and after the group terminates.

A strengths-based, psycho-educational approach is an effective design for school-based grief groups. For younger children, art creation, bibliotherapy, and game playing are effective support group activities (Heath et al., 2008). Activities such as these help reduce the negative impact of the death, provide steady "emotional holding" and support by someone who is not emotionally overwhelmed by the loss, bolster feelings of self-worth that may have suffered due to the loss, enhance confidence in one's ability to manage life difficulties, and expand the child's understanding of grief (Zambelli & DeRosa, 1992).

Since older children have a greater capacity for insight, it is important for the facilitator to listen to the group's needs and adjust the group content to address those needs. This is especially effective with middle school and high school students in order to encourage them to talk to each other, not just the group facilitator, and to elicit their ideas on the topic at hand. On the other hand, the facilitator will need to have some planned topics and activities to establish rapport among group members, to build trust within the group, and to encourage the sharing of feelings.

The following exemplifies the structure of a school-based group for middle school students who have lost a loved one through death.

Pre-group preparations: The facilitator invites students to a presentation about the grief support group to be held at the school. The facilitator shows an age-appropriate video about grief and explains the purpose and function of the group. Students are asked to fill out an intake form and mark if they are interested in participating in the group. This process normalizes the impact of loss, decreases feelings of isolation and stigma, and facilitates the invitation to receive support. A packet of information, including a parental consent, is given to each student who expresses interest in participating in the group. Upon review of the student's intake form and receipt of the signed consent form, the student is officially enrolled in the group.

Group 1: In this introductory session, students participate in activities designed to help them get to know each other. The facilitator guides the students in the collaborative creation of group guidelines and an extensive discussion about confidentiality. Students are reminded that group attendance does not exempt them from doing their academic work. Members briefly tell who died in their life and when and how the deaths occurred.

Group 2: The focus of this session is to allow each group member to tell the story of the death. It is often helpful to provide an art activity members can do individually that elicits the feelings they had upon learning about the loss. Upon completion, group members take turns sharing their creation and telling their story of loss.

Group 3: In this session, group members discuss behavioral, emotional, cognitive, physical, and spiritual changes that they have experienced due to their loss. The facilitator provides education about the bereavement process and normalizes expected grief reactions. This can be a beneficial time to process issues of guilt and regret that the students may have in relation to their loved ones.

Group 4: During this session, members discuss coping skills that they have used to help them deal with their grief. The facilitator provides information about additional coping skills that could be useful to group members. In addition, the group leader can facilitate a discussion about life-enhancing (healthy) versus life-depleting (unhealthy) coping behaviors. Members should be encouraged to bring a picture of their loved one for the next session.

Group 5: This session is devoted to giving group members a time to memorialize their loved one in the presence of a supportive audience. Students can complete a worksheet that prompts them to identify their favorite memories, least favorite memories, characteristics about their loved ones, things they would like to say to their loved ones, and other aspects related to their relationship with the deceased. Members take turns sharing their pictures and telling the other members about their deceased loved ones.

Group 6: The final group session focuses primarily on termination. Members can be asked to evaluate the group and review its benefits. The leader may want to help students identify safe people and resources that can give them support outside of the group. Students may also participate in an exercise designed to use their experience for the benefit of others. For example, they can make a brochure that explains "What adults need to know about teens who are grieving" or "How to help a friend who is grieving."

Grief support groups provide a safe environment for students to tell their story of loss, which is often an important component of the healing process. In some instances, the traumatic nature of the loss may lead to disturbing stories that are brought out in the group setting. Though it can be very healing for the student to review the details of the trauma in a supportive atmosphere, doing so may arouse anxiety in other group members. Thus, students with traumatic losses (e.g., homicide, suicide, violent death) are better served with a combination of individual and group counseling. In the event that a group member tells the details of a traumatic event, it is crucial that the facilitator be aware of the potential for this to have deleterious effects on the other group members. Facilitators should follow up with any student who appears distressed and provide additional services and referrals as appropriate.

Classroom Interventions Classroom-wide interventions may be appropriate when an entire class has been touched by a loss, such as the death of a teacher or classmate. Classroom interventions can take a myriad of forms and should be adapted to the specific circumstances. They may include crisis debriefing, teaching coping skills, providing information about loss, or facilitating a memorial ritual among students. The school-based practitioner can also work with teachers to integrate helpful information about grief and coping skills into the class curriculum and assignments. For activities that focus on a specific student, such as sending cards to a terminally ill classmate, the parents of the classmate who is ill should be informed of the intervention and their consent should be obtained prior to initiating the activity. The parents of children who are not directly affected should also be kept informed of the situation and the classroom activities that address it. Parents should be encouraged to discuss any concerns with their child's teacher. Successful class-wide interventions require collaboration between the helping professional, the classroom teacher, and the parents.

Interventions for School Personnel   Another example of a mezzo-level intervention includes services targeted at school personnel. These may include crisis debriefings, informational sessions, memorial rituals, or training sessions for how to handle grief reactions in the classroom. Research has confirmed that, though teachers rate loss as a prominent issue for their students, they feel uncomfortable and unsure of how to assist students in this area (Holland, 2008; Reid & Dixon, 1999). When faculty are provided with resources that enhance their knowledge, understanding, and personal coping capacity, the students are likely to benefit as well. For example, many bereaved students can vividly recall their first day back at school following the loss. They often feel discounted, disconnected from others, awkward, ashamed, unsure, and different. Teachers should receive guidance on how to appropriately interact with such students upon their return. They should also be enabled to assist the student's classmates with appropriate responses. Such training and skill-building can provide valuable experiences for the entire school community and minimize distressing feelings for the bereaved child (Holland, 2008).

MACRO-LEVEL INTERVENTIONS

Often school-wide tragedies require macro-level interventions that involve the entire student, teacher, and parent populations of the school community. A school-wide intervention may be necessary in the event of a large-scale traumatic event that impacts the entire school population. Often this takes the form of memorials or rituals that bring the community together and allow for the expression of thoughts and emotions. Such activities can help reduce feelings of isolation and affirm a supportive atmosphere within the school environment. In addition, school-wide interventions may also serve to bridge the gap between the need for mourning the loss and the need for proceeding with regular school functions (National Association of School Psychologists, 2002). Given the traumatic nature of these events, it is important for the school to have an implementation plan if such an event does occur. Haviland (2008) recommends a series of specific steps that allows the school community to "reset a proper balance between grieving and teaching and learning" (p. 62). His ten suggestions are summarized as follows:

1. Establish a group of personnel to make decisions regarding how the school will respond to the tragedy. This group should include administrators from both the individual school as well as district-level administrators. The response that is developed should be made with guidance from other resources in the community, such as mental health professionals and other education agencies.

2. Communicate the events to school personnel, parents, and students as soon as possible. Delays in dispersing knowledge about the event impedes the ability of the community to coalesce and work together as they address the needs of students and families.

3. Assemble staff meetings soon after the tragedy and hold frequent meetings in the days following to share the plan of response, solicit suggestions for improving the plan in light of further developments, and give school personnel opportunities to support each other.

4. Communicate with parents via e-mail and letters sent home with students. Provide information about warning signs that may indicate a student is at risk. If the tragedy focused primarily on one or a few families, their requests can be shared with the wider school community.

5. Suggest that teachers use class time to talk about the event. While outside resources from the community can be made available to students, staff should honor student preferences to talk with people with whom they have a relationship, that is, teachers.

6. Offer various forms of support for students that are both short- and long-term. Establish a triage system that allows students to be assessed and then, if needed, referred to different types of support, including talking with other students and talking to a professional grief counselor individually or in groups. Attempts to return to the pre-crisis routine should be done incrementally with respect to the needs of the student body.

7. Chief administrators of the school and district should visit the bereaved families to express condolences, offer support, and clarify what information can be shared with the broader school community.

8. Recognize the stress experienced by teachers and others who are providing care to the school community. Offering a variety of short- and long-term resources both within and outside of the school enables school personnel to receive assistance in a manner that fits their individual needs.

9. Evaluate the school's response and continued needs and use the tragedy as an opportunity to learn and improve.

10. After a sufficient amount of time has passed, solicit views from the school community regarding the school's response. Use this

feedback to facilitate more effective plans and interventions should a similar event occur in the future.

By having a predetermined plan, school counselors, teachers, and administrators can respond quickly and effectively to a crisis, thereby enhancing the potential for positive outcomes from the experience.

While interventions should be put in place immediately following the event, school staff should also recognize that the effects of the tragedy will be long-term and may become worse with time. In addition, some students and faculty may exhibit a delayed reaction to the loss. While it is important that schools gradually transition back to a predictable school routine, support services and resources should be offered for a sustained period of time following the event to provide for the ongoing and changing needs of staff and students.

SCHOOL RESPONSE TO SUICIDE

School-based practitioners should be especially mindful of how a suicide within the school community is handled, as this tragedy differs greatly from other types of loss. Bereavement resulting from suicide is often more complex due to the social stigma surrounding suicide and tremendous feelings of guilt or responsibility that surviving loved ones often harbor (Hoff, Hallisey, & Hoff, 2009). While students and families mourning a suicide are at greater risk of having post-traumatic stress disorder (PTSD), depression, suicidal ideation, substance abuse, and a worsening of prior behavior problems, they are also less likely to receive sufficient social support to manage their grief reactions (Weekley & Brock, 2004). Consequently, there has been growing attention given to "postvention" interventions for survivors of suicide. The term *suicide postvention* is defined as "the provision of crisis intervention, support, and assistance for those affected by a completed suicide" (American Association of Suicidology, 1998, p. 1). Suicide postvention strategies go beyond serving the bereavement needs of those affected and are more closely related to responses directed at traumatic events and disasters (Wenckstern & Leenaars, 1991). Of greatest concern with postvention initiatives is the prevention of suicide clusters. The CDC (1988) defines a suicide cluster as "a group of suicides or suicide attempts, or both, that occur closer together in time and space than would normally be expected in a given community" (p. 2). Though suicide contagion is rare, it is most often seen among teenagers and young adults and is thought to be influenced by feelings of culpability, feelings of connection with the deceased, and the dynamic of imitation (Weekley & Brock, 2004). School-based practitioners should consult the Centers for

Disease Control for an extensive list of recommendations for suicide postvention strategies (CDC, 1988) and work with school administrators to implement the school's response to a suicide according to these guidelines. A summary of these guidelines is as follows:

1. Plans should be developed, reviewed, and agreed upon by all relevant community entities prior to a suicide. Doing so enables responders to immediately take advantage of opportunities for prevention during the first hours after the suicide.
2. All relevant community entities and agencies should be involved in developing a community-wide response plan. While it can be helpful for one agency to assume responsibility for notifying the responders and calling them to relevant meetings, the responsibility for addressing this issue should be done in a collaborative manner.
3. Pertinent community resources, including local media, should be identified and given a clearly defined role in the response.
4. The decision to implement the postvention plan should be made when a suicide cluster is present or when one or more traumatic deaths occur and the coordinators believe it may sway others toward suicidal behavior. The specific strategies to be implemented may depend on the degree of crisis currently present in the community.
5. If it is decided to implement the response plan, key persons should be briefed on the situation before informing the entire student body.
6. All efforts should be made to not glorify, vilify, or sensationalize the suicide victim and circumstances. School-wide memorials are discouraged as they may inadvertently influence high-risk students or encourage students to seek similar positive attention.
7. The response team should identify individuals deemed to be at high risk, have them assessed by an experienced mental health professional, and connect them with further assistance when necessary.
8. The handling of the incident by the media should be done in collaboration with the response team to ensure that accurate information is reported on a time schedule that aids other postvention strategies. Detailed information about the method of suicide should be omitted to discourage copycat suicides.
9. Attention should be given to aspects of the suicide location, method, and other characteristics so that increased monitoring can be done to prevent imitation of the suicide.

10. The nature of the suicide cluster should be assessed and analyzed so that relevant issues in the community can be addressed.

Even carefully planned and well-intentioned postvention plans can inadvertently promote an "atmosphere of romantic tragedy," resulting in an increase in suicidal gestures and attempts (Callahan, 1996). School-based practitioners and administrators, therefore, should seek expert consultation in such matters.

Working with the Professional Team

Because school is an integral part of a child's or adolescent's life, it provides many opportunities for intervening with those who have suffered a loss. Due to a young person's dependence on adults to access services, interventions that are school-based can help eliminate this barrier. Interventions may be orchestrated by school personnel, such as a school counselor, psychologist, or social worker or by professionals from the outside community. Regardless of who delivers the service, it is essential that the interventions have the clearance and support of the school administration. Doing so can help practitioners more smoothly find a suitable location within the school for service delivery, facilitate permissions for students to leave class for services, obtain parental consent, and manage other logistics inherent in working with the school system. Having the practical and moral support from school administrators can facilitate collaboration and cooperation from teachers and other staff members and thus, allow for services to be delivered more efficiently and effectively. When enlisting such cooperation, it may be helpful for school personnel to have information about loss and the intervention approach to be used. This can be accomplished by disseminating written information, speaking at staff meetings or in-services, or in casual conversations with school staff. Practitioners should approach the school with a willingness to be flexible and work within the constraints inherent in the school's bureaucracy. Identifying an ally from within the school, someone who supports the interventions being provided, can be a tremendous help in negotiating the school's existing systems in order to meet student needs. By demonstrating a respect for the other duties and functions required of school personnel, practitioners can forge strong collaborative relationships that will subsequently benefit the students (NASW, 2002).

Practitioners working from within the school system may find the protocol to be less cumbersome than for those who are outside the school community. The school social worker, for example, may have an established and trusting relationship with the administrators who must approve the services that are offered. In addition, school-based practitioners may be in the position of educating and advocating for system changes that can accommodate service delivery. School-based practitioners may also be put in the position of explaining and justifying services to school staff (NASW, 2002). If done with a collaborative spirit, school-based practitioners can successfully negotiate with teachers who may view a student's need for counseling as being in competition with class attendance and academic demands. Many times, well-meaning teachers focus on maintaining normalcy in the midst of a crisis, whereas students may need counseling before they can return to their previous functioning.

It is also important to remember that school personnel may be uncomfortable with topics related to death, dying, and loss (Westmoreland, 1996). This may be due to their own bereavement experience, a lack of experience with such situations, or their prior personal experiences with loss that are triggered by events at the school. Serving the needs of the students involves, in part, serving the school staff as well (Browder, 2006). Such assistance may include providing referrals, information, and supportive listening.

Ethical Issues

A code of ethics governs the behavior of both mental health professionals and educators. The National Education Association has a code of ethics for educators, as do many state boards of education. The ethical standards for both mental health practitioners and educators reflect similar values, such as belief in the inherent worth and dignity of all human beings, equal opportunity for all students, and protecting students from harm. In addition, both professions are bound by their respective codes of ethics as well as federal statutes to protect a student's right to privacy and confidentiality. While there are many different organizations with a code of ethics, some relevant examples can be found at the following Web sites.

- Texas Administrative Code for Educators: http://info.sos.state.tx.us/pls/pub/readtac$ext.TacPage?sl=T&app=9&p_dir=P&p_rloc=96032&p_tloc=&p_ploc=1&pg=8&p_tac=&ti=19&pt=7&ch=247&rl=2
- Texas Revised Code of Ethics for Educators: www.tcta.org/capital/sbec/codeapproved.htm
- Florida Code of Ethics for Educators: www.fldoe.org/edstandards/code_of_ethics.asp

- National Education Association Code of Ethics: www.nea.org/ home/30442.htm
- Association of American Educators: www.aaeteachers.org/code-ethics.shtml
- National Association of Social Workers Code of Ethics: www.social workers.org/pubs/code/default.asp
- National Association of School Psychologists, Principles for Professional Ethics: www.nasponline.org/standards/ProfessionalCond .pdf
- California Teachers Association Code of Ethics: www.cta.org/ About-CTA/Who-We-Are/Code-of-Ethics.aspx
- New York State Code of Ethics for Educators: www.highered.nysed .gov/tcert/resteachers/codeofethics.html#statement

Maintaining a student's confidentiality in the school setting can be especially difficult. Because the school-based practitioner serves as a liaison between students, families, the school, and the community, effective interventions often necessitate information sharing among colleagues (NASW, 2001a). When confronting the dilemma of confidentiality in the school setting, practitioners should ask, "How does this information impact the student's ability to learn and function appropriately in school?" If no relevance to academic and social functioning is determined, the practitioner should carefully evaluate the purpose (if any) of disclosing information (NASW, 2001a). School-based practitioners should also take the following actions to promote ethical practice among themselves and their colleagues:

1. Become familiar with state and federal laws regarding student confidentiality.
2. Develop and enforce policies within their schools regarding confidentiality.
3. Obtain informed consent from students and family members explaining the limits of confidentiality in the school setting (NASW, 1991).

Several individuals may unintentionally become aware that a student is receiving mental health services due to their role in helping the student access that assistance. For example, one social worker was invited by a child's parents and school staff to provide individual counseling to the student during school hours. The pass granting permission for the student to leave class stated, "Your therapist is here," and was seen by several people, including student office aids. Upon receiving the pass, the teacher unwittingly read the pass out loud, thus announcing to the entire class that the student was receiving mental health services and potentially subjecting him to stigmatization from his peers. While some general disclosures may be inevitable and beyond the therapist's control, practitioners should look for opportunities to minimize lax disclosure of student information and make suggestions as to how it can be handled in a more confidential manner. In this instance, for example, the therapist might ask that the pass specifically read, "You have a visitor in the counselor's office." Detailed information regarding the nature of the student's issues should be carefully guarded and, when it is absolutely necessary, only referred to in very general terms.

PROFESSIONAL BOUNDARIES

While the code of ethics for mental health professionals clearly delineates the boundaries expected between the client and practitioner, the educator's code of ethics addresses this vaguely or only in the context of a romantic or sexual relationship. While supportive and caring teachers are strengths in any school, the school-based practitioner may need to help teachers set appropriate emotional boundaries with their students. Some teachers may be so moved by a student's experience that they neglect their own needs, which negatively impacts their ability to function. They may over-involve themselves in a student's situation or over-extend themselves to help a student in need, perhaps even providing them with shelter, food, and money. This blurring of boundaries can be confusing to students, damaging to families, and a distraction from academic demands. It may also mean that a high-risk child is receiving inappropriate and unprofessional "counseling" that is beyond the capacity of the teacher. It also has the potential to develop into secondary trauma or burnout for the teacher. School-based practitioners should work with such staff, educate them about potential problems in their relationship with the student, and offer to work with the teacher to help the student in more appropriate ways.

Resources

While grief, loss, and bereavement are an important issue within a school setting, the school population as a whole will present with multiple needs of all types. Therefore, the school-based practitioner is often a generalist who possesses the ability to serve the basic mental health needs of students and faculty. To supplement this knowledge base and most efficiently serve students adequately, school-based practitioners should be well informed of grief-related community resources (NASW, 2002). Such resources can complement the practitioner's efforts by providing services to students and families, disseminating information and education to the school community, as well as providing consultation to the school-based practitioner. The types of resources may vary, including nonprofit agencies that provide mental health services, nonprofit and government agencies that provide tangible and practical support, experienced mental health specialists, advocacy groups, as well as members of the clergy and religious organizations. Some agencies and professionals will offer to train school-based practitioners in the development of knowledge and skills with a particular type of loss so that the practitioner may then independently serve the student population. Some districts have funds that can be used to pay outside professionals for their services. Many professionals willingly donate some of their services for the benefit of the school community. The school-based practitioner has an important role as the bridge between community resources and the school community (NASW, 2002). Time spent networking and developing relationships with outside professionals is valuable to maintaining and strengthening this link to the broader community. School-based practitioners can also help students and families identify their personal and environmental strengths, including existing resources they have or can easily develop and access.

Cultural Considerations

The concept of culture in the school setting can mean a variety of things. Practitioners will want to obtain knowledge, skills, resources, and understanding that will help them make referrals and implement services that are culturally relevant for students and their families (NASW, 2001). Without attention to issues of culture, interventions can easily be misunderstood and can even be unhelpful or harmful. Practitioners must be willing to let their students teach them about their culture and how it is manifested in their family. Most often discussed, with regard to culture, is the student's race, ethnicity, religion, and socioeconomic status. There may be instances where school rules are in conflict with cultural norms for a family. For example, the honoring of Muslim holidays and practices, including fasting and prayer at appointed hours often conflicts with the secular school schedule (Hodge, 2002). The practitioner can play a valuable role, advocating for the family and negotiating solutions that honor the family's traditions and viewpoints (NASW, 2001).

In addition to this concept of culture, practitioners should also seek to become aware of culturally relevant aspects of the student's family. Students' cultural and familial values may or may not be evident when they are among their peers, but they are no less important. Practitioners should strive to be knowledgeable about students' cultural influences, while also being aware of other influences in students' experience that may be in conflict with their family's culture. This is particularly relevant for adolescents who are in the developmental stage of forming their own identity and questioning their parents' beliefs, values, and traditions. This may also be relevant for immigrant families in which different members have different levels of acculturation and assimilation. In speaking of this dynamic with regard to Muslim students, Hodge (2002) states that when students are in "conflict with parents and their cultural heritage, social workers may be tempted to side with the adolescents' struggle for independence, especially if the youths affirm values that are similar to those held by workers" (p. 16). Practitioners must be mindful of this dynamic and thoughtful in their work so that cultural values are not undermined. Hodge (2002) recommends that the practitioner inform the family of the struggles their child is facing. Doing so allows for the emergence of solutions that are congruent with the family's value system. While it is important for practitioners to continually expand their knowledge of other cultures, it is virtually impossible to be completely competent in the multitude of cultures in our society. Therefore, practitioners should be open to learning about each family's unique background and to regard it respectfully (Pomeroy & Garcia, 2009).

Attention to culture is especially important for bereaved students and families. In times of loss, cultural mores, worldviews, and rituals can be a tremendous source of strength. One's cultural and spiritual orientation can be a life-enhancing resource in that it provides a protocol for mourning the loss, a context for understanding the loss, and a framework for finding meaning in the loss. In essence, when mourners feel as if their world has turned upside down, cultural and spiritual points of reference can furnish a modicum of safety, constancy, and security.

An individual's spiritual belief system is often an integral component of how students deal with loss, particularly loss due to death. Practitioners should always inquire about a student's spiritual views and not speak in a manner that presumes the student's beliefs are consistent with the practitioner's beliefs. For students who face a crisis of faith due to their loss, practitioners can validate the pain and discomfort this causes, normalize this experience in the context of loss, and help them connect to culturally relevant resources that will allow them to further explore their concerns.

A child or teen's peer group may have its own subculture. The power of peer groups should not be underestimated and can be a source of strength for students. Practitioners, therefore, must be careful not to minimize this influence and to demonstrate openness and acceptance of a student's peers, though not necessarily of all their behaviors.

Each school also has its own school culture. Boyd (1992) defines school culture as "the existence of an interplay between three factors: the attitudes and beliefs of persons both inside the school and in the external environment, the cultural norms of the school, and the relationships between persons in the school" (www.sedl.org/pubs/catalog/items/cha03.html). The nature of a school's culture can have a tremendous impact on how at-risk students are treated, the acceptance of mental health services in the schools, and the success or failure of efforts to support the emotional needs of students. School culture can play a role in how teachers view students, how they interact with students, and how they discuss students with other school staff. Unfortunately, students can easily become labeled with names such as "troublemaker," "drama queen," or "lost cause." Such labels have the effect of putting a child in a box, believing one can predict his or her behavior, and potentially obscuring one's view of the student's strengths and needs. Even labels with positive connotations, such as "perfect student," can obscure a child's or teenager's struggles and needs. Labeling as such can constrict the efforts, attitudes, and skillfulness with which interventions are delivered. Practitioners must be aware that they may unconsciously hold preconceptions about a student based on opinions and judgments made by other staff members. Honest awareness of this potential bias allows the practitioner to separate herself and consciously make herself open to hearing and seeing the student free from any preconceived ideas (NASW, 2001). This creates space for the practitioner to develop compassion and an enhanced understanding of the student, which consequently makes interventions more effective.

CASE EXAMPLE

Isaac Horsoff is a seven-year-old first-grader at Maple Ridge Elementary School. He is an average student with no previous history of academic or behavior issues. The school counselor, Janice, received a call that Isaac's father would be picking him up early that day because Isaac's four-year-old brother, Jonathan, had been run over and killed in a grocery store parking lot that morning. Janice instructed the father to ask for her when he arrived at the school's front desk and she would assist him in pulling Isaac out of class.

When Mr. Horsoff arrived, Janice invited him to sit in her office. Mr. Horsoff appeared very shaken and distressed and seemed very anxious to see Isaac. He briefly and tearfully told Janice the circumstances surrounding the accident, and she listened attentively. Janice asked Mr. Horsoff if he would like to walk with her to the classroom or have her bring Isaac to her office where she would allow them to talk privately or with her present. After some deliberation, Mr. Horsoff decided he would wait for Isaac in the office so that he would have a chance to think of how he was going to tell Isaac the news. Janice gave Mr. Horsoff a handout titled "How to explain death to children" and pointed out the succinct bullets that hit the highlights. Mr. Horsoff seemed grateful for this information and spent a few moments looking at it. Before leaving to get Isaac, she let Mr. Horsoff know that she would inform Isaac's teacher and other school staff. He nodded his agreement.

Janice got Isaac from class and instructed him to bring his things because he was leaving school early. On the way back to her office, Isaac kept asking why he was leaving early. Janice explained, "Your dad will explain it all to you. He is waiting for you in my office."

Janice let Isaac into her office, told Mr. Horsoff to take his time, and shut the door. She then informed the school principals, office staff, and Isaac's teachers, and reminded them of the policy to say nothing to the students until they had received further communication from the family. When a tearful Isaac and Mr. Horsoff emerged from Janice's office, she gave him her card, briefly explained how she could help, and asked permission to call the family in a few days. The principal also approached Isaac and Mr. Horsoff, expressed her condolences and offered support on behalf of the school. Before leaving, Mr. Horsoff accepted these gestures gratefully and told them he didn't know when Isaac would be back.

Later that day, Janice overheard a group of teachers and staff discussing the incident in the teacher's lounge. They were discussing their feelings about the tragedy and many were crying. Janice noticed that one teacher, Ms. Seller, was very quiet but appeared very upset. Ms. Seller abruptly stood up and left the room without saying anything. Janice contacted Ms. Seller the next day and learned that she had babysat for Isaac and Jonathan when they were infants. Janice made it a point to check in with Ms. Seller often and keep her informed of the family's arrangements regarding Jonathan's death. Janice also listened and gently offered guidance as Ms. Seller struggled with if and how to contact the family, what to say, and her own feelings of grief. She told Ms. Seller that she would be available to talk with her any time she needed support.

Janice met with Ms. Baldwin, Isaac's homeroom teacher, to discuss how to talk to Isaac's classmates and ways that she could lead the class in supporting Isaac. They decided they would have the class make condolence cards for Isaac, pending approval from the family. Janice agreed to talk to the class with Ms. Baldwin to explain the death and answer any general questions the students had. They also wrote a brief letter/e-mail to parents, informing them of the news and of their plans to tell the students the following day. The letter included information about how children at this age process death and listed reactions that might indicate a concern. Before school ended, Janice called the family and received their permission to tell Isaac's classmates. They also approved the idea of having Isaac's classmates send him cards and said they would call the school once funeral arrangements had been made so that school personnel could come in support of Isaac. Mr. Horsoff explained to Janice that they would sit shivah for seven days and that Isaac would be absent during that time. Janice communicated this to the attendance clerk so that Isaac's absences would be excused. The letter to Isaac's class parents was completed and sent home with the children. Janice also sent out an e-mail to all school staff, informing them of the tragedy and reminding them of the school policy regarding such issues and that her services were available if they needed personal or professional support in this matter.

Janice continued communicating with the family to offer support and assess their needs. As planned, Janice and Ms. Baldwin talked to Isaac's classmates. They read a book about death, talked about grief, and discussed ways to show that they cared to Isaac. The children asked for details about the accident. Janice answered those that she could and reminded students of ways they can stay safe around cars. Ms. Baldwin gave the children guidelines for making condolence cards in an effort to respect the Horsoff family's Jewish faith. Janice also explained that Isaac would be out of school for a few days but that he was safe and will return.

Upon learning from Mr. and Mrs. Horsoff that Isaac would be returning to school, Janice again met with Ms. Baldwin and discussed how she should best handle Isaac's return to school. Ms. Baldwin agreed to privately acknowledge to Isaac his return and to let her know if he became upset or uncomfortable. Ms. Baldwin also informed the students that Isaac would probably be returning the next day and suggested they be friendly, tell Isaac they were glad to see him, and to not ask lots of questions unless Isaac indicated that he wanted to talk about it. When Mrs. Horsoff arrived the next day with Isaac, he was clinging to her and attempting to stand still so as not to go to class. He appeared anxious and started screaming and clamoring for his mom when she tried to separate herself. After several minutes of unsuccessful attempts to get Isaac to let go of his mother, Janice invited them to her office. Janice correctly surmised that Isaac was worried something would happen to his mother while he was in school. Janice and Isaac agreed that he could come to her office anytime he felt too worried about his mom to stay in class. She also told him he could come to her office during recess if he wanted to call his mother. Though still very upset and tearful, Isaac went to his class. Janice then met with Mrs. Horsoff. She normalized Isaac's responses and suggested strategies that might help Isaac separate from her to attend school, including a special handshake and a touchstone object. She encouraged Mrs. Horsoff to not give in to Isaac's pleas to stay home as this could make it worse. Janice was grateful that Mrs. Horsoff was willing and able to digest this information and glad to be able to provide information before the issue had gone on for some time. Janice also listened while Mrs. Horsoff talked about how she was coping. Janice validated her pain and gave her some referrals for grief counseling. They agreed to work as a team to help Isaac adjust to the loss and she encouraged Mrs. Horsoff to contact her with any concerns she had.

Through the combined cooperation with Mrs. Horsoff, Ms. Baldwin, Isaac's other teachers, and Janice, Isaac was able to follow through with a plan to reenter the classroom situation and remain in school for the entire day. Though he still became anxious when his mother was not right at the school door when school let out, he and Ms. Baldwin "practiced being brave" while they waited for Mrs. Horsoff to arrive.

After a few months had passed, Mrs. Horsoff called Janice and informed her that due to their grief, she had been unable to work and that this was causing a financial strain on the family. Janice referred her to some community resources that could help, in addition to grief support groups that all members of the family could attend.

This case illustrates the varied and important roles of school-based practitioners and the carefully chosen skills used to work with children, families, and school staff who are experiencing loss. From the beginning of the crisis, the practitioner provides emotional support and information to the father and child, as well as the school staff. In addition, she disseminates information, teaches skills, and gives support to the other teachers who are directly involved with the grieving child. The practitioner also serves as a liaison between the school staff and the family. She makes accommodations for the child and family during the mourning period and assists with the child's assimilation back into school. She also attends to the needs and concerns of other students who were affected by their classmate's loss. These same skills can be used with other losses that affect the school community. In summary, the school-based practitioner can play a pivotal role in helping bereaved children and families.

Summary

The school-based practitioner will encounter many children and adolescents experiencing a myriad of issues that engender feelings of grief, from loss of a friendship to death of a family member as well as tragic events with peers. School counselors need to be knowledgeable about the signs and symptoms of grief in children and how it can impact school functioning. As a member of the school community, practitioners may collaborate with teachers, administrators, parents, and community members to provide life-enhancing structures, programs, and interventions for bereaved children. Maintaining a focus on the strengths that both the students and adults possess can effectively support successful adaptation to loss events. Strengths-based interventions can be beneficial during the recovery period and prevent students from falling through the cracks. Students who mask their grief and remain hidden may engage in life-depleting behaviors that ultimately lead to failure in the school setting. School-based practitioners need to be knowledgeable about community resources that can assist bereaved students and their families.

Schools and the communities that form around them offer an abundance of unique strengths, making them valuable to bereaved students. First, schools have easy access to students in need, regardless of their family income or their parents ability to access outside services. Second, attentive school personnel are often able to identify and intervene with bereaved children at the time of the loss. In this sense, they provide prevention of chronic difficulties with depression, anxiety, trauma, and delinquency. Third, schools are an environmental resource for students because they often function similarly to an extended family for the child. When the school community is able to rally in support of bereaved students, it can buffer the secondary losses that result from living with bereaved caregivers who are struggling their own grief reactions. Fourth, by convening groups of students with similar losses, schools help to normalize the bereavement process and can diminish the stigma that often accompanies loss and grief.

References

American Association of Suicidology. (1998). *Suicide postvention guidelines: Suggestions for dealing with the aftermath of suicide in the schools.* Washington, DC: Author.

Ayyash-Abdo, H. (2001). Childhood bereavement: What school psychologists need to know. *School Psychology International, 22,* 417–433.

Boyd, V. (1992). School context: Bridge or barrier to change? SEDL. Retrieved May 19, 2009, from http://www.sedl.org/pubs/catalog/items/cha03.html.

Browder, R. (2006). Teachers dealing with the death of students: A qualitative analysis. *Journal of Hospice and Palliative Nursing, 8*(1), January/February.

Callahan, J. (1996). Negative effects of a school suicide postvention program—a case example. *Clinical Insights, 17*(3), 108–115.

Centers for Disease Control (CDC) (1988). CDC recommendations for a community plan for the prevention and containment of suicide clusters. *Morbidity and Mortality Weekly Report 1988, 37,* Suppl. S-6.

Garrison, E. G., Roy, I. S., & Azar, V. (1999). *Responding to the mental health needs of Latino children and families through school-based services.* Clinical Psychology Review, 19*(2), 199–219.*

Haviland, J. E. (2008). *A season of sadness: Responding to tragedy in school. Education Digest.* March. Available from http://www.eddigest.com

Heath, M. A., Leavy, D., Hansen, K., Ryan, K., Lawrence, L., & Sonntag, A. G. (2008). Coping with grief: Guidelines and resources for assisting children. *Intervention in School and Clinic, 43,* 259–269.

Hodge, David R. (2002). Working with Muslim youths: Understanding the values and beliefs of Islamic discourse. *Children & Schools, 24*(1), 6–20(15).

Hoff, L. E., Hallisey, B. J., & Hoff, M. (2009). *People in crisis: Clinical diversity perspectives.* New York: Routledge.

Holland, J. (2008). How schools can support children who experience loss and death. *British Journal of Guidance & Counseling, 36*(4), 411–424.

Humphrey, G. M., & Zimpfer, D. G. (1996). *Counselling for grief and bereavement.* Thousand Oaks, CA: Sage.

National Association of School Psychologists (2002). Retrieved June 26, 2009, from http://www.nasponline.org/resources/crisis_safety/memorials_general.aspx.

National Association of Social Workers (NASW). (1991). NASW commission on education position statement: "The school social worker and confidentiality." Washington, DC: Author.

National Association of Social Workers (NASW). (2001a). Confidentiality and school social work: A practice perspective in practice update from the National Association of Social Workers. October, Vol. 2, No. 2. Washington, DC: Author.

National Association of Social Workers (NASW). (2001b). NASW standards for cultural competence in social work practice. Retrieved January 16, 2010, from http://www.socialworkers.org/practice/standards/NASWCulturalStandards.pdf.

National Association of Social Workers (NASW). (2002). NASW standards for school social work services. Retrieved January 12, 2010, from http://www.socialworkers.org/practice/standards/NASW_SSWS.pdf.

Pomeroy, E. C., & Garcia, R. B. (2009). *The grief assessment and intervention workbook: A strengths perspective.* Belmont, CA: Brooks/Cole, Cengage Learning.

Rando, T. A. (1993). *Treatment of complicated mourning.* Champaign, IL: Research Press.

Reid, J. K., & Dixon, W. A. (1999). Teacher attitudes of coping with grief in the classroom. *Psychology in the Schools, 36*(3), 219–229.

Schlozman S. C. (2002). The shrink in the classroom: When illness strikes. *Educational Leadership, 60*(1), 82–83.

Schlozman, S. C. (2003). The shrink in the classroom: Mental health specialists in schools. *Educational Leadership, 60*(5), 80–83.

Webb, N. B. (1996). *Social work practice with children.* New York: Guilford Press.

Weekley, N., & Brock, S. E. (2004). Suicide: Postvention strategies for school personnel. In National Association of School Psychologists, *Helping children at home and school II: Handouts for families and educators.* Retrieved June 25, 2009, from http://www.aamentalhealth.org/SCHOOLPERSONNEL_000.pdf.

Wenckstern, S., & Leenaars, A. A. (1991). Suicide postvention: A case illustration in a secondary school. In A. Leenaars, *Suicide prevention in schools* (p. 173–179). Bristol, PA: Hemisphere Publishing Corporation.

Westmoreland, P. (1996). Coping with death: Helping students grieve. *Childhood Education, 72,* 157–160.

Worden, J. W., & Silverman, P. S. (1996). Parental death and the adjustment of school-age children. *Omega, 33*(2), 91–102.

Zambelli, G. C., & DeRosa, A. P. (1992). Bereavement support groups for school-age children: Theory, intervention, and case example. *American Journal of Orthopsychiatry, 62*(4), 484–493.

CHAPTER SIX

Children, Adolescents, and Grief in Medical Settings

Barbara L. Jones and Mikki Tesh

Eight-year-old Joshua wakes from a deep sleep to his mother's shout, "Josh, wake up! We've got to go to the hospital." Josh hurls himself out of bed, yanks his portable game system from its charger, and throws it in his bag—the one he keeps ready for this occasion. In the car, Josh and his mom follow the ambulance carrying Edie, his five-year-old sister. Josh's mom sits up straight as she grips the steering wheel and focuses intensely on the road. Neither of them says much. After six years of Edie's struggles with leukemia, these middle-of-the-night trips to the hospital have become part of the routine. His mom is tense and alert but tries to pretend she is calm and that everything is under control. Josh thinks she is trying not to upset him. Josh's mom always brags on him for being such a "good helper" and "never giving me any trouble." Since it's just the three of them, there isn't much choice except for him to help and not make things any harder on his mom. Josh's dad left when he was six, and Josh rarely hears from him.

When they arrive at the hospital, Josh finds his usual spot and settles down with the remote to see if there is anything good on TV. The TV reception stinks, and he isn't allowed to turn the volume up very high, but it's something to do while he waits. His favorite nurse, Louise, is working tonight. She tousles his hair and says, "Hey, hot shot! You hungry?" He shakes his head no, but Louise gives him a granola bar anyway.

He throws it in his bag to join the three flattened ones he already has. Josh can hear his mother's voice in the distance, though he can't make out what she's saying. For a few moments, he begins to worry. His mother has explained to him that Edie could die at a young age. What if this is it? What if Edie doesn't make it this time? His stomach lurches at the thought, and he quickly pushes it away. Why would tonight be any different from all the other times?

Josh used to fantasize that his father would come swooping into the hospital, rush to Edie's side, and miraculously cure her with his love. But Josh is older now and mostly he feels angry. Angry with his dad, angry with the doctors, angry at his friends who have normal lives, angry at the stupid hospital TV. Sometimes he's even angry at Edie, but then he feels guilty. He's careful to never let anyone know he feels this way.

Josh turns from his video game to see his mom kneeling at eye level with him. He can tell by the look on her face that something is very, very wrong. He braces for what his mom is about to say.

Joshua is the face of a child's grief in the medical setting.

Introduction

This chapter addresses the unique needs of children facing grief in a medical setting. It includes children who are facing the death of a friend or family member and those who may be facing their own impending death. Hospitals can be frightening and confusing environments for many young people, and health-care professionals can be instrumental in helping children in these settings. Children are often excluded from the conversations about prognosis, treatment, and symptoms, and may wonder what is happening to their loved ones or themselves (Beale, Baile, & Aaron, 2005; Fitzgerald, 1992; Jones, 2006; Silverman, 2000). Children may respond to the affective responses of the adults around them and sense that something has changed, but not have the ability to discuss their feelings (Beale et al., 2005; Jones & Weisenfluh, 2003). Identifying the varying needs of grieving children in medical settings will allow us to offer more comprehensive, compassionate, and responsive support to them.

Overview of Grief and Loss in Medical Settings

Children can face a myriad of losses, including the death of a parent, grandparent, sibling, or close friend, that may bring them into contact with the medical setting. The death may occur after a lengthy illness or suddenly after a traumatic injury or disease. Children may also face their own declining health or life-threatening illness. Children are frequent visitors to loved ones in the hospital setting. Adult medical settings are not designed to address the unique developmental needs of children and often lack child-friendly rooms, toys, or books. Children's hospitals, on the other hand, are usually better equipped and staffed to help children understand and cope with their own or a loved one's hospitalization. Particularly in the adult setting, clinical staff can be so focused on the psychosocial and medical needs of the patient that the needs of the child may be inadvertently overlooked. Recently, there has been an increase in research on the psychosocial issues that children face at the end of their lives (Beale et al., 2005; Field & Behrman, 2003; Jones, 2006). However, there is still a dearth of literature on the needs of children with a parent, friend, or family member who is facing the end of life. While common themes exist for children and adolescents who encounter a loss in the medical setting, understanding the specific dynamics present with different types of loss can be helpful to the practitioner. The following section provides an overview of the variety of losses found in a medical setting and how they relate to and impact children and adolescents.

WHEN A LOVED ONE IS DYING

The dying process can be a frightening experience to adults, much less children. Children are often shielded from the family process and may be secluded and kept unaware of the activities, developments, and circumstances surrounding the person who is dying (Schoen, Burgoyne, & Schoen, 2004). It is understandable that families want to protect children; however, children who are informed in a developmentally appropriate manner are better equipped to cope with the dying process (Boyd-Webb, 2003). When informed and supported, children can be involved in simple caretaking roles such as bringing water, making pictures, hugging and cuddling, reading, talking, playing, and generally being encouraged to be around the person who is ill.

Families often look to professionals for guidance about helping their children through their grief. Children need opportunities to have an age-appropriate level of control over their participation in the end-of-life process. If the child is aware that someone is sick, then it is helpful for the child to make choices about visiting the dying person. During this process, however, children need to be told what to expect. Children need concrete, factual information about how their loved one looks, feels, smells, acts, and sounds. It is important to relay this information to the child before his or her visit. Children can be comforted by knowing that their loved ones are being taken care of by others and that what is happening to them is part of the disease. For younger children, it can be important to distinguish the concept of "getting sick" from the everyday occurrences of cold and flu. The practitioner may explain that "the person is very sick, a lot sicker than what happens to you or me."

Children need to be informed about physical, emotional, and behavioral changes evident in their loved ones prior to each visit. Children may display a range of emotional reactions from excitement to fear to curiosity. All of these reactions are normal and expected and may vary within hours for the same child. Assessment of the child's reactions and feelings needs to be ongoing and repetitive. For example, a six-year-old may show excitement about seeing her grandmother at the hospital and state that she wants to visit grandmother in her room. However, upon seeing her grandmother in a deteriorated state, she may change her mind and want to leave.

Finding effective ways to communicate with children is critical for their well-being during life-changing events (Rotheram-Borus, Lee, Lin, & Lester, 2004). Children understand the concept of illness and death when practitioners communicate in developmentally appropriate ways that explain illness with honesty and clarity, using simple words for small children, and more complicated words for older children. It is critical to avoid euphemisms and phrases that may be upsetting or confusing to the child. Children do not always understand certain cultural phrases like, "He passed," "She is in heaven," "God took him," or "She is an angel," and will sometimes need more concrete explanations. Although euphemisms are meant to ease the pain of an experience, they can also create more anxiety and confusion for a child. A typical example of a confusing statement might be, "He went to sleep," or, "He is with grandmother now." Adults can talk about the death of a family pet or other experiences of death in nature. Some children may need more than one explanation about what happened, and some children may need just one short or long explanation. It will depend on their age, maturity, and personality. Practitioners can support the adults in talking to their children and model ways to communicate information.

Not all children will react the same way. Some children may want to outwardly express their feelings; some may want to grieve quietly or in subtle ways. Some children may want a lot of information or details; some may not want a lot of information. Some children will want to visit the family member who has died; some may want to escape or play. Interestingly, children's reactions will at times mimic the reactions of the adults. Children may also delay mourning until they sense that the adults around them can handle their grief.

For children facing their own death, uncertainty and fear are common reactions that can be ameliorated by honest and caring information from medical staff and caregivers (Beale et al., 2005; Sourkes, 2005).

Children have a right to know what is happening to them and to make decisions about their end-of-life treatment and plan, which may include choices about where to die, how much palliative treatment to receive, who to see, and how they would like to be remembered. Telling children about their own illness trajectory may also help parents cope with their own grief and sense of helplessness (Kreicbergs, Valdimars-dóttir, Onelöv, Henter, & Steineck, 2004, Kreicbergs et al., 2005; Sourkes, 2005).

Children grieve as part of a family, and their unique family history, culture, and spirituality will have an impact on both the child's level of understanding and the ways that children can be involved. Throughout this process, the practitioner may assess both the family and the child's expressed desires, beliefs, concerns, and needs. Practitioners can help families identify when and how to involve the children by inquiring about the family's beliefs regarding illness and children. It is important to ascertain what the child has been told and by whom, how much the child comprehends about the situation, and how the child is responding to the changes occurring in his or her life.

SUDDEN DEATH

Sudden and traumatic death is known to complicate mourning for children and adults (Rando, 1993). Children may be even more affected than adults by a death that occurs suddenly. Because many of the adults are experiencing the typical responses of shock, disbelief, anger, horror, and fear, they may try to protect the children from information about the death. However, this can cause helplessness, anger, anxiety, confusion, self-doubt, and feelings of being unsafe for young people. Children need to know that their feelings of fear and confusion are expected and that they can express them safely. After a traumatic death, it is common for children to display their feelings behaviorally and affectively. Children may withdraw from family and friends, behave aggressively, have difficulty sleeping, display signs of anger or anxiety, express hopelessness, have physical symptoms, have tantrums, avoid school or peer groups, or regress developmentally. Children may report and display fear of their own death or of other loved ones. They may have anxiety about being alone or far away from their caregivers. These reactions are normal, and children need to have a wide berth of acceptance and unconditional love. If the reactions persist for a lengthy amount of time or impair functioning, it is important to provide more structured intervention and counseling.

Children who have experienced a sudden loss also need opportunities to express the myriad of feelings that they may be experiencing, including fear, anger, horror, guilt, sadness, and even post-traumatic stress reactions (Nader, 1997). Children may need extra assurances of safety and love. They will require patience from parents and caregivers with their increased need for attention and support. Very young children may have concerns that they somehow caused the death. For example, a child may conclude that his anger at a loved one resulted in the death. Children need frequent reassurances that neither their thoughts nor behaviors caused the traumatic death.

If the child was present or witnessed the event, such as in the case of motor vehicle crashes, shootings, and domestic violence, they may actually present to the hospital emergency room and need medical intervention as well. Health-care professionals and mental health practitioners can talk with the child about what she saw and heard. The opportunity to discuss the experience in the initial hours may help the child cognitively and affectively deal with the aftermath. Interventions that can help after a sudden or traumatic death include the use of facilitated groups, expressive arts, returning to normal activities, unconditional love and support, and opportunities for verbal and nonverbal expression of feelings (Clements, 2001; Hartley, 2004; Nader, 1997).

DEATH OF A PARENT

For children, the death of a parent may be one of the most life-changing events they experience and can introduce deep feelings of sadness, fear, isolation, and abandonment. The child's reaction may change over time, but the loss will remain a part of their lives forever (Silverman, 2000). Children need opportunities to speak with the dying parent and to participate in rituals surrounding the parent's life and death. Children benefit from honest and clear information about what is happening to their parent and what to expect during the bereavement process. Many children experience anxiety about who will take care of them after the parent's death and how their day-to-day living will be affected. Children facing the death of a parent need to be involved, informed, engaged, and supported throughout the time of the parent's life and death.

In many instances, it is assumed that children understand the critical nature of a parent's illness. In the case of a very young child, families often try to protect the child from the intricate details or the final hours or days of the parent's life. At these times, the child has no ability to say good-bye or experience any closure with the dying parent. This lack of inclusion often leads to misconceptions and fantasies about what has happened to the deceased parent. For example, Susie is a four-year-old girl whose father recently died of brain cancer. She was not allowed to go to the hospital during the last week of her father's life. She is angry, irritable, agitated, and encopretic. Six weeks after the father's funeral, Susie and her mother were driving by the hospital, when Susie screams,

"Stop! Stop! I want to see Daddy!" After talking with Susie, her mother realizes that Susie believes her father is still recovering in the hospital and has been awaiting his return home. The despondent mother realizes she needs help explaining the father's death to Susie and contacts a bereavement counselor at a local hospice. This case exemplifies the need for providing the child with accurate information and support both during the parent's illness as well as the bereavement period following the death.

DEATH OF A SIBLING

Siblings have intense emotional concerns when they are facing the death of a brother or sister or other relative close to their age (Davies, 1998; Gibbons, 1992). (The term *sibling* is extended to include cousins or other same-aged relatives who comprise a close-knit extended family unit.) Many siblings wonder if they are responsible for the illness in some way. If the illness or condition has been protracted, it is not uncommon for the sibling's needs to have been pushed aside as the family deals with the ongoing care of the terminally ill child. Siblings may feel anger and resentment about how they have been treated. They may have been angry with the dying sibling and now be faced with guilt about that anger. As death approaches, siblings should be offered age-appropriate choices about their involvement in the end-of-life care. In some cases, lack of involvement can complicate their loss experience (Davies, 1998). After the child dies, siblings may benefit from special, individualized attention. In some situations, siblings may experience survivor guilt and need safe outlets to express these feelings. They may experience a myriad of feelings that include jealousy, idealization, insecurity, low self-esteem, shame, rage, relief, and depression (Davies, 1991, 1998; Gibbons, 1992). Siblings may have increased death anxiety and somatic symptoms (Rolsky, 1992). Siblings often need extra support at a time when their parents have a diminished capacity to care for them. It is crucial to identify adults, both familial and professional, who can provide loving, consistent care to the sibling after the death of a child.

WHEN THE CHILD IS DYING

When the child is the person who is dying, he or she needs opportunities to speak honestly with family members, friends, and professionals (Beale et al., 2005; Jones, 2006; Sourkes, 2005). Children who are dying often understand more about what is happening to them than their parents and care providers may realize. Like grieving children, they tend to protect their parents from their grief and sadness. They may also worry about how their family will handle their death (Himelstein,

Hilden, Boldt, & Weissman, 2004). Practitioners need to have very honest conversations with parents and children about what is happening and what can be expected (Beale et al., 2005). Children benefit from knowing what is happening with their bodies and making plans for what they would like to happen after they die. Very young children may not understand fully what death means and will need to know that they will be kept free from pain and not be alone. Older children and adolescents will likely need to process more mature issues, such as the meaning of life, spiritual concerns, and the concepts of legacy and continued relationships (Jones & Weisenfluh, 2003). They can only do so if they understand what is happening and feel supported to express all of their feelings and wishes.

Practitioners can talk with parents and caregivers about how they would like children to receive information about their prognosis and medical status. Some parents prefer for medical staff to tell the child, some prefer to be the one to tell their child what is occurring, and others would like to do so in collaboration with the health-care staff. Professionals can help families deal with the painful work of telling a child that she or he may not survive her or his illness and then provide support to the whole family and the child in dealing with the myriad of emotions that follow.

Assessment

There are many factors that can influence how a child responds to loss in a medical setting. Some factors to assess include: age and developmental level of the child; previous history of loss; what the child is told and when; relationship with the person; cultural and spiritual background; level of inclusion/exclusion from the medical experience; level of understanding; suddenness of the loss; concurrent stressors; family history; sources of support and resilience; individual coping style; preexisting emotional state; and current behavioral, affective, cognitive, and spiritual reactions. When supporting children in the medical setting, the first level of assessment is to understand their age and developmental level and how that may influence their understanding of what is happening. Very young children may not understand the finality and permanence of death, while adolescents will likely struggle with the existential and spiritual aspects of the loss (Jones & Weisenfluh, 2003). Chapter 2 of this book provides an excellent overview of the developmental stages of children and grief.

Another important factor for assessment is to understand who is dying or has died, and how the child's relationship with that person may influence his or her grieving responses. Simultaneously, the practitioner should understand that the child may have very different reactions to a sudden versus anticipated death.

ASSESSMENT INSTRUMENTS AND TOOLS

There are no specific standardized validated instruments to measure childhood loss in a medical setting, but there are some tools that practitioners may find useful in working with children facing loss. Some children's grief centers have been utilizing the following measures developed by Shane R. Jimerson at the University of California, Santa Barbara, as part of Project LOSS: the Jimerson Youth Common Grief Reactions Checklist–Caregiver Report, the Jimerson Youth Common Grief Reactions Checklist–Youth Report, and the Jimerson Loss Outcomes Checklist–Youth Report. These three scales have between twenty-four and eighty-six items, and cover a range of common psychological, behavioral, and emotional sequelae of grieving children (Jimerson, 1997; Lehmann, Jimerson, & Gaasch, 2001).

Other centers utilize more projective measures, such as the "Child Drawing: Hospital," or CD:H (ages five to twelve), which has been used to measure anxiety in hospitalized children (Brewer, 2006). Clatworthy et al. (1999) examined the reliability and validity of the CD:H. This instrument is designed as a means of measuring the emotional status and anxiety of hospitalized school-aged children. The children are given a blank 8.5 x 11-inch sheet of white paper and a box of eight basic color crayons, and instructed to draw a picture of a person in the hospital. The clinician then scores the drawing using a scoring tool provided in the CD:H manual.

Another tool for measuring children's anxiety is the "Revised Children's Manifest Anxiety Scale: What I Think and Feel" (RCMAS) for children ages six to nineteen (Reynolds, 1978, 1985). This is a thirty-seven-item self-report instrument designed to assess the level and nature of anxiety in children and adolescents. The child responds to the questionnaire by circling "yes" or "no," depending on whether or not the given statements are descriptive of the child's feelings or actions. The "yes" responses are counted to determine a total anxiety score. The RCMAS has strong internal consistency and test-retest reliability. A recent study found that the RCMAS was a valid measure in cross-cultural research with Latino and Caucasian youth (Pino, Little, Knight, & Silverman, 2009).

For children who are facing life-threatening conditions such as childhood cancer, the Pediatric Quality of Life Inventory (Peds-QL) (child and parent) may be a useful assessment tool. The Peds-QL is a modular instrument designed to measure health-related quality of life in children and adolescents ages two to eighteen. It is a brief, practical scale that was first developed for use with children with cancer. It takes less than four minutes to complete and can be completed by the child or the parent. It includes items related to anxiety, worry, and pain, and focuses on multidimensional quality of life, including physical, emotional, and social. It is the standard measure of quality of life in randomized clinical trials conducted by the Children's Oncology Group (COG), the cooperative research group that studies childhood cancer treatment and quality of life. The scale has good internal consistency (alpha = .88) and has been shown to measure a unitary construct. Peds-QL has strong construct, criterion, and convergent validity (Varni, Burwinkle, Katz, Meeske, & Dickinson, 2002; Varni, Seid, & Murtin, 2001; Varni, Seid, & Rode, 1999).

The Psychosocial Assessment Tool (PAT2.0) is a brief screening device to be used with families of children with cancer. This measurement instrument assesses behavior symptoms, anxiety, acute stress, and family functioning. The foundation of this instrument is based on a prevention framework developed by the National Institute of Mental Health for examining psychosocial risk factors among families of children in the health-care system. It classifies families as the following: (1) distressed but resilient, (2) acute distress with risk factors present, and (3) persistent distress with high risk factors (National Institute of Mental Health, 1998). The PAT2.0 has been shown to have strong internal consistency for the total score (alpha = .81). In addition, the screening tool has been shown to have good criterion and content validity for a newly developed instrument (Pai et al., 2008). (Kazak et al., 2001).

It can be important to assess the history of losses that a child or adolescent may have faced, and to do so one might use the Children/Teen's Loss Inventory created by Khris Ford, LPC, director of My Healing Place, a center for grieving children (see the appendix). While this is not a standardized instrument, it can provide practitioners with an understanding of the full scope of losses that the child has faced.

Interventions

When a child is facing the loss of a loved one in a medical setting, there are a variety of ways that clinicians can provide therapeutic support and intervention. Providing information about common reactions of grieving children can greatly assist caregivers to help children cope with loss. Such information can include common psychological, behavioral, spiritual, social, and physical reactions related to the various developmental stages. Because it is common for children to shield their fears from their parents, practitioners can assist the family in identifying a trusted adult to whom the child can turn for support throughout the process. Research shows that children who receive consistent nurturance and support from adult caregivers cope more favorably over time and have less fear of abandonment (Wolchik, Ma, Tein, Sandler, & Ayers, 2008). Helping adults feel more confident in their ability to talk to their children can provide comfort for everyone involved.

In addition to working with parents or caregivers, developmentally appropriate interventions to children in the medical setting can enhance their ability to cope with the loss event. Activities such as therapeutic games and expressive arts may facilitate the children's abilities to comprehend what is occurring to them and their loved one (Boyd-Webb, 2003). These interventions can be adapted to various types of losses, including the death of a loved one or a child's impending death.

CHILD INTERVENTIONS

Children frequently seek ways to communicate their love and concern for a loved one who is facing illness or death. Children may express the desire to say good-bye to the person they love, whether that person is at the end of life or has recently died. It is critical that children have the opportunity to choose how, when, and where to communicate with the person they love. Practitioners in the medical setting can provide children with choices about who they would like to have with them during this time. Children can also be encouraged to express their feelings by writing a letter to the person, drawing a picture, or choosing a gift for the person. They can give items to the person directly or have them delivered. Letters, pictures and gifts can also be given to the person, placed on their bed, under the pillow, or read to them. Other ritual ways to communicate with a loved one include releasing balloons into the air, floating messages down a stream, placing handmade items in a casket, the child's pillow, or at the gravesite.

Transitional objects are commonly used to help mourn the loss of a loved one. Transitional objects are items that children or adults may cling to during times of grief and loss. Children will sometimes choose to wear a cap worn by the person they loved or cover their pillow with the person's shirt. Children or adults may wear a ring or carry a cell phone that belonged to the deceased. Some children may wear a locket with a picture or some ashes from the person who died, or have a picture printed onto a pillow or blanket. These objects can feel protective and help children feel close to the person.

Bibliotherapy, art therapy, and play therapy are all important life-enhancing techniques to assist young children who are experiencing anticipatory or current grief. Children who are facing a loss may express their feelings through art differently than children who have not experienced a loss (Findling, Bratton, & Henson, 2006). Artistic expression has been shown to be effective in reducing symptoms that children who may have been traumatized may display (Reyes & Asbrand, 2005). Drawings about feelings and experiences may reduce anxiety through a reduction of heart rate and autonomic arousal (Delue, 1998).

It is important to support children's expressions of grief and recognize the strengths of children's natural tendency to use reenactment and fantasy regarding the person who died. It is common for children to act out experiences they have had through talking to the deceased person on a toy phone, in a private conversation, or involve them in an imagined story. These are all life-enhancing and adaptive responses to loss, and caregivers need to know that these strategies signify strengths and should be supported. Other coping techniques for children include snuggling in a loved one's favorite chair, hugging a cherished pillow, talking to the stars, talking to a photograph or praying to the loved one. These continuing bonds with the deceased are generally adaptive and healthy (Silverman, 2000).

Children may discover their own ways to express and make sense of the loss. No matter what the interventions, it is most important that children feel supported and are given choices. Children need assurance that their needs will continue to be met and they will not be abandoned.

ADOLESCENT INTERVENTIONS

Adolescence is a particularly difficult time to face an impending loss due to the tension between the developmental need to differentiate from family and the need to be close during an illness or after a death. The natural dependence and closeness that occurs when a family member is dying may be in direct conflict with the adolescent's task of identity formation. The isolation of feeling different than peers is particularly painful for adolescents. Adolescents benefit from interventions that incorporate their developmental needs.

Like younger children, adolescents often express the desire to communicate with their loved ones. However, adolescents may also struggle with the larger spiritual and existential questions about why death occurs and what it means for their lives. Life-enhancing interventions include speaking directly to the person who is dying, talking to a peer who has been through a similar experience, or confiding in a safe adult whom they trust. After a death has occurred, adolescents can be invited to provide input to the funeral or ritual that is planned and to have a role in that public expression of mourning.

Adolescents may display reticence about openly expressing negative feelings of anger, sadness, regret, and loss. Creative expressions, such as journaling, poetry, music, letter-writing, art, dance, public speaking, and multimedia displays may be encouraged. Music can be a sophisti-cated style of expression that allows teens to share complex private feel-ings in socially acceptable ways. Music can provide an outlet for the expression of emotions and a means of connecting to others. Adoles-cents can benefit from expressive art interventions individually or in groups (Paone, Packman, Maddux, & Rothman, 2008; Register & Hilli-ard, 2008).

Peer support can be a beneficial grief intervention, particularly for older children and adolescents. The importance of being understood by peers cannot be overstated. Adolescents often use their friends as a diversion from the thoughts and feelings of grief that may be over-whelming to them. It is not uncommon for children and adolescents to experience PTSD and complicated grief (CG) symptoms, and avoidance is one protective mechanism that may temporarily help them cope (Melhem, Moritz, Walker, Shear, & Brent, 2007). While adolescents may need breaks from the intensity of their feelings, they also need opportu-nities to process their emotions in a constructive and life-enhancing environment. Age-specific grief groups help teens communicate with others who have experienced similar losses. A practitioner can teach strengths-based coping skills that are relevant to the teen's stage of development and be an objective listener with whom the adolescent can be authentic. In some situations, a practitioner may only be able to offer crisis intervention services. In such cases, the practitioner can supply families with information and referrals to resources that offer extended support.

FAMILY INTERVENTIONS

When someone is facing a critical illness, it affects the entire family. Family members may have different perceptions of the medical situa-tion and differing opinions regarding the care of their loved one. Family conferencing is an important tool for bringing family members together with medical professionals to create a plan of action (Curtis et al., 2001).

Following the death of a loved one, hospice practitioners, pastoral counselors, and funeral home employees will likely be involved with the family. They may assist families in planning funerals, memorials, burials, or cremations. Depending on the family culture, children may or may not be invited to the ceremony. The funeral may be a new expe-rience for the children of the family. It is important to prepare children for what they may see, hear, and feel. For example, tell the child that the person may not look as they remember him and that he may be cold to the touch but that the child cannot hurt him in any way. Depending on the circumstances, parents or caregivers may offer chil-dren a choice about attending the ceremony. If a child attends the rit-ual, it is beneficial to have an appointed person present to care for the child's needs during the ceremony. After the death, it is common for children to ask what will happen to the person's body. Practitioners can help families anticipate such questions and guide parents in providing answers that convey basic factual information in age-appropriate language that is congruent with the family's religious and cultural beliefs.

Working with the Professional Team

Delivering quality psychosocial services in a health-care setting requires collaboration and interdisciplinary teamwork. When a patient is dying, the need for care coordination and integration is paramount. Children and families are served by a variety of health-care professionals who are integral to their emotional support. The interdisciplinary team may include physicians; nurses; occupational, physical, and speech therapists; social workers; psychologists; child-life specialists; pharmacists; chaplains; music and art therapists; and many supportive staff. Each person may form a unique bond with the child or family and can be helpful in supporting them through the critical time. Social workers, psychologists, and child-life specialists receive specific training in providing therapeutic interventions to children and families facing life-threatening conditions.

The social worker often facilitates the collaborative efforts of the other health-care professionals on the team. While other health-care workers specialize in one particular area of the child's health, the social worker has a global perspective of the child and family's situation. Given the complexity of the health-care system, it is imperative that families have a trusted advocate who hears their concerns and can integrate all the information from various sources into a comprehensive and understandable care plan. In other words, the social worker helps bring the family on board as a crucial member of the team. By using her skills and knowledge, the social worker acts as an advocate, translator, mediator, and liaison between the family and the professional team. In turn, she also acts as an interpreter for the health-care team to engage the family's cooperation with medical recommendations and procedures.

As a social worker on an interdisciplinary health-care team, it is important to understand the various roles and power structures that exist in order to be the best advocate for the patient and family. Medical settings are traditionally physician-led institutions, but there is a growing trend toward truly collaborative, trans-disciplinary, family-centered practice.

Common Ethical Dilemmas

Helping children facing loss in a medical setting is challenging and presents many ethical dilemmas. One of the most common issues that practitioners face is how much to tell children about their own impending death or the death of a loved one. Families are understandably reluctant to talk with children about death and often seek the guidance of the professional care team. Families are frequently concerned that children will be too young to understand what is happening and that telling them will somehow create emotional damage. When the child is dying, parents struggle with how much to let the child know and how it will impact the child's hope and emotional well-being.

It is important to support all families' choices within their own cultural and spiritual traditions, but when the truth is hidden, children may become confused and may imagine stories that are sometimes more frightening than the actual truth. Children who are not told the truth often feel isolated, angry, resentful, or mistrustful of the adults in their lives. Telling a child the truth lets her know that she is part of a family, that she is loved and supported. Including children early in the illness trajectory or traumatic event can help them understand what is occurring and reduce their isolation (Boyd-Webb, 2003; Doka, 1995; Fitzgerald, 1992; Silverman, 2000). Issues of disclosure and truth-telling can create ethical dilemmas for the care providers who try to balance the needs of the family with the needs of the child. When the practitioner is faced with this type of ethical dilemma, every effort should be made to explain the benefits of truth-telling for the child as well as the family.

When a dying child confronts a practitioner with the question, "Am I going to die?" the practitioner should use this opportunity to explore the child's concerns, fears, and wishes regarding his health status. Such questions as, "What have you been told about your condition?" "How do you think about dying?" "What are your concerns or fears about dying?" and "Would you want someone to tell you if you were dying?" can help the practitioner assess the child's understanding of his health status as well as anxieties about death. Following this assessment, the practitioner explains to the child the importance of discussing these questions with his parents. The practitioner can then meet with the parents and relay the child's concerns about dying. This opens the dialogue about the importance of telling the child the truth about his condition. The practitioner may want to obtain permission from the parents to truthfully talk to the child about his prognosis or be present while the parents discuss these issues as a family.

Cultural Considerations

Culture plays a critical role in how individuals and families cope with illness and death. In fact, the constructs of health, illness, life, afterlife, and death are culturally defined and can differ greatly between groups. Consequently, mourning behavior that may be normative in one culture would be completely abnormal in another. Understanding how culture impacts a child involves understanding how that child makes meaning out of his or her cultural beliefs within the context of the family. It is critically important to ask the child and family how illness and death have been dealt with in the past and what would help them cope during the current situation. When asking about cultural beliefs in palliative care, it is important to consider the following issues (Lum, 2009):

- *Communication*: find out how the family would like to learn medical information and how they would like that shared with the child.
- *Unique cultural values*: ask honest and respectful open-ended questions about what is important to this family.
- *Locus of decision-making*: inquire about who needs to be consulted on decisions.
- *Translators*: use medical interpreters and avoid using children as interpreters for the family.
- *Understanding the patient and learning as a provider*: check in and ask for clarification on both what the patient and family understand and also what the provider has heard.
- *Ritualized practice and restrictions*: determine what specific customs, rituals, or prohibitions will be important and try to accommodate them.
- *Environment at home*: assess how ready the family is to receive help in their home. Understand that some cultures may feel stigmatized by hospice providers in the home.

The key is to approach the child and family from a stance of cultural humility, honoring that they are the experts in their own lives.

CASE EXAMPLE

Donny is an Anglo, sixteen-year-old tenth-grader at Sylvannia High School. He is an average student who loves sports and plays varsity football. He has a younger sister, Sally, who is in seventh grade and a brother, Billy, who is in kindergarten. Donny's parents, John and Karen, are very involved with the school's athletic booster club, and Karen volunteers at Sally's school library. In March of his tenth-grade year, Donny developed flu-like symptoms. When he failed to recover from the illness, Karen took him to the doctor. After numerous tests, it was determined that Donny had a rare form of lymphoma. He was hospitalized and treated aggressively with chemotherapy. During that time, the family's lifestyle changed dramatically. Karen spent most of her time at the hospital with Donny while John continued to work as an accountant, care for Donny's siblings, and manage the household responsibilities. Susan, the oncology social worker, recognized that the stress was taking a toll on the family. She also noticed that Donny had become despondent about missing school and his friends.

Susan met with Donny and his mother on a regular basis but initially had limited interactions with Donny's two siblings, who are only able to visit on weekends. Susan was able to arrange individual meetings with Sally and Billy shortly in order to assess their level of understanding about the cancer diagnosis and to clear up any misconceptions they may have had. Susan also used this opportunity to prepare both siblings for Donny's treatment and its side effects. She provided Karen and John with information about typical reactions for children who have a sibling with cancer and also recommended some national organizations that help siblings dealing with these issues. Susan made a point to get routine updates from John and Karen about the children's behavior and reactions to the changes in the family.

Susan encouraged Karen to spend time with each of the two siblings individually outside of the hospital. She explained to Karen that these times with Mom are important for maintaining strong emotional bonds with the children while she is spending so much of her time and energy caring for Donny.

As Donny's illness progressed and his health continued to decline, Susan continued to assess how the siblings were coping. Karen reported that Sally's school grades had dropped, and John said that she was spending most of her time alone in her room. Billy, the six-year-old, has been acting out with his various caregivers and has grown increasingly clingy in Mom's presence. Susan arranged weekly times to meet with each of Donny's siblings to provide them with support as Donny's disease progressed. She also spoke often with John and suggested ways he might support the children in the home.

At an interdisciplinary family meeting, the medical team informed John and Karen that, despite the aggressive chemotherapy, Donny's cancer was spreading. They also discussed the utility of further treatment and indicated that the family should prepare for Donny's death. Susan remained with John and Karen after the meeting to assist them in understanding and comprehending the devastating news. She supported the parents in their grief and also helped them strategize how to tell Donny and his siblings of the news.

Susan met with Sally and Billy individually and provided them with age-appropriate information on Donny's medical status. She engaged

Sally in an expressive art activity that allowed Sally to articulate her feelings of helplessness and guilt. She expressed her desire to do more for Donny and said she was frustrated by the limited time she is able to be with him. Sally also explained that she was having difficulty focusing at school while Donny is in the hospital. She said she remembers being pulled out of class by her father and taken to the hospital on the day of Donny's diagnosis and now feels anxious every time a call is made to the classroom, fearing that something has happened to Donny. Susan assisted Sally in sharing these feelings with her parents and together they brainstormed some ways to ease Sally's anxiety at school. As a family, they decided that Sally will only be contacted in her homeroom class, and any other updates will wait until after school. This would allow Sally to focus on school and know that she will not be pulled out for any reason. Susan reminded the family that they can revisit this plan and modify it as Donny's condition changes.

Susan also helped the family to create a schedule allowing Sally to spend more one-on-one time with Donny. It was also decided that Sally could assist Donny in communicating with his friends by returning e-mails and helping to update his social networking sites.

Susan engaged Billy in play therapy sessions and shared with him books about loss and cancer. Billy was also encouraged to spend more time at the hospital with Donny, and he created a collage for Donny's room that shows all of the fun things they liked to do together. Susan worked with John and Karen on ways to provide Billy with as much consistency and routine as possible. This included consistency in who took Billy to school, who picked him up, and a structured bedtime routine that included phone contact with Mom. Susan encouraged the parents to allow Billy choices throughout the day to help him regain some sense of control. They also offered him tasks to help him feel part of the team, such as making crafts and drawings to decorate Donny's hospital room.

As Donny's medical situation declined, the medical team, in conjunction with the family, focused on decisions regarding end-of-life care for Donny. Donny expressed his desire to die at home, and Susan introduced the family to the hospice team. Susan and the hospice social worker, Nancy, worked together closely to make the transition as smooth as possible for the family.

During the last few weeks of Donny's life, Susan and Nancy helped him with decisions about his care and who he wants to see. They also discussed his funeral preferences and helped him write letters to important people in his life. Concurrently, Nancy worked with Sally and Billy to have meaningful conversations about their relationship with Donny and to create memories with him by hanging out, watching movies, and telling funny stories together. Nancy helped each child choose a way to say good-bye to Donny. Sally decided to write a good-bye letter, and Billy chose to exchange a favorite toy, drawing, or memento with Donny.

Susan and Nancy helped Sally and Billy choose how involved they would like to be with Donny's death, including if they would like to be present at the time. Nancy provided them both with concrete information about the dying process and discussed their fears and concerns. Nancy suggested that the parents identify an adult who will be available for each sibling should they need to leave the home or choose to not be present at the time of death.

Donny died surrounded by his parents and siblings. The hospice nurse as well as Susan and Nancy arrived shortly afterward. Donny experienced no pain and knew that he was loved. Donny's siblings were very upset but also knew they had family, friends, and professionals who will help them as they grieve their brother.

Resources for Practitioners

There are a number of resources that can provide guidance and support to practitioners wishing to support children and families facing loss in the medical setting. Practitioners in any given area of the country can utilize local resources to support the work they do with families. Other national online resources that may be useful are the following:

CENTERS FOR GRIEVING CHILDREN

The following list presents only a few of the many that exist throughout the U.S.

> The Dougy Center
> PO Box 86852
> Portland, OR 97286
> (503) 775-5683
> toll-free (866) 775-5683
> www.grievingchild.org

> Fernside
> 4380 Malsbary Road
> Cincinnati, OH 45242
> (513) 745-0111
> www.fernside.org

> My Healing Place
> 2130 Guadalupe
> Austin, TX 78705
> (512) 472-7878
> http://myhealingplace.org

National Alliance for Grieving Children
PO Box 1025
Northbrook, IL 60062
(866) 432–1542
www.nationalallianceforgrievingchildren.org

ORGANIZATIONS THAT ADDRESS PEDIATRIC PALLIATIVE AND END-OF-LIFE
CARE

The Initiative for Pediatric Palliative Care (IPPC)
Center for Applied Ethics and Professional Practice (CAEPP)
Education Development Center, Inc.
55 Chapel Street
Newton, MA 02458–1060
(617) 618–2454
www.ippcweb.org/home.asp

National Hospice and Palliative Care Organization
www.nhpco.org

Social Work in Hospice and Palliative Care Network
www.swhpn.org

American Academy of Hospice and Palliative Medicine
www.aahpm.org

Children's Hospice International
www.chionline.org

OTHER RESOURCES

*Pediatric Medical Traumatic Stress Toolkit for Health Care
Providers*
The National Child Traumatic Stress Network (NCTSN)
www.nctsnet.org/nccts/nav.do?pid=typ_mt_ptlkt

Project LOSS (for the Jimerson measures)
http://education.ucsb.edu/jimerson/loss.html

Compassion Books (for books on grief, illness, and loss)
www.compassionbooks.com/store

Summary

Children need to be offered caring, interdisciplinary, culturally grounded, developmentally appropriate assessment, support, and life-enhancing interventions when they are facing loss in a medical setting. Children often have both the capacity and desire to be involved, informed, and engaged in their own and their loved one's medical treatment and emotional support. There are many ways to help children understand what is happening to their loved one and to empower family members to engage the child throughout the illness, injury, or dying process. Over time, children may need age-appropriate grief groups, identified adults to help them, and time to be a child and engage in normal activities. Building on children's natural adaptive capacities and strengths can ensure successful adjustment to losses experienced in the medical setting. Practitioners in the medical setting can play a critical role in reducing the child's sense of isolation, fear, and confusion, and in making the hospital a safer place for the child and family.

References

Adams, K., & Hyde, B. (2008). Children's grief dreams and the theory of spiritual intelligence. *Dreaming, 18*(1), 58–67.

Beale, E. A., Baile, W. F., & Aaron, J. (2005). Silence is not golden: Communicating with children dying from cancer. *Journal of Clinical Oncology: Official Journal of The American Society of Clinical Oncology, 23*(15), 3629–3631.

Boyd-Webb, N. (2003). Play and expressive therapies to help bereaved children: Individual, family, and group treatment. *Smith College Studies in Social Work: Special Issue on End-of-Life Care, 73*(3), 405–422.

Brewer, S. G., S. Syblik, D., Tietjens, M. Vacik, H. (2006). Pediatric anxiety: Child life intervention in day surgery. *Journal of Pediatric Nursing, 21*(1), 13–22.

Clatworthy, S., Simon, K., & Tiedeman, M. E. (1999). Child drawing: Hospital—An instrument designed to measure the emotional status of hospitalized school-aged children, *Journal of Pediatric Nursing, 14*, 2–9.

Clements, P. T., Benasutti, K. M., Henry, G. C. (2001). Drawing from experience: Using drawings to facilitate communication and understanding with children exposed to sudden traumatic deaths. *Journal of Psychosocial Nursing and Mental Health Services, 39*(12), 13–20.

Curtis, J. R., Patrick, D. L., Shannon, S. E., Treece, P., Engelberg, R. A., Rubenfeld, G. D. (2001). The family conference as a focus to improve communication about end-of-life care in the intensive care unit: Opportunities for improvement. *Critical Care Medicine, 29*(2), N26–N33.

Davies, B. (1991). Long-term outcome of adolescent sibling bereavement. *Journal of Adolescent Research, 6*, 83–96.

Davies, B. (1998). *Shadows in the sun: The experiences of sibling bereavement in childhood.* Oxford, UK: Taylor & Francis.

Delue, C. H. (Ed.). (1998). *Physiological effects of creating mandalas.* Philadelphia: Guildford Press.

Doka, K. J. (1995). Talking to children about illness. In K. J. Doka (Ed.), *Children mourning, mourning children.* Washington, DC: Hospice Foundation of America.

Field, M., & Behrman, R. (2003). *When children die: Improving palliative and end-of-life care for children and their families.* Washington, DC: Institute of Medicine, National Academy of Science.

Findling, J. H., Bratton, S. C., & Henson, R. K. (2006). Development of the trauma play scale: An observation-based assessment of the impact of trauma on play therapy behaviors of young children. *International Journal of Play Therapy, 15*(1), 7–36.

Fitzgerald, H. (1992). *The grieving child.* New York: Simon & Schuster.

Fredericks, E. M., Lopez, M. J., Magee, J. C., Shieck, V., Opipari-Arrigan, L. (2007). Psychological functioning, nonadherence, and health outcomes after pediatric liver transplantation. *American Journal of Transplantation, 7*(8), 1974–1983.

Gibbons, M. (1992). A child dies, a child survives: The impact of sibling loss. *Journal of Pediatric Care, 6,* 65–72.

Hartley, B. (2004). Bereavement groups soon after traumatic death. In N. B. Webb (Ed.), *Mass trauma and violence: Helping families and children cope* (pp. 167–190). New York: Guilford.

Himelstein, B. P., Hilden, J. M., Boldt, A. M., & Weissman, D. (2004). Pediatric palliative care. *The New England Journal of Medicine, 350*(17), 1752–1762.

Jimerson, S. (1997) *Jimerson youth common grief reaction checklist (CGRC).* Available from author at: http://education.ucsb.edu/jimerson/loss.html.

Jones, B. (2006). Companionship, control, and compassion: A social work perspective on the needs of children with cancer and their families at the end of life. *Journal of Palliative Medicine, 9*(3).

Jones, B., & Weisenfluh, S. (2003). Pediatric palliative and end-of-life care: Developmental and spiritual issues of dying children. *Smith College Studies in Social Work: Special Issue on End-of-Life Care, 73*(3), 423–443.

Kazak, A. E., Prusak, A., McSherry, M., Simms, S., Beele, D., Rourke, M., et al. (2001). The psychosocial assessment tool (PAT): Pilot data on a brief screening instrument for identifying high risk families in pediatric oncology. *Families, Systems, & Health, 19*(3), 303–315.

Kreicbergs, U., Valdimarsdóttir, U., Onelöv, E., Björk, O., Steineck, G., Henter, J. (2005). Care-related distress: A nationwide study of parents who lost their child to cancer. *Journal of Clinical Oncology, 23*(36), 9162–9171.

Kreicbergs, U., Valdimarsdóttir, U., Onelöv, E., Henter, J. Steineck, G. (2004). Talking about death with children who have severe malignant disease. *New England Journal of Medicine, 351*(12), 1175–1186.

Lehmann, L., Jimerson, S. R., & Gaasch, A. (2001). *Teens together grief support group curriculum: Adolescence edition: Grades 7–12.* New York: Brunner-Routledge.

Lum, H., & Arnold, R. (2009). Asking about cultural beliefs in palliative care: Fast facts and concepts (Vol. 216). Available from http://www.eperc.mcw.edu/fastfact/ff_216.htm.

Melhem, N. M., Moritz, G., Walker, M., Shear, M. K., & Brent, D. (2007). Phenomenology and correlates of complicated grief in children and adolescents. *Journal of the American Academy of Child & Adolescent Psychiatry, 46*(4), 493–499.

Nader, K. O. (1997). Childhood traumatic loss: The interaction of trauma and grief. In C. B. Figley, B. E., Mazza, N. (Eds.), *Death and trauma: The traumatology of grieving* (pp. 17–41). Washington, DC: Taylor and Francis.

National Institute of Mental Health (1998). *Priorities for prevention research: A national advisory council workshop on mental health disorders prevention research.* Bethesda, MD: NIMH Publication, No. 98–4321.

Pai, A. L. H., Patino-Fernandez, A. M., McSherry, M., Beele, D., Alderfer, M. A., Reilly, A. T., et al. (2008). The psychosocial assessment tool (PAT2.0): Psychometric properties of a screener for psychosocial distress in families of children newly diagnosed with cancer. *Journal of Pediatric Psychology, 33,* 50–62.

Paone, T. R., Packman, J., Maddux, C., & Rothman, T. (2008). A school-based group activity therapy intervention with at-risk high school students as it relates to their moral reasoning. *International Journal of Play Therapy, 17*(2), 122–137.

Pino, A. A., Little, M., Knight, G. P., & Silverman, W. K. (2009). Cross-ethnic measurement equivalence of the RCMAS in Latino and Caucasian youth with anxiety disorders. *Journal of Personality Assessment, 91*(1), 58–61.

Rando, T. A. (1993). *Treatment of complicated mourning.* Champaign, IL: Research Press.

Register, D. M., & Hilliard, R. E. (2008). Using Orff-based techniques in children's bereavement groups: A cognitive-behavioral music therapy approach, *Arts in Psychotherapy, 35*(2), 162–170.

Reyes, C. J., & Asbrand, J. P. (2005). A longitudinal study assessing trauma symptoms in sexually abused children engaged in play therapy. *International Journal of Play Therapy, 14*(2), 25–47.

Reynolds, C. R. (1978). "What I think and feel: A revised measure of children's manifest anxiety." *Journal of Abnormal Child Psychology, 6,* 271–280.

Reynolds, C. R. (1985). "Multitrait validation of the Revised Children's Manifest Anxiety Scale for children of high intelligence." *Psychological Reports, 56,* 402.

Rolsky, J. T. (1992). *Your child has cancer: A guide to coping.* Philadelphia: The Committee to Benefit Children, St. Christopher's Hospital for Children.

Rotheram-Borus, M. J., Lee, M., Lin, Y. Y., & Lester, P. (2004). Six-year intervention outcomes for adolescent children of parents with the human immunodeficiency virus. *Archives of Pediatrics & Adolescent Medicine, 158*(8), 742–748.

Schoen, A. A., Burgoyne, M., & Schoen, S. F. (2004). Are the developmental needs of children in America adequately addressed during the grief process? *Journal of Instructional Psychology, 31*(2), 143–148.

Silverman, P. R. (2000). When parents die. In K. J. Doka (Ed.), *Living with grief: Children, adolescents, and loss.* London: Taylor & Francis.

Sourkes, B., Frankel, M. D., Brown, M., Contro, N., Benitz, W., Case, C., et al. (2005). Food, toys, and love: Pediatric palliative care. *Current Problems in Pediatric Adolescent Health Care, 35,* 350–386.

Varni, J. W., Burwinkle, T. M., Katz, E. R., Meeske, K., Dickinson, P. (2002). The Peds-QL in pediatric cancer: Reliability and validity of the pediatric quality of life inventory generic core scales, multidimensional fatigue scale, and cancer module. *Cancer, 94,* 2090–2106.

Varni, J. W., Seid, M., Murtin, P. S. (2001). Peds-QL 4.0: Reliability and validity of the pediatric quality of life inventory version 4.0 generic core scales in healthy and patient populations. *Medical Care, 39,* 800–812.

Varni, J. W., Seid, M., Rode, C. A. (1999). The Peds-QL measurement model for the Pediatric Quality of Life Inventory. *Medical Care*, 37, 126–139.

Wolchik, S. A., Ma, Y., Tein, J.-Y., Sandler, I. N., & Ayers, T. S. (2008). Parentally bereaved children's grief: Self-system beliefs as mediators of the relations between grief and stressors and caregiver-child relationship quality. *Death Studies*, 32(7), 597–620.

APPENDIX: CHILDREN/TEEN'S LOSS INVENTORY

Place an "x" beside the life events you have experienced.

_____ death of a parent

_____ change in group of friends

_____ death of brother or sister

_____ change in schools

_____ death of another family member (who? ———)

_____ destruction/loss of property

_____ death of a friend

_____ school failure

_____ death of a classmate

_____ loss/change of physical ability

_____ death of the parent of a friend/classmate

_____ serious medical diagnosis

_____ a move to a new city (self)

_____ broken relationship (friend, coach, family member)

_____ serious medical diagnosis (family member)

_____ close friend moved to a new city

_____ incarceration of parent

_____ a parent who returned to work

_____ incarceration of other family member

_____ a parent who lost their job and is no longer working

_____ a parent whose work schedule changed significantly

_____ incarceration of self

_____ death of a pet

_____ loss of foster parent (change in homes)

_____ divorce or separation of parents

_____ separation from biological parent

_____ parent no longer living in the home

_____ sibling moved out of the home

_____ physical abuse of self

_____ new child in the home

_____ sexual abuse of self

_____ new adult living in the home

_____ emotional abuse of self

_____ parent with serious illness or injury

_____ lack of adult supervision and protection

_____ other family member with serious illness or injury

_____ physical abuse of parent

_____ home destroyed by fire/tornado/flood, etc.

_____ violence or abuse within the home

_____ physical assault of family member

_____ physical assault of self

(Developed by Khris Ford, LPC)

CHAPTER SEVEN

Grief and Youth in Crisis

Pamela A. Malone, Renée Bradford Garcia, and Elizabeth C. Pomeroy

Twelve-year-old Olivia wakes up to the clanging of pots and pans and a bright light trying to sneak under her eyelids. She groans as she pulls the pillow over her head.

"You might as well get up, Olivia," her mother says. "I've got to get to the welfare agency soon, and you need to get your sister ready." Olivia grunts discontentedly but rolls off the couch, sorts through her clothes in the trash bag, and stands outside the bathroom waiting for her uncle to finish. Olivia begins to hop around, "Can you please hurry up? I've got to go real bad!" she hollers at the door. A few minutes later the doorknob turns and her uncle emerges. "You better watch your attitude, girl. You're lucky to even have a bathroom to wait in line for. How about showing some respect for all I've done for you and your family!" Olivia says nothing, darts into the bathroom, and quickly locks the door. She is tired, hungry, and very grumpy. "I don't know how much more of this I can take," she says to herself.

Olivia's mom and six-year-old sister had to move in with her uncle after Hurricane Beulah hit her town. The four of them have somehow managed to squeeze into his one-bedroom apartment. Her dad is three states away, staying with a friend. There was simply no place that had room for all four of them, and her parents decided they needed to save the little money they had to get their own place . . . somewhere. Olivia wonders where they will end up and if they will ever find a home of their own again. It has already been four months, and "the plan," according to her mother, changes every week. Olivia wonders if there even is a plan. "Hurry up, Olivia," her mother calls. "Get Desiree ready. I've got to get to the bus stop in fifteen minutes."

"All right, already!" Olivia yells back. She knows her voice is dripping with attitude and she doesn't want to be mean to her mother, but she can't help it. It takes everything she has not to burst into tears—tears of anger, tears of fear, tears of sadness. She's been trying to hold it together, but it's hard. She can't even vent to her friend Lelah, because she doesn't know where she is. Did she go to a relative's house some-where far away? Is she staying in the shelter back home? She hasn't been answering her phone. It's probably underwater. She's terrified something horrible happened to Lelah in the storm. Every time she closes her eyes, she sees the rush of water coming underneath the front door of their house that was torn away by the hurricane. She again feels the panic of the stampede to get out and the scream of her sister in another room. She thought they were all going to die.

She hears her mother calling her again and moves slowly to the kitchen to get Desiree only to find her sitting in a puddle on the floor. "Desiree, what is wrong with you? Why did you pee on the floor?" Olivia quickly washes and dresses her so that her mom won't be late for the bus. As her mom runs for the bus stop, Olivia shouts, "Hey, Mom, what's for breakfast?" Her mom glances over her shoulder and says, "Get some noodles out of the cupboard and don't be late for school." Olivia heaves a big sigh and swears under her breath. *Geez, something's gotta give*, she ponders. *I'm drowning.*

Olivia is the face of a child's grief in a crisis.

Introduction

This chapter addresses bereaved youth whose loss results from aban-donment, domestic violence, natural disaster, and other crisis events. While dealing with a major life crisis is difficult for adults, it can be devastating to a child's stability and sense of well-being. Often these youth are facing unknown and uncertain futures while attempting to cope with dramatic changes in their lives. In addition to the traumatic nature of the crisis itself, the child can be overwhelmed by feelings of grief and loss. On the other hand, adults often focus on the immediate concerns such as living arrangements, legal issues, and securing and maintaining physical safety. They may overlook the emotional needs of youth due to the urgency of the critical situation. Practitioners working with youth in crisis need to be competently aware of the dynamics of loss and the ensuing grief reactions that youth may develop over the first few weeks and months following the crisis. Assessment and intervention techniques for working with grief issues of youth in crisis will be provided.

Overview of Grief and Loss

Grief and loss come into the lives of youth in many forms and with more frequency than adults realize. There are the obvious crises such as the death of a parent, sibling, friend, or other family member. Children and adolescents who are victims of abandonment, intrafamilial (domestic) violence, interpersonal violence, community violence, serious accident, and other emergency situations may experience indescribable grief and loss. The crisis event may take the form of a natural disaster such as a hurricane, flood, wildfire, avalanche, or earthquake. It may occur through a technological, or human-made disaster such as a shipwreck, plane crash, building collapse, toxic spill, or nuclear reactor leak. There are times when these crises may overlap, producing multiple and varied losses. Disasters tend to happen to many people simultaneously and invariably involve extreme danger, suddenness, a magnified sense of helplessness, as well as significant degrees of loss (Miller, 1998). The crisis might be violent in nature and may occur in the home, school, neighborhood, or community. Examples of crises that may elicit less obvious grief responses in children and adolescents include the impact of exposure to media coverage of catastrophic events such as 9/11, the devastations of the Iraq war, or the impact of Hurricanes Katrina and Ike.

The experience of grief and loss in childhood and adolescence "constitutes a risk factor for concurrent and sometimes chronic distress" (Currier, Holland, & Neimeyer, 2007, p. 253). Children and adolescents exposed to trauma and crisis events may exhibit impairments in academic, peer, and family functioning. Recently acquired developmental growth and achievements are particularly vulnerable to disruption in the wake of a crisis. Reactions to trauma may appear immediately after a traumatic event or in the following weeks or months. Crisis events can shatter hopes, destroy confidence, and cast children and adolescents into despair that could last a lifetime.

During the aftermath of a crisis, reminders of the trauma may contribute to intense psychological and physiological reactivity, which can provoke and maintain distress (Saltzman, Steinberg, Layne, Aisenberg, & Pynoos, 2001). Chronic distress may take the form of physical, emotional, social, and cognitive grief reactions, as outlined in table 7.1.

TABLE 7.1
Types of Grief Responses

Physical	Emotional	Social	Cognitive
Trouble eating	Dazed	Feeling different from peers	Decline in school performance
Sleep disturbances	Numbed	Perception of peers being intolerant of their grief	Paranormal (hallucinatory) experiences
Headaches	Shocked	Social isolation	Preoccupation
Stomachaches	Afraid	Isolation from family	Thoughts of own death
Joint pain	Frustrated	Risk-taking behavior	Sense of presence of the deceased
Muscle pain and tension	Depressed	Increased sense of maturity	Realization of the permanency of death
Being ill more often	Alone	Experience of unkind remarks from peers	Disbelief
Lump in throat	Anxious	Avoidance of reminders	Confusion
Tightness in chest	Guilty	Antisocial	Distraction
Aching arms	Uncomfortable when happy	Withdrawal from normal activities	Difficulty with concentration
Muscle weakness	Sad	Change in peer group	Intrusive thoughts
Dry mouth	Irritable	Self-destructive behavior	Lowered self-esteem
Lack of energy	Vulnerable		Memory problems
Eating disturbances	Angry		
	Aggressive		

Children's Grief Reactions to Crises

Children's grief reactions to crises can be as varied and unique as children themselves. Often following a disaster, adults notice how extraordinarily quiet some children are in comparison to the level of distress evidenced in adults and mistakenly assume they are coping well. The

inhibition of children's normal spontaneous activity is typically an indicator of underlying stress (Miller, 1998). Other children may demonstrate their grief with excessive crying, clinging, and regressive
behavior. They may cry or act out as a means of informing adults that
they are in pain (Schuurman, 2008). In addition, children intuit and
absorb the distress of the bereaved adults around them, which
increases their level of fear, uncertainty, and distrust.

The preschool tasks of sharing and cooperation with other children
may be impacted by a child's withdrawal, emotional constriction, and
problems with impulse control (Pynoos, Steinberg, & Goenjian, 1996).
Play that reflects or reenacts the crisis may limit and disturb the typical
fantasy play of a preschool child. This may lead to the child being
labeled as "deviant" by other children, parents, and teachers (Pynoos
et al., 1996). Preschool children are typically able to organize narrative
material into a beginning, middle, and end. This is a crucial developmental task that allows for competency in reading, writing, and communication skills. Exposure to a crisis may interfere with this developmental
task, resulting in a more chaotic narrative construction (Pynoos et al.,
1996). A crisis may also lead to the child's inability to cognitively and
emotionally process the loss in a healthy and resilient manner. Also,
school-age children exposed to crises may have difficulty developing
appropriate emotional regulation, which is necessary and critical to
functioning with family, peers, and within school settings (Pynoos et
al., 1996).

Grief reactions among school-age children may include increased
attachment behaviors, such as clinginess toward parents or caretakers
due to worries about the safety of family members and themselves.
Childhood is a time for transitioning to more involvement with peers
and development of friendships. A crisis may jeopardize this necessary
transition, adding frustration to the child-parent relationship and creating further difficulties for the child (Pynoos et al., 1996). In contrast,
some children may strive to accelerate autonomy and pursue activities
beyond their developmental capabilities, becoming emotionally distant
from parents in the process. All of these behavioral responses are indic-
ative of the significance of the loss and ensuing grief.

Adolescent Grief Responses to Crises

Adolescent grief reactions do not necessarily parallel the grieving of
adults. Notably, adolescent grief may involve mourning that comes and
goes, and the overall process may extend over a long period (Hogan &
DeSantis, 1992). Adolescent grieving is paradoxically both continuous

and intermittent (Balk & Corr, 1996). The experience of a crisis can cause significant distress, which may take the form of avoidant behaviors in adolescents. They may restrict their normal daily activities as a way to avoid confronting reminders that strongly evoke disturbing images and reactions (Saltzman et al., 2001).

The major task of adolescence is identity formation, with an emphasis on themes of separation and connectedness. Identity tends to shift away from parents and family, although attachment to parents is still vital, and move toward forming an identity among peers (Noppe & Noppe, 2004). Adolescents are exploring who they are and who they might become. This developmental period is important for the formation of self-esteem, the determination of self-efficacy, the absorption of others' perceptions, and the acquisition of the ability to manage life's demands and unexpected changes (Steese et al., 2006). Adolescents perceive themselves as members of a peer culture. They use their peers and the popular culture to provide feedback and to formulate their identity. Crises and "traumatic experiences may skew expectations about the world and the safety and security of interpersonal life. Such expectations map onto a schema of risk, danger, injury, loss, safety, security, protection, and intervention, which once organized, may be incorporated into the developing personality" (Saltzman et al., 2001, p. 45). Adolescents have not developed the social or emotional maturity to fully incorporate and process bereavement into a coherent worldview (Rowling, 2002). In addition, traumatic experiences and crises can upset or complicate an identity still in formation (O'Brien, Goodenow, & Espin, 1991).

Adolescents tend to seek out one another when they have experienced a crisis and may feel most comfortable talking with other teens who have experienced the same crisis. Yet, simultaneously, they can feel different from and misunderstood by their peers (Ringler & Hayden, 2000). They may feel discomfort talking with parents or other adults about their feelings and are often disappointed in parents' reactions (O'Brien et al., 1991). Many adolescents expect more support from parents and other adults than they actually receive. Parents are often unsure how to react to their adolescent. The disenfranchised nature of adolescent grief is a phenomenon "that is shaped fundamentally by grieving rules of parents, other adults, and peers, all of whom create the grieving norms of an adolescent's world" (Rowling, 2002, p. 276). Adolescents are often perceived as resilient and not seriously affected by the crisis, especially if it is a disaster experienced by the entire family or community (Ringler & Hayden, 2000). Adolescents' perceived lack of parental or adult support makes it difficult for them to find adults whom they can trust and with whom they can discuss their grief.

Adolescents can experience a multitude of emotions resulting from a crisis (Webb, 2002). These bereavement reactions may include a sense of bravado, denial, anger and rage, shock, numbness, fear of one's own death, nightmares, insomnia, loneliness, survivor guilt, school problems, great sadness, substance abuse, and suicidal ideation (Rheingold et al., 2004; Ringler & Hayden, 2000). Adolescents are typically reluctant to show strong emotions, making it difficult to assess the nature and depth of their emotional pain. Their natural and expected self-absorption can make it difficult for them to connect with adults (Goodman, 2002).

Adolescents are often invested in projecting an image of independence and control over their lives. They often want to appear as if they don't need adult guidance or support. They may delay or repress their grief in order to maintain this appearance. Adolescents can look like adults in physique, body development, and attire, and yet will struggle with the emotional immaturity of their age (Noppe & Noppe, 2004). The adults in their lives may react to this pseudo-sophistication with unrealistic expectations for emotional control. These adolescents may look like they are doing well but may in fact be postponing their grief reactions, which can reemerge later in adulthood (Kandt, 1994). Many adolescents endure an overwhelming sense of being permanently changed by their loss experience and grief. This "changed self" does not reflect their previous carefree, invulnerable self and, instead, is more fearful and reflective (Lattanzi-Licht, 1996).

Disoriented Grief

Children and adolescents who experience a crisis that leaves them devoid of home, family, pets, and a life that they were familiar with may exhibit symptoms of disoriented grief (Malone, Pomeroy, & Jones, 2009). Disoriented grief is characterized by a paralyzing effect, a pervasive feeling of uncertainty and fear, a perceived lack of motivation, and an enduring sense of living in survival mode. Disoriented grief is composed of categories that include displacement, destruction, death, and distress.

Displacement encompasses the loss of family members, friends, pets, employment, school, and identity. Being displaced means leaving behind all that was familiar. Loss of identity involves a sense of isolation, not knowing where one belongs, and a feeling of being an outsider in one's current location.

Destruction includes the physical loss of a home, material belongings, and neighborhood. Children and adolescents may experience the death of family members, the death of their friends, and/or the death of their pets. They may also exhibit or express fear of their own death.

Distress entails the witnessing of traumatic events to which children and adolescents would not ordinarily be exposed. This type of distress may include a loss of hope about the future and about life in general. It also includes a loss of innocence and childhood. Another cause of distress may be the stigma, or "blaming of the victim," that may result from the crisis.

These components of disoriented grief lead to a paralyzing effect that makes it difficult for children and adolescents to move forward in their lives beyond the crisis experience. They are often left with a pervasive feeling of uncertainty and fear, unsure of what the future holds for them and whom they can trust. Teachers and mental health professionals frequently perceive a lack of motivation on the part of these children and adolescents, whose main purpose is an enduring sense of living in survival mode.

Assessment Methods with Youth in Crisis

When assessing youth in crisis, it is important to obtain information from the child or adolescent as well as the parents or caregivers in order to obtain a thorough evaluation. To accurately and thoroughly assess grief in youth who have experienced a crisis, practitioners must take into account the wide range of potential responses in the aftermath of the event, especially after a sudden or violent loss (Crenshaw, 2008). In addition to the grief assessment outlined in chapter 2, a crisis assessment can be divided into three categories: assessment of the situation, tasks of the assessment, and treatment goals (Goodman, 2002).

ASSESSMENT OF THE SITUATION (GOODMAN, 2002; WEBB, 2002)

- Personal thoughts and beliefs about the crisis
- Family's thoughts and beliefs about the crisis
- Relationship with any person(s) involved in the crisis or loss event
- Memories of the crisis event
- Relationship with any survivors
- Current emotional state and functioning
- Personality traits
- Family, social environment, and social supports
- Adaptation to life changes resulting from the crisis

TASKS OF THE ASSESSMENT (CHRIST, 1999; GOODMAN, 2002; LIOTTA, 1996)

- Assessing symptoms, thoughts, and feelings related to the crisis
- Normalizing the grieving process

- Allowing nonverbal and verbal content to be revealed at the child's or adolescent's own pace
- Encouraging trust
- Respecting all expressed emotions
- Aiding adjustment to changed family relationships
- Supporting mastery of events and emotions
- Promoting continued age-appropriate development, reengagement, and reinvestment in activities and peers

TREATMENT GOALS (GOODMAN, 2002; GOODMAN, WILLIAMS, AGELL, & GANTT, 1998)

- Establish a trusting relationship
- Express feelings in a safe environment
- Explore memories of the crisis
- Understand and adjust to the life changes following the event

Further assessment involves a comprehensive evaluation that addresses a tripartite etiology of the crisis, which should include (1) a clear delineation of the objective features and a thorough description of the child's or adolescent's subjective experience of the crisis; (2) a determination of the type and frequency of distressing reminders to include both external and internal cues; and (3) a detailed accounting of current secondary stressors that the child or adolescent may be facing, as well as potential adversities or ongoing hardships (Pynoos et al., 1996). The practitioner needs to gather precise information regarding the speciyfic objective features of the crisis which include (Pynoos et al., 1996):

1. Extent of exposure to direct life threat
2. Any injury to self, including extent of physical pain endured
3. Witnessing of mutilating injury or grotesque death, especially to family members or friends
4. Any perpetrating of violent acts against others, especially to family members or friends
5. Hearing unanswered screams for help and cries of distress
6. Smelling noxious odors
7. Being trapped or without assistance
8. Proximity to violent threat and violence
9. Unexpectedness and duration of the trauma or crisis event
10. Extent of violent force and use of a weapon or injurious object
11. Number and nature of threats during any violent episode
12. Witnessing of atrocities, to include torture, rape, and murder
13. Witnessing of dead bodies, especially family members or friends

14. The relationship to the assailant and other victims
15. Use of physical coercion
16. Violation of the physical integrity of the child or adolescent
17. Degree of brutality or malevolence

All of these factors may contribute to the onset and persistence of potential problems with grief and trauma in youth (Pynoos et al., 1996).

Interventions with Children and Adolescents

It is imperative that grief interventions for children and adolescents who have experienced a crisis meet developmental and age-appropriate needs. Conflicts and issues that are specific to the developmental tasks and transitions of early-, middle-, and late-adolescent development are important to consider (Balk, 2008). Since the "symptomatology is like a blanket covering the mourning" (Rando, 1993, p. 587), the impact of the crisis must be addressed prior to grief and loss issues. The goal of interventions for grief reactions related to trauma and crisis is to ameliorate chronic distress symptoms, enhance coping and adaptive behaviors, increase family support, and help children and adolescents resume activities that promote normal developmental growth and progression (Saltzman et al., 2001).

PSYCHOEDUCATION ABOUT GRIEF AND LOSS

Interventions for youth in crisis must incorporate a psychoeducational component regarding age-appropriate reactions to trauma, grief, and loss. This approach is essential in order to assist children and adolescents in identifying the physical, emotional, social, and cognitive symptoms they may be experiencing related to the crisis and loss. While children may perceive their reactions to the event as wrong, abnormal, bizarre, or related to personal shortcomings or faults (Saltzman et al., 2001), the psychoeductional approach utilizes a strengths-based perspective to normalize their grief reactions. This method also involves teaching children and adolescents the vocabulary for communicating about the crisis and their experiences of bereavement.

SYMPTOM MANAGEMENT AND REDUCTION

The following are some symptom management and reduction techniques that practitioners can utilize with children and adolescents during individual, group, or family therapy sessions. Symptom reduction and management can be taught to children and adolescents as a skill set to be used at any time and is an extremely important component of crisis intervention and ongoing therapy. These methods include (Saltzman et al., 2001):

- Relaxation techniques to include graduated muscle tensing and relaxing, and creating safe-place imagery
- Thought-stopping as a cognitive strategy designed to increase the ability to monitor disturbing or dysfunctional thoughts and replace them with more calming and adaptive thoughts
- Self-talk to counter negative and distorted thinking and to replace with positive and rational thinking
- Breathing retraining as a method of taking deep and focused breaths as a calming technique (also increases the child's or adolescent's awareness of when they stop breathing as a maladaptive method to reduce upsetting feelings)
- Interpersonal skills training to increase knowledge and awareness of interaction with others
- Grounding techniques to be used during sessions when the child or adolescent is overwhelmed or not able to stay in the moment:
  —Focusing on bodily sensations
  —Listening to practitioner's voice
  —Touch on the hand

GROUP THERAPY

Group therapy is an intervention that can work well for both children and adolescents. Many participants in bereavement support groups report experiencing more freedom in expressing feelings, being more in control of their lives, and being more confident, happy, and better able to connect to others (Tedeschi, 1996). An effective, developmentally appropriate group teaches symptom reduction and management, increases life-enhancing coping strategies, identifies and minimizes risk factors, and identifies and maximizes strengths. Risk factors may include the experience of previous losses or crises, isolation, few friends or close relationships, problematic relationships with friends or family, substance use or abuse, low self-esteem, and poor school performance (Balk & Corr, 1996). Strengths may include good relationships with friends and family, a sense of connection to the school community, involvement in extracurricular activities, a healthy level of self-esteem, good school grades, and parental involvement.

Group therapy goals may include creating a sense of safety, identifying and embracing the emotions of grief, commemorating or remembering the crisis event, acknowledging ambivalence, and recovering and preserving positive memories and thoughts about oneself and others that may have been lost during the crisis (Schuurman, 2008). Group therapy allows children and adolescents the knowledge that there are others who understand their feelings, thoughts, and behaviors. The following tasks can be incorporated into the group sessions by the group practitioner (Heegaard, 1990):

- Teach basic concepts about death, loss, and grief
- Help children and adolescents recognize, accept, and express feelings
- Provide opportunities for taking risks and problem-solving
- Encourage open communication and opportunities to learn from each group member
- Give support and encouragement
- Discover life-depleting misconceptions

Each of these tasks can be addressed through group activities, sharing times, and the dynamics of the group process (Dane, 2002). In addition, the use of games and communication exercises may help children and adolescents express feelings and thoughts about the crisis event or loss.

Group therapy for youth can offer opportunities for emotional connection and safety. It can alleviate the sense of loneliness that many children report following a crisis. Children may also receive validation for who they are, what they feel, and what they experience (Schuurman, 2008). Groups provide a setting for children to learn how to express and share emotions that they may feel overwhelmed by, ranging from anger and self-pity to relief and panic (Schuurman, 2008). The range of emotionality can be random in nature and confusing for both the child and the family. Groups can help children and adolescents begin to move through the bereavement process.

Group therapy as a modality of intervention for adolescents has historically been utilized for a wide variety of issues and concerns that have an impact on this population (Gitterman & Shulman, 2005; Malekoff, 2004). Groups provide a framework toward understanding the impact of grief and loss (Balk & Corr, 1996) and effectively build support, mutuality, and connection among group members (Gitterman & Shulman, 2005). There is a positive connection between social support and the adjustment of adolescents, which is understandable given the importance of peer relationships in the development of cognitive and social skills during adolescence (Tedeschi, 1996). This makes group therapy especially significant for adolescents since grief and trauma can be isolating, private experiences for many teens (Lattanzi-Licht, 1996).

ART THERAPY

Integrating art therapy into grief interventions helps children and adolescents communicate, understand, and cope with bereavement issues (Goodman, 2002). Art therapy includes drawing, painting, modeling with clay or Play-Doh, writing or journaling, as well the creation of memory boxes. Art creation can provide direct access to a youth's world and can be achieved through his or her imagination. It is through this medium that thoughts, ideas, and emotions connect with factual information (Goodman, 2002). Therapeutic communication may be easier and at times more direct "through the use of symbols or images rather than through the complex world of spoken language" (Goodman, 2002, p. 299). "Symbols restore a sense of unity by integrating and connecting emotions, perceptions, and thoughts not previously brought into juxtaposition and, in so doing, create a complex subjective experience that is deeply moving and cathartic" (Lewis & Langer, 1994, p. 232). Art therapy provides young people with a safe channel to express their inner pain in a manner that gives them mastery over the crisis.

PLAY THERAPY

The use of formalized (directive) and free-form (nondirective) play therapy creates an environment that can elicit the stories, fears, thoughts, and concerns of children who have experienced a crisis. Initiating play therapy with children is an approach that allows for the reinterpretation and modification of traumatic impressions and emotions. "Using directive methods while recognizing the child's own rhythms, timing, needs, strengths, and weaknesses, the practitioner can expedite the child's resolution of difficult aspects of traumatic response and experiences" (Nader, 2002, p. 218). Directive play may elicit deeper levels or variations of painful emotions such as rage or fear, and may require further sessions that focus on the specific crisis event (Nader, 2002). Nondirective play is led predominantly by the child. For example, the child may assign a role to the practitioner such as family member, victim, perpetrator, witness, rescuer, or other relevant actor (Nader, 2002). The activity gets played out at the child's own pace, with the child directing the actions.

Role play with adolescents involves conscious exploration of the inner turmoil that the adolescent is experiencing. For example, an adolescent who survived a school shooting may be fearful of returning to the hallway where his classmate was killed. Role play may involve rehearsing the first day that the teenager returns to school and walks down the hall to his locker. The practitioner might role play an interaction between the adolescent and the other students and practice the use of life-enhancing coping skills.

The therapeutic environment room needs to be well equipped with toy people, stuffed animals, various people puppets and animal puppets, buildings and blocks, clay and Play-Doh, toy weapons, and an array of drawing materials (various sizes and colors of paper, crayons, markers, and colored pencils). Nader (2002) outlines the following guideline for play therapy at various ages:

- Preschoolers: the practitioner focuses on play while verbalizing reactions and sequences for the child.
- Younger school-age children: the practitioner uses a combination of play and drawing with cognitive review and discussion.
- Adolescents: the practitioner emphasizes discussion along with some role play and/or demonstration.

THE USE OF TRAUMA NARRATIVE CONSTRUCTION

Children and adolescents can be "assisted in constructing a coherent, temporally organized trauma narrative that includes objective and subjective features of the traumatic experience, and the worst moments of extreme fear, horror, and helplessness" (Saltzman et al., 2001, p. 52). With the practitioner's guidance, the youth explores his or her thoughts about what occurred during the traumatic event, including thoughts about what could have been done to prevent the injurious or lethal consequences by any of the parties involved (Saltzman et al., 2001). The worst moments of the crisis get explored, with connections made between those moments and traumatic reminders they experience. This initial narrative allows the practitioner insight into the range of possible coping mechanisms used by the youth, such as avoidance of painful reminders, which can then be used in creating a life-enhancing coping plan. This form of therapy is described in detail in *Treating Trauma and Traumatic Grief in Children and Adolescents* (Cohen, Mannarino, & Deblinger, 2006).

Interventions with Families

Children and adolescents are highly influenced by how those around them respond to a loss (Rosen, 1991). Many children and adolescents who have been exposed to a crisis exhibit a loss of trust in adults and maintain a fear that the event will reoccur. If a family constructs a taboo against discussing the crisis, then many children and adolescents lose the opportunity to inform anyone about their thoughts, beliefs, and feelings. Included in their ensuing silence will be questions about their own safety, their belief about what actually occurred, and their imagined guilt, as well as their own grief (Rosen, 1991). Also, if following a crisis the functioning of the family or adult caregivers is impaired, children and adolescents may be further traumatized (Miller, 1998). Interventions with families need to focus on assisting children and adolescents in regaining a sense of safety, while validating their emotional reactions, as opposed to discouraging or minimizing them.

FAMILY THERAPY

Families may benefit from family grief therapy that focuses on the loss resulting from the crisis. An initial assessment should be made to determine the family dynamics, strengths, and motivations for intervention. It is imperative to assess how the family copes with loss as well as the family's thoughts and beliefs about the crisis. How the family makes meaning of the event provides a framework for assessment and a direction for intervention (Nadeau, 2001).

Finding or making meaning is critical for a family's successful adjustment to a crisis (Armour, 2003; Davis, 2001). Appraising personal losses and attributing meaning to them prompt movement toward grief resolution. Family therapy can help this process by allowing children and adolescents an emotionally safe environment to find positive meanings and mitigate negative aspects of the crisis. The focus of family therapy is a process of meaning reconstruction. For example, experiencing a crisis can lead to a growth in character, a shift or gain in perspective, a strengthening of familial relationships, or an increased sense of connectedness with others (Davis, 2001).

Another important focus of family therapy is to assist parents and caregivers in creating an environment that reduces the frequency of painful reminders and unnecessary reexposures, including graphic depictions of the traumatic event (Pynoos et al., 1996). This serves to reduce parents' own reactivity to those reminders that may accentuate their children's anxieties (Pynoos et al., 1996). Practitioners can help families identify triggers related to the crisis in order to anticipate them and to increase the family's ability to cope with them. These interventions can rebuild parents' confidence in their own ability to protect their children.

THE USE OF RITUAL

Rituals can be very powerful and rich in meaning. Funerals, loss anniversaries, and remembrance or memorial ceremonies are common examples of rituals. Rituals provide guidance about behavior, time, and emotions in response to death and loss. They organize emotional expression and pattern behavior during a chaotic period of transition (DeVries, 1996). Rituals allow for both collective and individual expression of loss. The significance is both social and personal (Doka, 2002; 2008). Grief therapy with families can focus on creating an appropriate and meaningful ritual to commemorate the loss. Practitioners can offer ritual as a form of intervention and can help the family create a therapeutic ritual that emerges from the narrative of the family's experience of the loss event. It is imperative that children and adolescents be included in planning the ritual because it empowers them to be part of the healing process. Doka (2002) outlines various therapeutic rituals beyond the funeral ritual:

- Rituals of continuity identify the importance of the ongoing presence or impact of the death. An example is the lighting of a candle on an anniversary, holiday, or birthday to commemorate a person or event. This offers an opportunity to grieve.
- Rituals of transition indicate movement or growth since the occurrence of the crisis. This may include a child moving from elementary school to middle school, an adolescent graduating high school and going on to college, or children welcoming a stepparent.
- Rituals of reconciliation allow people to offer or accept forgiveness or to complete unfinished business regarding the crisis.
- Rituals of affirmation acknowledge the lessons learned or growth gained from the experience of the loss.

Working with Schools and the Community

Practitioners can work effectively with school and community leaders to provide post-disaster interventions, to include large or small group interventions, didactic sessions, and one-on-one counseling with children and adolescents. The provision of this service addresses crisis events that occurred within the community, such as the violent and sudden death of a peer or teacher, a local disaster, or urban violence. The school environment is an excellent setting for the delivery of support and crisis intervention because the school can provide a "developmentally appropriate environment that encourages normalcy and minimizes stigma" (Pfefferbaum, 1997). The school setting can aid children and adolescents in returning to a pre-crisis level of functioning and routine. It is important that schools and students be assisted to understand that all reactions are normal, because there is no one response that is appropriate for all people. Chapter 5 provides a complete review of school-based interventions for children and adolescents.

Common Ethical Dilemmas

Confidentiality is a critical component of working with bereaved and traumatized children, adolescents, and families. Confidentiality with children and adolescents can be complicated and has its limits. The limitations of confidentiality need to be explained to all family members prior to the beginning of any intervention. Children and adolescents need to feel secure that they can speak freely without fear of retribution. While the practitioner keeps the information discussed in sessions with the youth confidential, she also explains to both parents and the youth that she will be providing general information to the parents. Parents, on the other hand, should be informed of the limits of what is shared with them regarding session content and educated about how this enables effective therapeutic interventions. While some information between the practitioner and the adolescent can remain confidential, it is important to inform the teen of information that needs to be shared with her or his parents or caregivers. In such cases, the practitioner should communicate to the adolescent the specifics of what she will share and discuss any concerns the teen has prior to talking with the parents. Finally, the practitioner makes it clear to all family members that any safety concerns will be shared with the appropriate adults in the family.

Practitioners have the ethical responsibility of pursuing knowledge and remaining educationally current about evidence-based practice in the area of grief, crisis intervention, and trauma. They must be knowledgeable about the spectrum of interventions and treatments for traumatized children and adolescents, and be aware of the scientific evidence that validates their potential effectiveness (Raphael, Minkov, & Dobson, 2001). Practitioners must possess proficiency in the developmental issues as well as the bereavement process of youth in crisis, and have the ability to assess who is at risk for life-depleting grief reactions.

Cultural Considerations

Culture places people in a protective and supportive system that provides norms and values, lifestyles, and knowledge. Disruption of culture through disasters and other crises can lead to a deep sense of loss of people, place, and coping mechanisms. Culture can create a meaning system that explains the causes of disasters (DeVries, 1996). "Cultural customs and rituals help individuals control their emotions, order their behavior, link the sufferers more intimately to the social group, and serve as symbols of continuity" (DeVries, 1996, p. 405).

Consideration must be given to how grief and loss is confronted and explained within each family unit, social setting, and cultural context. Culture influences the experience, expectations, and expression of grief and loss in response to a crisis. In addition, different cultures come with unique strengths, which can be utilized in the recovery process. It is important to explore and know what children and adolescents have been taught and what they believe about grief and loss, death, and disasters. Culture also influences patterns of attachment and defines the meaning of different types of losses, as well as the extent of who grieves (Doka & Martin, 2002). Cultural expectations also define appropriate support and interventions. Cultures differ in how support is offered and accepted, as well as the applicability of interventions such as group, individual, or family therapy.

CASE EXAMPLE

The following example illustrates how a crisis impacts an adolescent and the treatment that effects positive change.

Jennie was fifteen years old when she witnessed the violent murder of her eighteen-year-old cousin, Paul. They had been at a dance club and were leaving when Paul was verbally accosted by a group of young men with whom he had had some previous problems. There was arguing, yelling, and some pushing and shoving. Paul and Jennie got away and ran into the parking lot to Paul's car. Jennie got into the passenger seat and Paul got behind the steering wheel, where he was promptly shot in the face by one of the young men.

Prior to Paul's murder, Jennie had been an A/B student who was outgoing, very social, and well-liked by her peers. Following this crisis, she quickly became a C/D student and refused to go anywhere with friends. For months afterward, Jennie complained of headaches and stomachaches, and became both nauseous and unable to move whenever she heard sirens. It became difficult for her to go to school or to leave home because of her fear of hearing sirens. In addition to her somatic complaints, Jennie also mentioned having difficulty concentrating on her school work. Often while she was reading, she would hear the gun shot and then begin to tremble and cry.

Jennie was brought to the initial assessment session by her mother, who was visibly distraught over her daughter's failing grades and fear of her former life. Her mother stated that the entire family was mourning the loss of Paul and that they saw him as "in a better place" since he had been hanging out with a tough crowd that "only predicted more trouble down the road." It had been three months since his murder when Jennie's mother sought help for her.

Jennie's visual memory was of "red, red, just everything covered in blood, sticky blood," and of her cousin Paul's face "just completely blown away." She described a persistent auditory memory of hearing her screams mixed with the sound of sirens. Jennie was first taught some relaxation techniques as a way of calming and controlling her somatic symptoms. This included breath retraining, where she learned to inhale slowly and deeply, while clearing her mind, and envisioning her breaths as a healing force throughout her body. Thought-stopping was also utilized in getting Jennie to recognize when disturbing thoughts and images began to run through her mind. She learned to clear her thinking, take a deep breath, and replace thoughts of danger with thoughts of safety. She was able to ground herself in the moment by observing her surroundings and telling herself that she was safe. This was her life-enhancing coping plan designed to assist her throughout the bereavement process.

During individual treatment with Jennie, the focus was initially on assisting her in the construction of a trauma narrative by helping her to identify links between the crisis of witnessing Paul's murder, her reactions at the time, and her current life-depleting behavior of attempting to avoid hearing sirens by staying home and not socializing with friends. In constructing the trauma narrative, Jennie had to explore and describe the worst moments of this horrific experience while utilizing her coping techniques. She gained insight into her range of painful reminders and avoidance behaviors. Over subsequent sessions, she was able to increase her tolerance of trauma-related thoughts and reactions by improving her use of life-enhancing techniques.

Psychoeducation about grief and loss reactions and reactivity was a component of therapy with Jennie. She needed to understand the interplay between trauma and grief, and have her thoughts, feelings, and behaviors normalized and validated. She learned to recognize loss reminders and to identify the ways in which her trauma and loss disrupted her life.

Eventually, the focus of therapy became aiding Jennie to recall pleasant and positive memories and aspects of Paul. Jennie was able to remember Paul's smile and sense of humor. During one session, she described how he liked to try new things and would tease her about doing things "out of my comfort zone." She quickly retreated into tears and stated that this is what got him killed and her so traumatized, "going outside the safety of home." She was able to successfully ground herself in safety by using her coping techniques and then proceed calmly with the session. Therapy continued to focus on Jennie's use of loss reminders to understand the impact and personal meaning of losing her cousin Paul. It was necessary for her to live her life without Paul present and to construct a non-traumatic image of him with which she could reminisce.

She needed to hang on to the sound of his laughter and remember his playfulness and ability to live fully in the moment. Jennie created a memory box of Paul that included a photo of them together as well as a picture of a red corvette, which was something he always wanted to drive. She wrote a poem about him that she included in her memory box and plans to continue to add positive mementoes about Paul.

One of the difficulties in Jennie's bereavement process involved the fact that she witnessed the murder of her cousin but could not identify his killer. The faces of the group of young men were a blur to her. However, she feared that these young men would stalk and pursue her. This, coupled with the blending of her screams and the sound of sirens, impaired her ability to venture far from home. She was eventually able to hear sirens as a helping response but still got knots in her stomach whenever she heard them. Her grades gradually returned to As and Bs, and she began socializing with a select group of friends.

Summary

Youth can be seriously affected by crises and the aftermath of grief. It is important for practitioners to be able to identify grief and trauma in youth, particularly when children and adolescents have been victims of abandonment, violence, serious accidents, or natural disasters. Practitioners who intervene with youth who have experienced tragedies have the opportunity to build on the youth's individual and environmental strengths to promote life-enhancing skills that eventuate in healing. These strengths-based methods can aid in the development of interpersonal growth with lifelong benefits. Understanding grief and trauma from a strengths-based perspective can provide the practitioner with the necessary tools to implement interventions effectively. Using the strengths-based tenets outlined in chapter 1 along with the techniques described in this chapter, the practitioner is well-equipped to work with children and adolescents who have experienced a traumatic loss (Pomeroy & Garcia, 2009).

The aftermath of a crisis overwhelms an individual's coping capacity and ability to draw on the strengths and resources inherent in the individual. The practitioner plays a vital role in assisting the individual mobilize their internal and external strengths to promote life-enhancing coping skills (Pomeroy & Garcia, 2009). This is particularly true for children and adolescents who depend on adults to provide care and support. The goal of grief counseling with young people is to minimize the life-depleting behaviors and maximize the potential for recovery.

Resources for Practitioners

Association for Death Education and Counseling
www.adec.org

1111 Deer Lake Road
Suite 100
Deerfield, IL 60015
(847) 509-0403
adec@adec.org

The Dougy Center
www.dougy.org
PO Box 86852
Portland, OR 97286
toll-free (866) 775-5683
help@dougy.org

References

Armour, M. (2003). Meaning making in the aftermath of homicide. *Death Studies*, *27*(6), 519–540.

Balk, D. E. (2008). The adolescent's encounter with death. In K. J. Doka & A. S. Tucci (Eds.), *Living with grief: Children and adolescents* (pp. 25–42). Washington, DC: Hospice Foundation of America.

Balk, D. E., & Corr, C. A. (1996). Adolescents, developmental tasks, and encounters with death and bereavement. In D. E. Balk, & C. A. Corr (Eds.), *Handbook of adolescent death and bereavement* (pp. 3–24). New York: Springer Publishing.

Bouton, B. L. (2003). Schools, children, and public tragedy. In M. Lattanzi-Licht & K. J. Doka (Eds.), *Living with grief: Coping with public tragedy* (pp. 151–164). New York: Brunner-Routledge.

Christ, G. H. (1999). *Healing children's grief.* New York: Oxford University Press.

Cohen, J. A., Mannarino, A. P., & Deblinger, E. (2006). Treating trauma and traumatic grief in children and adolescents. New York: Guilford Press.

Crenshaw, D. A. (2008). Grief therapy with children and adolescents: An overview. In K. J. Doka & A. S. Tucci (Eds.), *Living with grief: Children and adolescents* (pp. 217–231). Washington, DC: Hospice Foundation of America.

Currier, J. M., Holland, J. M., & Neimeyer, R. A. (2007). The effectiveness of bereavement interventions with children: A meta-analysis review of controlled outcome research. *Journal of Clinical Child and Adolescent Psychology*, *36*, 253–259.

Dane, B. O. (2002). Bereavement groups for children: Families with HIV/AIDS. In N. B. Webb (Ed.), *Helping bereaved children: A handbook for practitioners* (pp. 265–296). New York: Guilford Press.

Davis, C. G. (2001). The tormented and the transformed: Understanding responses to loss and trauma. In R. A. Neimeyer (Ed.), *Meaning reconstruction & the experience of loss* (pp. 137–155). Washington, DC: American Psychological Association.

DeVries, M. W. (1996). Trauma in cultural perspective. In B. A. van der Kolk, A. C. McFarlane, & L. Weisaeth (Eds.), *Traumatic stress: The effects of overwhelming experience on mind, body, and society* (pp. 398–413). New York: Guilford Press.

Doka, K. J. (2002). The role of ritual in the treatment of disenfranchised grief. In K. J. Doka (Ed.), *Disenfranchised grief: New directions, challenges, and strategies for practice* (pp. 135–148). Champaign, IL: Research Press.

Doka, K. J. (2008). The power of ritual: A gift for children and adolescents. In K. J. Doka & A. S. Tucci (Eds.), *Living with grief: Children and adolescents* (pp. 287–295). Washington, DC: Hospice Foundation of America.

Doka, K. J., & Martin, T. L. (2002). How we grieve: Culture, class, and gender. In K. J. Doka (Ed.), *Disenfranchised grief: New directions, challenges, and strategies for practice* (pp. 337–347). Champaign, IL: Research Press.

Gitterman, A., & Shulman, L. (2005). The life model, oppression, vulnerability, resilience, mutual aid, and the mediating function. In A. Gitterman & L. Shulman (Eds.), *Mutual aid groups, vulnerable & resilient populations, and the life cycle* (pp. 3–37). New York: Columbia University Press.

Goodman, R. F. (2002). Art as a component of grief work with children. In K. J. Doka (Ed.), *Disenfranchised grief: New directions, challenges, and strategies for practice* (pp. 297–322). Champaign, IL: Research Press.

Goodman, R., Williams, K., Agell, G., & Gantt, L. (1998). Talk, talk, talk, when do we draw? *American Journal of Art Therapy, 37*(2), 39–42.

Heegaard, M. E. (1990). *Coping with death and grief.* Minneapolis, MN: Lerner.

Hogan, N. S., & DeSantis, L. (1992). Adolescent sibling bereavement: An ongoing attachment. *Qualitative Health Research, 2*(2), 159–177.

Kandt, V. E. (1994). Adolescent bereavement: Turning a fragile time into acceptance and peace. *School Counselor, 41*(3) 203–212.

Lattanzi-Licht, M. (1996). Helping families with adolescents cope with loss. In C. Corr & D. Balk (Eds.), *Handbook of adolescent death and bereavement* (pp. 219–234). New York: Springer.

Lewis, L., & Langer, K. C. (1994). Symbolization in psychotherapy with patients who are disabled. *Journal of Psychotherapy, 48*(2), 231–239.

Liotta, E. J. (1996). *When students grieve.* Alexandria, PA: LRP Publications.

Malekoff, A. (2004). *Group work with adolescents: Principles and practice.* New York: Guilford Press.

Malone, P. A., Pomeroy, E. C., & Jones, B. L. (2009). *Disoriented grief: A lens through which to view the experience of Katrina evacuees.* Manuscript submitted for publication.

Miller, L. (1998). Out of nowhere: Natural and technological disasters. In L. Miller, *Shocks to the system: Psychotherapy of traumatic disability syndromes.* (pp. 140–156). New York: W. W. Norton & Company.

Nadeau, J. W. (2001). Meaning making in family bereavement: A family systems approach. In M. S. Stroebe, R. O. Hansson, W. Stroebe, & H. Schut. (Eds.),

Handbook of bereavement research: Consequences, coping, and care (pp. 329–347). Washington, DC: American Psychological Association.

Nader, K. (2002). Treating children after violence in schools and communities. In N. B. Webb (Ed.) (2002). *Helping bereaved children: A handbook for practitioners.* New York: Guilford Press.

Noppe, I. C., & Noppe, L. D. (2004). Adolescent experiences with death: Letting go of immortality. *Journal of Mental Health Counseling, 26*(2), 146–167.

O'Brien, J. M., Goodenow, C., & Espin, O. (1991). Adolescents' reactions to the death of a peer. *Adolescence, 26*(102), 431–440.

Pfefferbaum, B. (1997). Post-traumatic stress disorder in children: A review of the past ten years. *Journal of the American Academy of Child and Adolescent Psychiatry, 36*, 1503–1511.

Pomeroy, E. C., & Garcia, R. B. (2009). The grief assessment and intervention workbook: A strengths perspective. Belmont, CA: Brooks/Cole, Cengage Learning.

Pynoos, R. S., Steinberg, A. M., & Goenjian, A. (1996). Traumatic stress in childhood and adolescence: Recent developments and current controversies. In B. A. van der Kolk, A. C. McFarlane, & L. Weisaeth (Eds.), *Traumatic stress: The effects of overwhelming experience on mind, body, and society* (pp. 331–358). New York: Guilford Press.

Rando, T. A. (1993). *Treatment of complicated mourning.* Champaign, IL: Research Press.

Raphael, B., Minkov, C., & Dobson, M. (2001). Psychotherapeutic and pharmacological intervention for bereaved persons. In M. S. Stroebe, R. O. Hansson, W. Stroebe, & H. Schut. (Eds.), *Handbook of bereavement research: Consequences, coping, and care* (pp. 587–612). Washington, DC: American Psychological Association.

Rheingold, A. A., Smith, D. W., Ruggiero, K. J., Saunders, B. E., Kilpatrick, D. G., & Resnick, H. S. (2004). Loss, trauma, exposure, and mental health in a representative sample of 12–17-year-old youth: Data from the National Survey of Adolescents. *Journal of Loss and Trauma, 9*(1), 10–19.

Ringler, L. L., & Hayden, D. C. (2000). Adolescent bereavement and social support: Peer loss compared to other losses. *Journal of Adolescent Research, 15*(2), 209–230.

Rosen, H. (1991). Child and adolescent bereavement. *Child and Adolescent Social Work, 8*(1), 5–16.

Rowling, L. (2002). Youth and disenfranchised grief. In K. J. Doka (Ed.), *Disenfranchised grief: New directions, challenges, and strategies for practice* (pp. 275–292). Champaign, IL: Research Press.

Saltzman, R. R., Steinberg, A. M., Layne, C. M., Aisenberg, E., & Pynoos, R. S. (2001). A developmental approach to school-based treatment of adolescents exposed to trauma and traumatic loss. *Journal of Child and Adolescent Group Therapy, 11*(2/3), 43–56.

Schuurman, D. (2008). Grief groups for grieving children and adolescents. In K. J. Doka & A. S. Tucci (Eds.), *Living with grief: Children and adolescents* (pp. 255–268). Washington, DC: Hospice Foundation of America.

Steese, S., Dollette, M., Phillips, W., Hossfeld, E., Matthews, G., & Taormina, G. (2006). Understanding Girls' Circle as an intervention on perceived social support, body image, self-efficacy, locus of control, and self-esteem. *Adolescence, 41*(161), 55–74.

Tedeschi, R. G. (1996). Support groups for bereaved adolescents. In C. A. Corr & D. E. Balk (Eds.), *Handbook of adolescent death and bereavement* (pp. 293–311). New York: Springer.

Webb, N. B. (Ed.). (2002). *Helping bereaved children: A handbook for practitioners.* New York: Guilford Press.

Therapeutic Activities for Practice

Renée Bradford Garcia

Initially, it can be difficult to engage a youth in conversation about sensitive subjects until a degree of trust and safety has been established with the practitioner. These activities are designed to provide youth with a comfortable means of expressing their feelings in the therapeutic setting.

There are a limitless number of activities that can help children and adolescents process their grief. In this section, a sample of activities and techniques to assess and intervene with youth are outlined. These activities have been utilized in grief counseling practice and have proved to be effective tools. Practitioners can modify these activities according to the setting, age, emotional functioning, cognitive functioning, and the unique needs and circumstances of the youth. Some of these activities can be completed individually in a group setting and then shared with group members.

Constructing the Feeling of Loss

Materials needed: Construction paper in various colors and glue.

Instruction: Instruct the youth to use the paper and glue to create something that represents how she felt at the moment of learning about the loss. Explain that she may want to choose different colors for different feelings or tear or fold the paper in different ways. Explain that the creation may be abstract in nature and clarify that the goal is not to produce a work of art but to create something that represents her inner experience at the time.

This same activity may be used with different prompts that are more relevant to the youth's needs and experiences. For example, youth with divorced parents can be asked to create something that represents their thoughts and feelings about family.

Making Masks

Materials needed: Card stock cut into the shape of a face or a box available with an attached lid, such as a cigar box; markers, crayons, and colored pencils. For boxes: various craft items that can be glued to the box such as sequins, pipe cleaners, Popsicle sticks, colored paper, magazine pictures, and so on.

Instructions: Explain how we often show the world a certain side of ourselves while what we feel inside may be different. Instruct the youth to use one side of the mask (or the outside of the box) to create something that represents what he shows others. On the other side of the mask (or the inside the box), he should create something that represents the feelings or thoughts that others don't see.

Grief Scavenger Hunt (for Groups)

Materials needed: Paper, envelopes in two different colors, pens, a prize to give to winning team. Identify a plan of locations for where to find each survey question. For example, location A is the secretary's desk, location B is the vending machines, and so forth through E. In each envelope include a survey question, such as the following:

1. "Make a list of the names of the people who died." (Place this envelope at location A.)
2. "List the date of death for each person." (Place at location B.)
3. "Name eight feelings associated with grief." (Place at location C.)
4. "List at least six things that can be helpful to a grieving person." (Place at location D.)
5. "How many people on your team are dealing with an expected death versus an unexpected death?" (Place at location E.)

Make a list of locations for each team. For example, the blue team list has the locations in ABCDE order. The yellow team list has the locations in EDCBA order.

Instructions: Divide the group into two teams and explain that they are to work as a group to find each envelope and record the answers to the survey questions. Explain the following rules for the scavenger hunt: (1) you must go in order to find the envelopes; (2) stay together; (3) answers must be complete; (4) only open the envelopes that respond to your team's color. The first team that returns to base with every question answered wins. When everyone is done, take turns sharing and comparing survey answers.

Anonymous Discussion Bucket (for Groups)

Materials needed: One set of 5 x 7 index cards with prompts for each group member. Prompts can include statements such as the following:

- "The hardest part about my grief when it comes to dealing with my friends is . . ."
- "The hardest part about my grief when it comes to dealing with my parents/guardian is . . ."
- "Talking about my loss makes me feel . . ."
- "One way I am different since my loss is . . ."
- "I hate it when people say _____ when talking about my loss."
- "My biggest fear or concern about my future is . . ."
- "Something else about my grief that I would like to discuss is . . ."

Instructions: Instruct each group member to complete the statements on the cards. Let them know that they will not have to identify themselves with their answers, and thus they should answer the prompts openly and honestly. Have members fold each card and place all cards in a large bucket or box. The facilitator randomly chooses a card out of the bucket, reads it, and invites group members to discuss the comment on the card as it relates to their own grief experience.

Memory Bracelet

Materials needed: Different colored beads and leather string.

Instructions: Have the youth choose beads that represent memories or characteristics of the loved one or lost object. Instruct the youth to string the beads into a bracelet so that she can carry "a piece" of the loved one with her. For example, green may represent a camping trip or orange may represent the person's love of basketball (McWhorter, 2003).

Strengths Bracelet

Materials needed: Different colored beads and leather string.

Instructions: Instruct the youth to choose beads that represent his strengths, including positive things about himself and resources that are available to him. For example, red can represent courage, pink can stand for patience, brown may represent a football coach. Encourage the youth to look at or touch the bracelet when feeling upset as a reminder of his strengths that can help with the current problem.

Balloon Message

Materials needed: Lightweight paper, pens, markers, colors, and a helium-filled balloon.

Instructions: Have the child draw a picture or write a private message to their loved one. Allow the child to release the balloon and watch it ascend into the sky as a way of "delivering" the message to the loved one.

More Of/Less Of

Materials needed: 8 x 10 papers with a grid of boxes on them; colored pens, pencils, and markers.

Instructions: Have the youth fill in the blank boxes of the grid with things she wants more of in her life and things she wants less of in her life. Use stamps or markers to identify "more of" items and "less of" items. In this activity, the practitioner can gain a better understanding of what is important to the child and how life changes may have affected her.

(Contributed by Art Prennace, LPC, Round Rock, Texas.)

Paper Hand

Materials needed: Construction paper, glue, craft sticks, markers, and pens.

Instructions: Assist the child in tracing his hand on a piece of paper. Cut out the imprint of the hand and have the child write (or assist the child in writing) the name of the loved one or lost object on the palm of the hand. On each finger, encourage the child to write a memory of the loved one or lost object. Glue the paper hand to a craft stick and give it to the child to "wave" to the loved one or lost object (McWhorter, 2003).

Feeling Heart

Materials needed: Paper and coloring crayons or pens.

Instructions: Have the youth draw a heart that fills the paper. Instruct the youth to identify four or five feelings and assign a color to each feeling. Instruct the youth to color the heart according to how he or she feels. (Older male youth may prefer to use a shape other than a heart) (Hayes, 2005).

Bridge Drawing

Materials needed: Paper and crayons, colored pencils, or pens.

Instructions: Have the youth draw a bridge, real or imagined. Instruct the youth to mark where he is in the drawing using an X or a figure. The practitioner can ask the following questions as a way to learn about how the youth is processing her current life transition.

1. Which direction are you moving in?
2. What is holding up the bridge? (support system)
3. Where are you going?
4. What are you leaving?
5. How long is the bridge?
6. What could make the bridge fall down? How strong/weak is the bridge?
7. Tell me about what is under the bridge.
8. Tell me about the weather around the bridge.
9. Do you want to get off the bridge? How?

10. Do you want someone else on the bridge with you? (Hayes, 2005).

Beaded Animal

Materials needed: Bead kit from arts and crafts store that contains small beads and instructions for making beaded animals.

Instructions: Assist the child in making the beaded animal of their choice. Explain that the child can hold the animal in his hand and rub the beads when he is feeling upset. The child can also count the number of different colored beads that make up the animal as a way to distract him from his worries. This is a tactile activity that can be soothing to a child who is experiencing distress. The animal is also portable and could be helpful to children who have to move, who are in transitional situations (divorce), or who need a stable object to take to school (Hayes, 2005).

Memory Box

Materials needed: Shoe box, colored paper, glue, foam decorations, pictures, magazine cutouts, and other decorative materials.

Instructions: Have the youth decorate the box so that it symbolizes memories of her loved one. The youth can take the box home and fill it with mementos or reminders of her loved one. The box may contain pictures, letters to the loved one, or other objects the youth associates with the loved one.

Letter-Writing

Materials needed: Paper and pencil or pen.

Instructions: Have the youth write a letter to his loved one. Explain that this is the chance to say things that he didn't have a chance to say or to express regrets. The youth can place the letter in the memory box (see above), or if in a camp setting, the youth can burn the message on the campfire and symbolically send the message to the loved one.

Self-Esteem Box

Materials needed: Shoe box, colorful paper, decorations, crayons, colored pens, markers, pictures of the youth, glitter, glue, stickers, magazine clippings, and so on.

Instructions: Have the youth decorate the box to portray her own unique personality, including a picture of herself on the box. The box is meant to be clearly associated with each specific youth (if doing this in a group setting). Ask supportive adults in the youth's life to write positive comments to the youth and place them in the box. The practitioner should view these comments to ensure that only positive sentiments are expressed. Practitioners can also add notes about the youth's progress in treatment. Send invitations to a box-opening party to significant people and have the youth open the box and read the comments out loud. Instruct the youth to use the comments in the box as reminders of her worth when having a difficult time. Continually add items to the box, which remains with the youth regardless of changing locations. The box of comments serves as a resource for the youth's positive sense of self and as a tangible support system (Wilke-Deaton, 2007).

Remembering Worksheet

Materials needed: "Remembering" worksheet (see the appendix at the end of this section) and photographs of loved one brought by the youth.

Instructions: Have the youth complete the statements on the worksheet and share these along with the picture of his loved one. This can serve as a catalyst for the practitioner to ask questions about the loved one and allow the youth to share additional information. This activity can be useful in groups with middle school and high school students as a way to memorialize loved ones.

Grief Public Service Announcement (for Groups)

Materials needed: Possible media for this activity are numerous, including visual arts, print, film, audio, and theater. The best medium for a particular group will depend on the group's time together and available resources.

Instructions: Give the group the task of developing a public service announcement on the type of grief that is most relevant to them (i.e., death, divorce, terminal illness, etc.). Guide them in designing, planning, and making the PSA. Discussions might include issues such as the message of the PSA, who their audience will be, the tone of the PSA, and how it could be helpful to others.

Worry Wall

Materials needed: A wall or door in the session setting; paper, markers, crayons, tape, and envelopes.

Instructions: Invite the youth to draw or write down a worry, place it in an envelope, and tape it to the "worry" wall according to the intensity of the worry. The major worries are placed higher on the wall and the smaller worries are placed lower on the wall. The youth can move the worries on the wall to different locations from week to week as the intensity of the worry changes. When the youth is no longer concerned about a worry on the wall, he may choose to take the envelope off the wall and throw it away, tear it up, or give it to the practitioner. The practitioner can celebrate with the youth his successful resolution of that issue. This provides youth a way of safely communicating their concerns and placing them outside of themselves.

Mandalas

Materials needed: Mandala coloring pages printed from the Internet; markers, colored pencils, colored chalk, or crayons.

Instructions: Provide the youth with a mandala outline and tell her to color the mandala according to how she feels or how she feels about the loss. This can be a soothing activity and a technique for initiating conversation in a non-threatening way.

Feeling Card Game

Materials needed: Pictures of faces showing different feelings pasted onto 2 x 4 card stock or index cards. These cards can be laminated to ensure durability. One feeling face is pasted onto each card, and some cards have blank faces. One die with the 5 and 6 covered with masking tape so that players can roll no higher than a 4.

Instructions: Place all the cards face down on the table or floor. Each player takes turns rolling the die and choosing a card. According to the number on the die, the player must describe the number of times he has had that feeling. If the player draws a blank face, he may choose any feeling or allow another player to choose the feeling that he will describe.

Feeling Balloon Game

Materials needed: An inflated balloon and permanent marking pens.

Instructions: Write six or seven feelings on the balloon. Take turns tossing the balloon to the other player who catches it. The feeling nearest the catcher's right thumb is the feeling she will talk about based on recent experiences (Shapiro, 2003).

Life Book

Materials needed: Bound paper or scrapbook; various art supplies, the youth's memorabilia, photographs, magazine pictures or art, decorations, and so on.

Instructions: The life book is a historical archive of the youth's memories using words, pictures, memorabilia, and so on. It can chronicle the life of the youth (in the case of a foster child) or it can be used to chronicle the life of a lost loved one. The youth can add to the life book over time, making it a consistent comfort and memory holder.

Body Map

Materials needed: Butcher paper on a roll, marking pens, and Band-Aids. (Alternative: legal-size paper with body outline drawn on it.)

Instructions: Have the youth lie down on the paper while the practitioner traces the outline of her body. After discussing how grief can be expressed physically, have the youth color in the body according to how she experiences grief. Discuss such questions as, "In what areas of the body do you feel sadness and grief?" "How does the grief get expressed?" "How intense is the grief?" "What areas are most affected? Least affected?"

For younger children, the practitioner can give the child Band-Aids and have her place them on the body map where it "hurts." The practitioner can explain that the hurt spot will heal with loving attention and time.

Tell a Story Game

Materials needed: Index cards with story prompts, pens, and tokens.

Instructions: The practitioner writes story prompts on 5 x 10 cards. Examples for prompts are: "A person who loses something important,"

"An animal that is lost," "A circus that gets hit by a storm," and so on. Cards are placed faced down, and the youth chooses a card. Using the prompt on the card, the youth attempts to tell a story that must have a beginning, a middle, and an end. In addition, the youth is asked to identify the moral, or lesson, of the story. Complete stories (beginning, middle, and end) can be rewarded with tokens as can the identification of the story's moral. This activity can assist the practitioner in understanding the youth's perspective on a problem, assessing emotional functioning, judgment, insight, values, organizational skills, worldview, and coping mechanisms (either life-enhancing or life-depleting). Practitioner can take turns drawing cards with the youth and use the storytelling as a means of teaching new perspectives and healthy coping skills (Shapiro, 2003).

Time Line

Materials needed: Butcher paper or newsprint and markers.

Instructions: This activity is most effective with older youth. Have the youth make a time line of his life from birth to present day, noting the major events, changes, losses, positive experiences, and any other significant life events. The time line provides the practitioner and the youth with a visible overview and history of major life transitions and a starting point for discussions.

Superhero Capes

Materials needed: Cloth capes that can be cut out of material and fabric markers.

Instructions: Suggest that the child pretend she is a superhero. Have her choose the superhero's name, design the cape, and identify her special powers. Invite the child to act out being the superhero she has created with the practitioner playing the role as partner or ally. As an alternative, encourage the child to write a story about her superhero.

References

Hayes, P. (2005). *Art therapy and anxiety: Healing through imagery.* Brentwood, TN: Author and Cross Country Education, Inc.

McWhorter, G. (2003). *Healing activities for children in grief.* Fort Worth, TX: Author.

Shapiro, L. E. (2003). *The secret language of children.* Naperville, IL: Sourcebooks, Inc.

Wilke-Deaton, J. (2007). *Over 75 quick, on-the-spot techniques for children with emotional and behavioral problems.* Eau Claire, WI: PESI, LLC.

APPENDIX

Remembering . . .

- I am here to remember . . . (name, when and where he died, age)
- What was her work? or How did she spend her time?
- A place he liked to go was . . .
- Her favorite food was . . .
- One quality or characteristic he had that made him special was . . .
- A gift she gave me, or a possession of hers I value is . . .
- My favorite memory of him was when . . .
- If she were here now she would say to me . . .
- Something I want to say to him now is . . .

Index